PENGUIN BOOKS

T0294772

A COUNTRY TOO FAR

A COUNTRY TOO FAR

WRITINGS ON ASYLUM SEEKERS

EDITED BY ROSIE SCOTT AND TOM KENEALLY

PENGUIN BOOKS

PENGUIN BOOKS

UK | USA | Canada | Ireland | Australia
India | New Zealand | South Africa | China

Penguin Books is part of the Penguin Random House group of companies
whose addresses can be found at global.penguinrandomhouse.com.

Penguin
Random House
Australia

First published by Penguin Group (Australia), 2013
This edition published by Penguin Random House Australia Pty Ltd, 2016

1 3 5 7 9 10 8 6 4 2

Cover design by Alex Ross © Penguin Random House Australia Pty Ltd
Cover photograph from shutterstock.com
Typeset in Adobe Garamond Pro by
Samantha Jayaweera, Penguin Random House Australia Pty Ltd
Colour separation by Splitting Image Colour Studio, Clayton, Victoria
Printed and bound in Australia by Griffin Press, an accredited ISO AS/NZS 14001
Environmental Management Systems printer.

National Library of Australia
Cataloguing-in-Publication data:

A country too far : writings on asylum seekers / edited by
Rosie Scott and Tom Keneally.
9780143574132 (paperback)

342.94083

penguin.com.au

CONTENTS

INTRODUCTION

The idea of this anthology was to ask some of our most admired Australian writers to bring a different perspective and depth to the public debate on asylum seekers.

The language of this discussion has been debased to such an extent that spin-doctor flacks and people on the extremist fringes of Australian politics are largely responsible for the tone and direction of one of the central moral issues of our time.

Even senior politicians have used inflammatory and inaccurate descriptions – detainees throw their children overboard, they are terrorists and fraudsters, and people smugglers are lower than paedophiles.

The fact that they are talking about the most marginalised people on earth – deeply traumatised refugees who have lost their countries, homes and families through disasters of every kind – is lost in this storm of venom and cliché.

We believe that the best writers can get to the heart of things in a way that almost no one else can because of the truthfulness, power and clarity of their language.

We were looking for these qualities in our choice of writers and the result has been extraordinary. Some of Australia's most distinguished novelists, poets and thinkers have focused their forensic intelligence on this issue.

What has become clear from these writers is that the Australian attitude to asylum seekers, their down-to-earth, personal experience of it is quite different from that of the artificial world of spin. The stories and poetry in this anthology confirm that the experiences of seeking asylum – the terrible journeys of escape from death, starvation, poverty and terror to an imagined paradise – are part of our mindset and deeply embedded in our culture and personal histories.

Les Murray's poem about his wife's journey from Hungary as a child immigrant during the war is so tender and perfectly observed that boat people of any age or time would recognise and respond to it.

Geraldine Brooks' and Sue Woolfe's stories, both about fathers who remained illegal immigrants all their lives, are poignant portraits of the millions of people around the world who live daily with the fear of discovery.

Judith Wright's daughter Meredith McKinney describes how her mother was haunted by her meeting with a young Jewish man desperate for asylum from the Nazis. Wright wrote about this experience in a painfully truthful section of her autobiography *Half a Lifetime*.

In writing about their personal histories these writers through the power of their language illuminate the larger picture of asylum seekers with eloquence, depth and compassion.

Passionately imagined fiction from writers like Gail Jones, Rodney Hall, Debra Adelaide, Kathryn Heyman, Christos Tsiolkas, Eva Hornung and Anna Funder memorably conveys the pain, joy and pity of asylum seekers' lives.

Each of these stories achieves an intensification of reality, an authentic glimpse into the interiority of an individual life in a way that only the best fiction can. In each story we are introduced to new, often startling worlds whose authenticity and originality are radiantly apparent.

Cogent and knowledgeable pieces on Australian policies for asylum seekers by Alex Miller, Raimond Gaita, Tom Keneally, Anna Funder and Elliot Perlman argue convincingly and passionately for a more humane approach. Kim Scott analyses the connection between Indigenous experience and that of asylum seekers in his lyrical and thoughtful essay. Fiona McGregor draws a deft and incisive portrait of a dancer and humanitarian forced to flee from his home in Sri Lanka.

Stephanie Johnson's sardonic dystopia throws a whole new light on Australia–New Zealand relations; Arnold Zable and Denise Leith tell moving and insightful stories of what it means to be a survivor; Bella Vendramini vividly describes an epiphany she goes through when she and her boyfriend help some Somalis to escape detention.

Haunting poems like John Tranter's lament on the damage of war and the dispossession of the battered people of Europe, Judith Rodriguez's sensitive portrayal of asylum seekers, Dorothy Hewett's evocative vision of the horrors of families fleeing from war, Ouyang Yu's ironic take on the cultural meaning of 'boat people' and Judith Wright's celebration of love in a threatening environment express the world of asylum seekers in unforgettable images.

In the beginning we approached these writers with apprehension, knowing they all had large workloads and were deluged by requests. Worse, a topic like asylum seekers is so fraught it is not easy to write about. Yet the majority of writers accepted immediately with enthusiasm and modesty.

It was inspiring to find such a communality of feeling and generosity among Australian writers.

Australians have a reputation for plain speaking, irreverence and sympathy for the underdog. Only a generation ago bipartisan support allowed thousands of Vietnamese refugees to be resettled here without fuss or acrimony, and at present count there are more than one hundred Australian organisations giving help to refugees. So it's not too much to hope that we can meet this crisis with compassion and optimism instead of cruelty and despair, constructiveness instead of damage, honesty instead of lies.

In this rich anthology the writers have made their contribution to the debate by addressing the lives of refugees with truthfulness and grace. Their stories show how closely our own histories mirror those of asylum seekers and how our fate is only a heartbeat away from theirs. These writers prove through the power of their language that workable and compassionate ideas about this human tragedy are not only possible but essential for us as a nation.

— Rosie Scott, 2013

MOONLIGHT
RODNEY HALL

Afloat on the empty night it is the sea itself that amazes him. The sea as a place of the living. There are no dead here. Gazing around, entranced and awestruck, he murmurs under his breath, but the words of his landlocked language do not seem adequate. That noble language of his forebears, having been shaped by gritty plains and harsh rocks, the dignities of work, even high notions of the sacred flame, has no voice for this . . . this continent of water. His heart opens with an ecstasy of unreadiness and yearning.

There is so much sea. Even as a modern, educated man he is unprepared. He can hardly breathe for the jostle of a million dancing moon-shards programmed to rise and subside with breathtaking restlessness. Thus, the strange name *ocean* (strange perhaps in every tongue) delivers for him, at last, its reality: the greatest beauty of creation. Nothing else on earth so vast or dazzling. Not rivers, not lakes, nor even snow-covered mountains.

Head tipped back he opens his voiceless mouth. Whether this is anguish or longing no one else on board is awake to witness or wonder – none, at least, among his own people. The only intruder on his privacy is one of the boat's resident cockroaches, exploring his hand for some minutes before being brushed off by the other. In the darkness he can make out just enough. Prow dark, deck crowded, feeble lamps for riding lights. The passage makeshift. A commandeered fishing boat and humble. The battered leaky hull not built for this. Cabins? None. The hold? An open slimy fish room. Unusable. The entire timber frame shuddering with the efforts of a clapped-out motor that hammers its wedge of noise into pure space – where scattered constellations stand tipped on their heads in the ambiguous, radiant and impending night – yet it is this stumbling thumping pulse that comforts him. Long since, were harbour lights. Dwindling, they sank behind the risen horizon. The last of the land left far behind. Observations, lost under a flood of time. Nothing remains to mark the distance travelled, nothing but shortlived hissing bubbles. So it is that the smooth-shifting slithering sea with its trickle music of folded water brings tears of relief to his eyes.

As for the promised destination, somewhere remote, on the far side of night, beyond the glittering floor . . . well he clings to his belief. Because the need is overwhelming. Easy to believe whole nations of refugees have successfully passed this way unharmed. Escaped without trace into the twinkling emptiness. Sea near. And sea far. Waves interlocked and heaving with sinister elasticity. Sinister? No, he corrects himself. This is, at last, an interval of hope. Himself almost at peace. He gazes over the side. To glimpse, past glassy fractures, a liquid abyss. Always and forever the abyss. Seen now and then for an instant only. Water vertiginous as the inverted sky in that towering transparency. Triggered alarm flashes lightnings through his uprooted tree. He recollects an ancient warning against casting oneself on the waters. Defiantly, he has done so. They have done so.

The moon, heavy as marble and miraculously airborne, hurtles overhead.

Can he yet reassure his wife and child? Can they afford his promise that this is the final leg of their journey? After so much treachery? The decision taken at home in a bombed-out water cistern a thousand years old? Once begun, the thing has been to keep going. History rewarding them with this. Escape in the wind. Beyond reach of killers – a leaky boat with greasy rails, stinking hold, and hammering engine. He buries the hollow memory: how everybody waited and watched when he handed over the last of his money and at long last the crew arrived. Then the voyage got under way. Small men, quiet and capable, took charge, light on their feet and deft with their hands. There is no choice but to trust them. That they also know their way.

Carved waves advance and break against the boat. Not quite real, though absolute, they shatter to diamonds and fold aside with a slump of heaviness.

The head turns on his wooden neck. His dragging eyes check the wheelhouse. From where he sits a steersman can be made out behind blurred cabin windows, the centre pane with a windscreen wiper, face like a boxing glove. Apparently this man has confidence in the course he sets, though the night emerges strange as Africa, secure on his perch and cooled by the steady hum of an electric fan. He seems unperturbed when, periodically, the motor chokes at some internal obstacle, no doubt relying on the child mechanic down in the engine room whose job is to attend to such problems. And the rhythm recovers.

He props his back against the rail. Mesmerised by this heaving net of moonlight stretched over the world like a membrane, he fights to stay awake. He must keep watch till dawn. Just for a moment another boat, this one without lights at all, comes ghosting the opposite way, a dark patch among the glitters. Looms stealthy as a bat. Almost motionless, then of a sudden sweeps past murmurously to slip astern as if still unnoticed, carrying with it the faint cadence of a routine prayer. Plaintive and devout. The gigantic night is left to settle again, in its seat, on the bedded waves. He must definitely stay awake, shielding the devastated wasteland behind his eyes.

He will keep watch. This is his duty, as husband and father. Darkness penetrates him at every pore. He would prefer to smoke a cigarette to soothe his agitation, but cannot spare one. Nor does he dare risk interrupting the dreams of others by lighting up. Waking them to fears of the unexpected in their flight from persecution. Though a freak swell intervenes to lift the battered boat bodily. Eerie as a passing monster. Arrives and subsides. Leaving the keel to dip down in a trough, deck tilted, ropes slatting and a dislodged chain clattering. The superstructure creaks and complains.

His son's head settles deeper in his lap – a bone ball – burdened by anxiety even while unconscious, filled with the weight of atrocities no child should ever have witnessed. Poor boy . . . his sisters were murdered a few days before their seventh birthday: shot because, when ordered to stop crying, they couldn't. Neighbours helped cover them in a grave scratched from dirt while their mother turned to stone. Yes, and it is she, intermittently deaf since then, who cradles the boy's feet in open hands while she snatches rags of sleep. Such a skeleton she has become. Muffled in black. Rocking toward safety as the hull lunges over lesser bumps of moonbright hazards. He can make her out, though vaguely . . . and reaches to touch her cheek. On second thoughts, his fingertips make do with the billowing contact of her headscarf. And, in the sultry salt-drunk air, his nose detects a hint of that perfumed modesty praised by poets. How has she managed it? Astonished, he inhales with love.

Will she ever be granted the blessing of oblivion? Maybe not. His doubts become a prayer.

Hours have passed. The old tub glides among little rocking moons as the crew improvise to keep it on course. Bare feet. Bare knees. An oldish one among them steps past and nods to him, realising he is awake. He does not respond. Contact somehow disallowed, disallowed because putting at risk the agreement. The secrecy. Nor can he afford any lapse in his duty to protect his family. He has no room left. Though what *is* the family, all said and done? Three skeletons. Three among a hundred others cramming the deck with hinged and hobbled awkwardness. Among the shadowy neighbouring faces some let show the glint of an eye and some a tooth. His people. His exiles. His history. Their purpose his. Their courage inspiring. Stars hail down around his head in a glitter of extinguished fires. He tries guessing how the future will be.

Is this what I am doing with my life? he asks, coming to himself. Reminded of his origins. He sits in his body. He is an architect, an out-of-work architect. The paradox astonishes him. Who builds buildings any more? And how does a spoiled career distinguish him from his fellows? Without these others the journey would be unthinkable, the distance too vast, direction lost and language incomprehensible. Without them his damaged family could never have fled so far. He and they are in this together, a huddle of refugees, a community in misery, already having thrown themselves on the mercy and trust of strangers. It cuts both ways. The crew at risk too. Far behind them, the terrifying thud of drums, remembered like rhythmic reminders of gunfire.

The knobs of his spine bump painfully when the boat rolls.

Could anyone feel at home on the open sea? What ease and sheer grit would that require? What aimlessness, in the scheme of things? What changeability? What longings for firm ground underfoot? The infinite ocean fills his soul with its seductive ruffles and with the equilibrium of revolving planets aloft. He focuses on the promised sanctuary ahead. Determined, once there, to be a better man. His wide eyes gather what light the darkness offers. Nearby, a shadowy something suggests itself – standing – and is gone. One of his neighbours snores, then stops and speaks in his sleep, asking if the goat has been milked yet, and snores again. Oddly, an answer comes, considerately, from elsewhere: 'She has.'

The spoken word a mystery at the threshold of eternity, a reminder of the perils of the heart-stopping risk of escape, the slog across mountain passes and deserts, themselves a ragged cavalcade wending its way in among strangers with their own ferocity of desperation, craving food when no food could be had, now and then bouncing along in the back of a truck under blanketing dust through treacherous poppy fields, being chased from a train by officers with guns, crouching while swift shadows of aircraft passed over with a snicker of bullets, plus themselves briefly behind bars, detained at roadblocks and photographed while under arrest for purposes of identification: uncertain of the difference between permission to pass, temporary detainment, a simple trap, or (worst by far) the threat of deportation back home to a violent death among all that has been left behind but which still remains.

Was there ever a time of peace? There must have been, because his memories include childhood games and flowers, the old town granaries and stables, brilliant mornings and laughter round a table piled with fruit in preparation for some feast or other.

He lets another breath escape. He feels his soul flutter naked to the soft intimate wind. What does he know? What does he know that matters? His paramount fear is that he might *lose* his fear, leaving loved ones exposed. Lose, even, the fear of shame. The sky flies away into outerspace. Life, he assures himself, will take us . . . as this boat is taking us . . . there. The hushed and lovely end to a year of terror. Chaos brought under control. He leans to dip one hand in the surge – that's how overloaded the boat is – the passing water blood-warm. When the hand emerges he finds it sheathed with a moonbright glove of transparency.

He snatches his breath again. Doubts gnaw at him as progress ploughs noisily from nowhere to nowhere. With no means of measuring the distance covered, the old tub might as well be wallowing on the spot, expending its claptrap force in wasted noise. A frantic exaggeration of first impressions. To his exhausted eyes shapes coagulate and flux, mutating as hollows in the emptiness. He accuses himself of vanity, of stubbornness and ignorance where the big things are concerned. And the little things, too. Of having lost his profession. Condemned to earn money as a builder's labourer. And never enough of it. The cold comfort, his will to fight, emerging. A vanity called individualism.

The steersman's face can be made out behind glass, a lonely dictator in the wheelhouse. Night sky shudders across glass. And not so

much a face either, more a skin mask, a remote ghost-moon of a pro-
file, advancing against the artificial wind from the fan. What does that
face see as night mounts – and mounts solid as a cliff about to break
apart to overbalance into the thunder of an avalanche? Who can guess?
This is a question without answer. Even when the fellow takes a swig
from his water bottle and the clear plastic gleams hints of the modern
world. The boat blunders on, stressed and trembling. Steady progress
nothing less than a pledge of faith. Well, he recaptures his suspicion
of a moment ago, the boat might indeed be travelling in circles – an
eternally pointless journey. As an educated man he is used enough to
questioning the evidence. Or was. In happier times. It seems impossible that he has ended up as helpless as he is. He will never recover from
the price already paid: his little daughters' lives.

The clanking motor, driven to repeat itself or die, an abstract
torture. Yet that lowgrade pain helps obliterate others. And now its
bat-bat-bat-BAT-bat ebbs whenever his eyes close, mysteriously
muted by sightlessness.

He is numb. Lulled and numb. For brief moments feeling himself
subtly airborne . . . gliding, weightless and without substance, sliding south, away from the remembrance of weeks in prison . . . to rise,
till nothing but the weight of his son's grief anchors him to reality.
Finally, he can almost admit he is done for. He shakes off the drowsi-
ness. And the sleeping boy knows – head lolling and nestling deeper
into comfort. Some loose piece of equipment moans, giving out a solitary unearthly note. A deep flute. Again. The head in his lap murmurs
sleepy utterances. He strokes it to smooth that silky, sticky, sweaty
hair. Moon and moonlight blur . . .

Himself now glaringly awake – did he doze off, then? – he recoils
from phantom shapes bounding his way . . . deckhands? . . . leaping . . . they fling open the wheelhouse door . . . a rectangle of dark on
darkness. To slip inside. The door swings shut, but not before three or
four words escape. Urgent words, somehow disembodied even as they
are uttered – suspended in a pocket of air – and incomprehensible.

He feels his life as an event approaching over the tropical sea, scintillant and dangerous, advancing and advancing.

What price reassurance? What price certainty? The desperate voyage can only be vindicated by reaching safety in a country without guns. Though he knows that no arrival is final. His wife could not survive being arrested again and sent back. And nothing is impossible to those corrupted by authority, wherever they are. As no fear can be fully left behind either. Cosmic emptiness his limit.

Caring for the head in his lap preoccupies him. Suddenly shaken by violent shame. As a father he bows over his duty, gazing down into the mystery of the child's hollowed face. Have we come so far? he asks the sleeping boy. Did no one spy on us? Did no one betray us while we trudged over the mountains? Were we never spotted, exhausted as we were, taking refuge at the back of that cave, that bomb crater in the dust, that broken tomb? Can you forgive me for the world we brought you into? He makes promises to the sleeping boy. Even so, eyes wavering, mind warped, his memory stumbles into an unanticipated void somehow happening to somebody else. And therefore almost the truth.

The vessel pushes on across night's immense and glamorous desolation toward some point among twinkling moon-shards at the edge of oblivion. But he must . . . he must . . . keep himself from nodding off again, buoyed high above the rocky seabed – a seabed passing as far below as land passes beneath an aircraft. The risk a measure of madness. Only the motor gasps. Plugging away. Only the stubby hull makes sense of what they are doing. Yet he seems to lift off, once again free of the flesh. Between being and non-being the last knot of fatigue unravels. All things considered, life has no meaning whatsoever.

The night coalesces to a wing-shaped shadow aslant above the fugitive moon.

The wheelhouse door bangs open for half-seen figures to flit out, past and away, out from inside, and from there to the side where – incredibly – they escape over the rail. Seeming to leap into the sea. Despite the abyss. The tiny cabin left empty has a larger meaning. Its humble abandonment he clearly observes. Also the dim glow of navigation instruments. No one at the helm. The wheel turns eerily by itself. Yet the motor sounds easier, as if coughing clear of the effortful obstacle it has struggled against since leaving port. Fluid and universal, the dome of stars turns to meet the prow. Silver-bladed water streams past into flattened hollows and sleek pockets of darkness.

He is afire with nerves. Unaware that his mouth is already a fixed hole around a speechless cry. He need not think – he knows the truth. His startled blood knows it. He shakes his wife's shoulder. Instantly alert, she helps him lift the boy upright. Between them they hold him, precious as he is. Others of the crowd wake. The boat alive and seething with agitation. The motor chokes and, quiet as an apology, stops. A life raft bobs out of reach with, to all appearances, several men clinging on. The horizon lurches as the deck tips to one side. Something falls and rolls their way. The cockroaches on deck are suddenly fighting uphill. The deadly clarity of space tilts its stars. A silky sheath of water folds in over the rail.

THE SINGER
AND THE SILENCE
GERALDINE BROOKS

I'm pretty sure that for much of his life my father was an illegal immigrant. His papers may have been in order when he arrived here from Honolulu in the 1930s, on tour as the vocalist with a dance band. But things went awry for him in Adelaide when the bandleader absconded with the musicians' pay. Dad was left without the means to pay for passage home, so to earn a fare, he hired on with an Australian ensemble, and was singing with them the night news came through that Paris had fallen to the Nazis.

He and the Aussie musos – who'd become his mates – went out drinking after their gig. I can just about hear those slurred voices as the beer flowed: 'Bloody well gunna enlist in the morning. Bloody well fight those Naaaazi baaaaastards.' My dad concurred. He too would enlist, along with his mates, because that is what mates do. And so he became, perhaps, the only US citizen to serve in the AIF in New Guinea and Palestine.

At the end of the war, he returned with his unit to Australia, where he met and married my mother and settled down in suburban Sydney to a life far removed from the big bands and hula skirts and the

Hollywood ballrooms of his earlier career. But he never got his immigration status sorted. He was in his seventies when someone finally noticed that an American had been voting in every Aussie election since the end of World War II. The resulting blizzard of bureaucracy amused us. Dad didn't need to take an oath administered by the local mayor to make him an Aussie. This bloke, who stood by his mates, was passionate about a fair go, who followed every bat-stroke of every Test, who marched on Anzac Day and who loved Australia with a fierce, belligerent, lefty patriotism, needed no certificate to tell him which country was his own.

But I don't think he'd recognise us now. If my sister and I hadn't scattered his ashes over Barrenjoey – a view he loved when he settled, on his retirement, on the northern beaches – he'd be spinning in his grave. Aussies don't lock up kiddies. They don't drive desperate people to the edge of despair, pushing them into depression and madness. They don't stick people out in the desert or on faraway islands where no one can hear their voices.

There has been an ugly brilliance to this silencing. Whoever devised the gulag system for asylum seekers understood very well that the Australian heart was too big to withstand the truth about the people who risked everything to come here. But if the truth is silenced, lies can fill the space. And that is what happened.

I wanted to tear out my hair in frustration, one cab ride home from Sydney airport, after I'd spent months as a foreign correspondent covering the violence and injustice in many of the countries from which our asylum seekers had fled. The cabbie, himself of Middle Eastern descent, informed me that half the people in detention were convicted criminals in their home countries. Yes, I said, that was true: many of the Afghans had been convicted by the Taliban of sending their daughters to school, or owning some music cassettes. Many of the Iranians had been imprisoned for taking part in democracy demonstrations. And some of the Iraqis had been not only jailed, but tortured, for brave acts of dissent against Saddam Hussein.

The lies, the lies. The lies of the shock jocks, but worse than that, the lies of our own elected leaders. The big lie about 'queue jumpers' when in fact many of the asylum seekers came from countries that had no queue to join. Where merely indicating a desire to leave the country was to sign a death warrant.

It is true that our ancient, thin-soiled, fragile continent cannot take everyone. There is an absolute imperative to consider limits to growth in the calculus of immigration. But if we can't take everyone, then let us consider who we are – who we were – when we decide who is to be turned away. A country founded on the sweat of the poorest, most despised outcasts of nineteenth-century society, a country that saw those people come together to forge one of the best and fairest and most prosperous nations the world has ever seen, might make a different choice, a radical choice. Such a country might do away with millionaires' business visas and stop the cherry picking of the educated elite that strips the talent from the developing world. Such a country might make a more generous choice, and take the people more like our forebears – the despised poor, the desperate, the brave, driven people who risk everything they have to get here and give their kids a better life.

That would be a policy my dad would recognise.

HOMELAND
JOHN TRANTER

My beautiful cities
lost in the whirlwind.
Douse the lights of Europe; some of us
were devotees of the beast, now
we will be born again.
Some were devoured, and shall rise up.
The pale coast clears. This life is a crooked
song, or a myth about climbing and falling.

A passage, a movie ticket,
everything moves backwards,
a gramophone bothers the afternoon.
Forced now to the journey by slang, through
broken tunnels under the community's memory.

The sky is huge, growing up from
sheets of water wobbling on the horizon.
They bring to a patched place
their bags of books, boxes of crockery,
the wind sneaking around the tents.

Cruel idleness
chatter patter

With his old camera
he'd captured Europe in its wreck,
but the grey bribe, the food gone rotten,
black-market poison, betrayal and tears
and fire along the artery, at the
end of talent's alley, a poor schooling,
those things were never photographed.

He'd shot his neighbour at night, he said;
a thing too terrible to speak about,
children, a deed not done, the orphans' home –
thin bread perishing in the rain . . .
I ask you men in front, in another tongue,
Did you see the heap of red?
One of our own race
under the car, the tank,
the slot,
the fire – just
one blade forged and beaten,
sharpened for the throat, now
snapped.
Rub out my name, erase the digits,
I wasn't there.
I don't remember.

They damned me, but hope is the drink
and the dialect.

He tries to read the faded snapshot
of a girl smiling in a vegetable garden –

a bean plant strung up against a stick –
he squints through the watery light –
now there's a skyline wavering into smoke, and
his dead family squabbling in his X-ray visions.
The old delirium: The police have seen us!
Then rivers full of bones rise up,
flooding the cobbles and the town square . . .

He was born high, and great minds
gilded his dinner table.
Fade then, memory.
Perhaps the idea of luxury is European,
and in this disarray of landscape, a crime.
He doesn't fit in, he's all
fractures, his shadowy advantage –
The wheel turns backwards,
and he's washing floors, such waste,
a philosopher among yokels.

A quicksand religion, they'll eat you up.
At nightfall people come calling,
fear and hatred spill off their lips,
young couples follow, and old widowers,
pitiful, the endless histories,
the happiest memories the most painful,
exhaustion, looking through a blurred lens.
See, the couples dressed up, there
in the background of the village wedding photo
mostly dead now,
shot and murdered,
among the beasts in that stadium, some escaped
and grew, learning enough cunning to survive.
And the place is every dirt road,

lit by smoking flares. Yet
there is kindness.
And this
fetch of disparate peoples
assigned to come possessionless into massive
light.

WHILE THE DRUM BEATS, 'STOP THE BOATS'
ELLIOT PERLMAN

It took me almost six years to research and write my most recent book, *The Street Sweeper*, a novel that deals with, among other things, history and various kinds of racism. One of the things I did for my mental health as much as for my physical health during those six years was to jog or at least walk, pretty much every day.

One morning, unusually early for someone so frequently in the merciless, tepid yet unforgiving grip of insomnia, I was pounding my way down the road when I noticed a tradesman of some kind inside the cabin of his ute with a fork in his hand, focusing his attention on the fork and the contents of a transparent plastic container. The man had black hair and brown skin. He looked thin. There are so many places on earth he could have come from and now he was in my neighbourhood.

As I got closer I tried to see what it was he was eating. It was early enough for it to be the man's breakfast, but the dust already on his clothes allowed the possibility that, even that early, he had been working for some time. So perhaps it was his morning tea? And I wondered, what was that in the transparent container? Was it a traditional dish from whatever far-off place he had come from that he was savouring in the early hours of the morning, temporarily away from the worksite of his employer whose house the black-haired, brown-skinned man could never even aspire to for himself and his wife?

As I drew level with the driver's door, I looked into the cabin of the dark-skinned tradesman's ute to see precisely what he was eating. Going too fast to satisfy myself with any certainty as to his food, I was there just long enough to see the man's face. And that's where I saw the sequelae of the disease we identify as racism.

Having seen me coming as I ran on the road towards him, his face was a cocktail of embarrassment, apprehension and defiance. Why was he embarrassed? Because, I surmised, he'd been caught eating his 'wog' food, some kind of weird concoction we don't yet eat. Why was he apprehensive? Because a white man was running towards him, possibly with hostile intent. Why was he defiant? Because he'd been in Australia long enough to know that he had to be?

He'd been here long enough to organise a car and a job, so whatever his first language, whatever difficulties he had with English, he'd heard strident rants perhaps on a building site and cascades of invective about the foreigners on talkback radio. Perhaps, like the rest of us, he hears simple language used over and over to frighten us, used like a drum that never stops beating. 'Stop the boats! Stop the boats!'

He knows it's not really the boats that are the problem. Why has a nation of some 23 million been obsessed for the last ten years or more with a problem that sees, at most, 6000 desperate people caught trying to come to Australia without permission? It can't be the number itself because 6000 out of 23 million is insignificant. Let's be honest with each other. We know, just as the man in the ute knows, it's the kind of people who are trying to get here. What kind of people are they? They're brown, they're Asian, sometimes they're black, they don't speak English. This is not really a national problem deserving of the almost relentless attention it's been getting in the Australian media for more than ten years: more attention than the Indians who get bashed and sometimes murdered on our streets; more attention than the massive disparity in life expectancy, educational and employment opportunities between indigenous Australians and the rest of us; more attention than the fact that our farmers are getting squeezed till they can barely afford to stay on the land and the country towns they're from are losing their young; more attention than the fact that 47 per cent of adult Australians are functionally illiterate; more attention than the exporting of jobs offshore; more attention than the destruction of our manufacturing sector to the point where we don't really make anything here but lattes and hairdressing appointments; more attention than the disguised unemployment that sees just under two million people wanting to work full time now or in the next four weeks having either no work or too little; more attention than the more than two million Australians who live in a household where no one has a job. These are among Australia's real problems. These problems really matter. Then there are the environmental problems that are just our own and the existential problem we share with the rest of the world – climate change.

But despite these very real and pressing problems Australia faces, we're more likely to wake up to the chant in the media: 'Stop the boats! Stop the boats!' And we keep hearing that because both major parties find these other problems so difficult they don't even acknowledge the existence of most of them. But they know that there are votes in the exploitation of the latent xenophobia in most of us. And so they compete with each other in their exclusion of the weak and persecuted with a different skin colour or different religion.

A few mornings after I first saw the brown-skinned workman eating something in the cabin of his ute, I was pounding the streets when I saw him in his ute again. This time there was a child beside him, a little boy looking every inch the boyhood version of his father. While his father instinctively looked away as I came towards the ute, the little boy's attention was captivated by the person running in a regular rhythm and getting closer and closer as I came towards them. Children are not born hating or fearing other groups. We teach them that. In fact, children don't even know who's in their group and who isn't. Ask a six-year-old to name the kids in his or her class and he or she will give you a list of names that includes many nearly unpronounceable ones without realising that any of those names are unusual.

The little boy's black eyes widened as I drew level with him and his dad inside their ute. He smiled, and when I waved he gave me a cheery wave back. Will he grow up with an experience of life in Australia engendering a ready-made expression of embarrassment, apprehension and defiance whenever a stranger looks at him? Or will he keep smiling and waving? The default expression he acquires, between now and the time he grows up will be determined by us. Which is it going to be? It's entirely up to you.

THE MASTER SHAVERS' ASSOCIATION OF PARADISE
DEBRA ADELAIDE

Early on the morning of the final day, you are ready to leave. You have already packed your belongings into the government-issue striped carryall. One for each person but one is too much. You could have fitted your cousin's and your uncle's possessions in your carryall alone, but it is too late for that. As it is, the fat blue-and-red stripes sag somewhere around the middle, whereas those of others who have already left seemed to have contained enough to make a firm, proud rectangle. You look around the room. You could take the blanket off the camp stretcher, or the stretcher itself, which dismantles and folds into a package. But these items belong to the camp, to the contractors, or to the government. You compromise by taking the towel. Grey-blue, the colour of marine paint, it is still damp. It will not dry before you leave. You fold the towel and place it on the top of the carryall, and then turn to face the open doorway. The little sign – a piece of cardboard with chalked lettering that you propped up every day next to the doorway – has already been taken down.

You sit on the step and look across the quadrangle, empty apart from puddles gleaming in the early light, to the huts in the row opposite. Their doors are held open with cabin hooks to comply with the regulation airing, their windows already shuttered with plywood. Beyond is a line of palms – you can just see the tops of them brushing against the morning sky – and beyond that is the hill that slopes down to the water and although the beach is bounded by a wall of rocks and barbed wire and you have never once felt these waves lap at your bare feet or even seen the colour of the water or the sand, you have heard the sea, day and night, and you hear it now, slapping at the shore. They cannot stop you hearing.

A good hour previously, you had gone outside and stepped down the long muddy pathway between the tents, careful to avoid the potholes from the rain, to the shower block at the end of the row. At that hour it was still dark, but it was better to wash alone in the dark than jostle at first light with the other men. The men were fewer, as it was the last day, but the showers had never been sufficient, as if two or three years back the camp were expecting a dozen men, not hundreds.

But the water was very clean. There were plastic rain barrels at each end of the larger sheds. These were bright blue, stamped MAUSER BIOFUEL, which some of the men said meant toxic but you'd never been sure. All the tents had buckets parked at the corners to catch the drips. And when you moved into your uncle's hut you took it with you in case the men were right about BIOFUEL – not that it would have made any difference, not after all this time. Unfortunately your bucket was bright pink, but then so were many others so you could tolerate the joking, though you would have preferred grey, or blue. Even yellow would have been preferable. Nevertheless in your pink bucket you still collected Paradise's purest, even up to today, the very last day, for it rained frequently.

You took this bucket to the shower block. There were meant to be plastic bowls set all along the wooden bench that ran opposite the latrines, but most had gone missing, which was a shame. A bowl would have been so much better for your business, these past few months. The conveniences were not very convenient. Men crouched there unconcernedly in the stalls, separated by a flimsy plywood panel not even waist height, and no doors. They stared back at you from the far end of the block, rising and hitching their trousers afterwards without so much as a glance back at their mess, barely breaking eye contact with you, the flies descending greedily the second they left. They were the kind of men who never came to you as clients, never spoke to you, never glanced at you except those times in the shower block, when they would stare so hard you would understand, without the need for words, the precise nature of your status in the camp. These were the men who would do nothing day after day but lie on their camp stretcher beds and smoke. From time to time one of these men would, as if on a roster system, throw himself at the fence screaming obscenities about the guards' mothers or sisters, and then be taken off to solitary detention with a look on his face as if he were an avenging angel who had stormed the gates of hell.

You did not shave, this last morning, as there were no more razors. Fortunately you had shaved cleanly a week before they were banned altogether and now you have produced a neat new stubble beard. You set your bucket on the bench and scooped some water out to rub over your face and neck. The day before there had been a sliver of soap like a cuttlefish bone, but in the dark you could not find it. You rubbed and rinsed with Paradise's purest, saving the last bit to clean your teeth and rinse your mouth. Your toothbrush was in the side pocket, velcroed, of your cargo pants. You were meant to hand this in every night but somehow yours had gone unnoticed despite the extra vigilance. Or maybe the guards no longer cared, now that it was the final day. As you examined it, holding it out in the growing light, you saw how the bristles were all flattened. Over the months you have so chewed and worn it down that how it could ever be turned into a weapon puzzled you. But then you had seen a man slash himself with one carefully cultivated thumbnail, slicing across his other wrist as if he were cutting through banana skin. You had seen men tattoo each other with

iron nails filed back to fine points. You once saw a man stitch his lips
with plastic thread teased from a rope and a needle made from a dried
chicken bone.

You dried your face and neck with the grey-blue towel and scraped
your damp hair back with your fingers, pressing the curls as flat as
you could. Now that there was only you, the last member of the
Association, you did your best with what you were left.

The day you arrived your uncle took you around the camp and ate his
evening meal with you and sat on a stool in front of your tent until
the other men had gone to sleep, when he left for his hut in the second
row, across the quadrangle. And the next morning he appeared again
to stand with you so you would not be confused or bullied. Before
breakfast he took you to the shower block, where the guard distrib-
uted plastic disposable razors. Like lollipops, they were handed out
one at a time, each recorded in a book with a pencil tick. Your uncle
grabbed you by the arm and took you to the bench inside.

Ten minutes, he said, they will collect them again in ten minutes.
You have to be quick.

How will we know? you said. No one here had a watch.

They'll ring a bell. And if we're not done a guard will take it off us,
mid-stroke if necessary.

You laughed. But maybe he was right. You looked around. The
showers were a long open-sided building with a low tin roof and
blue plastic sheeting attached to one side, to protect from rain, you
assumed. A long wooden bench contained a stack of plastic basins.
Two stainless steel sinks were covered in plywood, the taps above them
wrapped in plastic bags.

They've never worked since I've been here, your uncle said.
Instead of a mirror, a polished steel sheet was screwed onto the timber walls above the bench. Opposite were the doorless stalls with low
dividers and lower toilets with no seats, also steel, but not stainless,
rather they were very stained. There were two men in the cubicles

staring at you as if shitting were an act of aggression. The three stand-ing at the trough next to them were pissing at the one spot on the wall as if in competition.

Come on. Your uncle grabbed your face, then after staring a few seconds laughed and thrust your chin away, slapping your cheek.

Puppy, he said. You are just a fuzzy pup.

You felt your face. It was true. Your struggling beard still shamed you. It was like baby's hair.

That's what Mr Kondappan used to say, you said to your uncle. He would not believe I was fifteen already.

And then the mention of Mr Kondappan made your words clog somewhere in your throat. You stood very still willing your face to remain immobile. Your mouth threatened to become too loose. Your uncle opened wide his arms and embraced you.

My boy, he whispered, my boy. We must be only grateful that you are safe.

Over his shoulder you squeezed your eyes so hard to stop the tears it hurt. When you opened them one of the shitting men was staring right at you. He brought his cigarette to his mouth and inhaled and exhaled slowly then let out a long loud fart into the bowl he was squat-ting over.

You do me then, your uncle said. Let's be quick.

That you could do. This is where you were skilled, where you could take charge. You would never see him again but you would make Mr Kondappan proud. You placed your uncle's towel over his chest and standing there beside the wooden bench rinsed the razor in the cold pure water then rubbed the soap into your palms.

No lather, you said.

It's all we have, he said. You'll get used to it.

You soaped his face then applied the razor. It was white, with an orange head. It said Bic. The blade was spotted with rust. You scraped down one cheek then the next.

Careful of my moustache, he said.

It needs a trim, old man, you told him. He nudged you. Later, he said. I think I can find some scissors.

He rinsed and dried while you washed your face and as you were both combing your hair the shitting man pushed past you. His beard was rough and tangled. The guard appeared with his box and book just in time, and your uncle handed the razor back and had his name ticked again. The box was tin, with a lid and a lock. Inside were about a dozen disposable razors. The guard snapped the lid shut and took it away.

You began to notice the number of men walking around badly or half shaven, or scraped all over their faces. Some men were like Janus, with half a beard on one side of the face, a stubbly but clean face on the other. Conversing with these men was improbable, like talking to a circus freak. Shaving was permitted every five days. Your uncle joined you most of those mornings, to line up, be checked on then off, and you shaved him, and it was always a scrappy soapy mess but you did your best. Sometimes the Bic disposable was too rusted. There were also some blue Gillette Double Blades in the locked tin and once or twice you were lucky enough to get these. As you shaved him your uncle stared at you and you at him. You were his mirror. You tried not to notice how like your mother's were his eyes, how the eyebrows arched then tapered past the eyes towards his hairline in the same way. Soon you began using your own bucket, and the grey-blue towel that was finally issued two weeks after your arrival in Paradise.

After a month you stopped asking what there was to do. The first time your uncle laughed at you and then, uncharacteristically savage in a low voice so Mani could not hear, told you, Stay sane. And shut up. Just shut up. He was afraid of the guards but also of the shitting men, the ones who would hurl themselves at the fence screaming. The same men who refused food, for weeks if they could. They would still line up in the mess hall but then, not breaking eye contact with the orderly, would tip the contents of their plates onto the floor and then the plates, before turning and walking out. But you ate the breakfast – porridge, bread, margarine and jam – and washed your plastic plate along with the others and returned it to its place in the mess hall, and walked around the quadrangle, like the others. Like all the others you sat in the opening of your tent and stared at the others sitting at the opening of their tents. When you moved to the hut you sat with your uncle and Mani in the doorway, and stared at the other men sitting in their doorways. When it rained you sat and watched the rain. If it was not raining you walked around the quadrangle in the mud. Your pair of running shoes was soon filthy, but like all the others you set them aside and went barefoot. You sat and waited for lunch – ham in perfect squares, sometimes sausages, and bread – walked some more and waited for dinner. Rice, pasta, sloppy mince in gravy. Potatoes, boiled, mashed and often in their skins and still gritty. Once a week you had an orange, or a banana.

Sometimes you and your cousin would sit in a corner of the quadrangle, or behind the kitchen shed, or up by the gate. Mani was twelve, large for his age, unlike you – still growing at sixteen, still sporting a laughable beard at seventeen – otherwise he might have been sent with the other children to the mainland. We are the lucky ones, your uncle said again and again, you and me and Maniyarasan, we are lucky, we must be grateful. Mani would stare at his father at this. You knew how much he hated hearing these things, though he did not contradict him.

Mani and you would speak in whispers. The water, the hunger, the parching heat and of course the thirst when there was water all around. He was in the water, along with your uncle and seven other men, rescued after a night and most of the following day. They were lucky, your uncle says, because they had a lifebuoy to share. Mani did not care that the beach on Paradise was forbidden. He would be happy never to see the ocean again. Sometimes sitting at dusk by the gate a quietness descended as if the whole island was asleep, and then you were aware of the slap of waves down on the forbidden beach.

Mani sometimes clamped his hands over his ears and walked back
to his hut. He spent a lot of time on his camp stretcher bed with the
blanket over his head.

After your first three months you had walked the perimeter so thor-
oughly you knew every rut in the path, every puddle after rain, every
rock, every weed. You couldn't lie and smoke and stare like the others.
After the tenth or hundredth game of playing cards you thought you
would die of boredom. Your uncle would patiently deal the cards, so
worn they were barely readable, sitting on the stool in front of his hut,
using your upturned pink bucket for a table.

For six months the Red Cross ran a weekly afternoon discussion
group. They served Cheezels while men practised the new language.
*Cheezels are made from cheese. Cheese is made from milk. Milk comes from
a cow.* There was also orange cordial from a large orange plastic barrel
with a big M on the top. You pronounced the words, *orange, drink,
thank you, thirsty*, and held the Cheezels up to your eye before popping
them in your mouth. They tasted good but not of cheese. You did not
say you had been learning English since you commenced school, nor
that your school had been closed down when you were eleven, when all
the teachers disappeared and the buildings shot up one night.

The Red Cross worker left a year ago. There was also a library, in a
converted Kombi van. The library volunteer set out plastic crates with
magazines, *National Geographic*, and *Reader's Digest*, plus English
language primers and comics for beginners, and an entire set of Ian
Fleming's James Bond books, *Casino Royale* to *Octopussy* and *The
Living Daylights*, with clever covers: a bullet shooting a hole into the
title page; playing cards fanned out against green cloth. One day your
English would be good enough to read them, but before that time
arrived, the volunteer stopped appearing every Thursday afternoon.

The men began their own smoking club, down behind the mess
hall late at night, where hidden packets of favourite cigarette brands or
tobacco would be mysteriously produced and traded. Longbeach and

Champion were the most prized brands, if they could be obtained. White Ox tobacco and Ventti papers, sometimes handed over, one at a time, in return for favours, information, documents, signatures, anything, even promises. One packet of cigarettes for a name that would give you a passage to freedom. You did not smoke, and your uncle never participated, retreating to his hut doorway and playing cards laid out on the upturned bucket. The Red Cross parcels that brought Champion and White Ox also brought essentials and other small indulgences: Lux and Palmolive soap, Cadbury's chocolate, dried fruit, socks, writing materials, sunscreen.

The camp rule forbade long beards. It was better to shave badly, or to use the scissors, than fight it. The guards were meant to supervise a proper trimming. All the scissors were aluminium bladed, with bright green plastic handles, however if a man was lucky he would get a new pair and it would not tug as much, at least for the first few times.

You had no need for the scissor option. Your beard, what Mr Kondappan had kindly called incipient, straggled down the sides of your face like a delicate weed. You still trimmed it and rubbed oil down your cheeks to make it shine. Meanwhile you made yourself useful, for the men who wanted a shave but did not have your patience with the rusty Bics. The guard handing out the razors got to know you every few days and after several months the ten-minute rule was not quite so rigid.

In the shop Mr Kondappan had had a cutthroat razor and a leather strop and he had begun to teach you the art of proper barbering. You had long and steady fingers, he said. You were his best apprentice by far and although your job, when you were not sweeping the floor, was to whisk the badger-hair shaving brush in the cup of soap to make the creamy foam just as he liked it, you had already learned a great deal. It was when you were out the back rinsing the brushes and combs that you heard the van as its tyres squealed to a stop. You heard shouts, then shots, then the squeal of the van again, and in seconds it was over and you were left staring out into the street that had been busy five minutes before, empty now but for the smell of burned rubber. And no one had seen a thing. It was not that people were unsympathetic. Just unwilling to get involved. When you left, bewildered, you were still holding the badger-hair brush so tight your knuckles were white. You took it with you when you fled. It was in the backpack along with everything else at the bottom of the Indian Ocean.

Once, lawyers came. At least your uncle thought they were lawyers, but on reflection no one was sure. They could have just been government officials, secretaries, bureaucrats, policy makers. They were driven up to the camp gate in 4x4s and set up an office in an empty shed, with their boxes of papers wheeled in on a trolley. You were called in one by one, five or ten minutes each. The men all waited sitting at their doors as usual and when your uncle filed back you saw there were tears in his eyes.

What happened? Will you be freed? you said, but he pushed past you shaking his head and gathering Mani inside he shut the door to your hut. You waited your turn in the corner of the quadrangle where the queue lined the perimeter. When the guard called your name you were parched in the mouth, but not from the heat. The guard, like all the others, had AIDS emblazoned on his shirt and it had taken you weeks before someone explained it did not stand for the disease but for the immigration detention service of the country you yearned to go to.

The man two places before you in the queue began crying. I wanted my children to be free, he said. I only wanted them to go to school and learn as I had learned and not be frightened that the next lesson would come from the barrel of an automatic. He cried again, a sniffling noise that made the man in front of you turn around and snigger. And then they took my wife and daughters anyway, he said, and so I left with my sons. They have drowned.

The man in front stopped sniggering but now had a look of contempt on his face as if to say to you, Only drowned? He should be so lucky. There was no room for compassion here in the camp.

When you went in, the look on the faces of the three lawyers or officials was profound boredom. In the corner behind them sat an oscillating fan. On the trestle table desk, large pebbles held down folders of papers that protested in the breeze as the fan rotated back and forth, back and forth. The questions were fast. No, you had no papers, no passport, nothing that would prove who you are. They had all gone in your only backpack, lost when the boat capsized. You had even kept your indentured papers from Mr Kondappan.

Can I get another passport? you said. Can I get a visa? Can I leave this place? Please sirs, when can I leave?

They looked at each other. The fan's rotating head caught a flurry of papers in its wake. One of them, loosening his tie, said, Steady on mate, where do you think you are?

Where? Somewhere that gave you a bed to sleep in, and shelter from the rain and the sun. Where there were beautiful meals, white bread and gravy mince, three times a day and a banana on Tuesdays. Where you could drink the water, which never ran out. Where men walked round rubbing their hands over their clean chins, wearing clothes that no longer stank of diesel fuel and rotting fish and salt water. Where there were no corpses of your mother, your sisters, your friends, to be hauled out and tossed away. Where the waves could not swallow you or worse: spit you out and let you live a little longer under the unblinking sun. Where there were no men to point their weapons at your groin, your head, your heart, simply because someone somewhere once decided that your corner of your country, your language, your religion, were subordinate to theirs.

You did not care that this was the place where men threw themselves at the chain link fence screaming, where men stitched their lips and were taken away for refusing food for more than a week, this to you was a place that had saved you from hell, and you told them so. Paradise, you said. I am in Paradise.

Parcels would come. From Red Cross, from Amnesty International, from the Coalition of Christians for Refugees. Allowed to help unpack and distribute them, you examined the labels, sounding out the strange names of so many worthy groups. The Asylum Seekers' Action Group, Lions clubs, the Salvation Army, the Women's Peace and Green Party. An organisation called the Young Matrons' Welfare Association of Ginninderra ACT, which you later learned was in the political heart of the country that sent you here, if heart was the right word. The parcels contained toiletries, handkerchiefs, snack foods. Once there was an entire box of Lux soaps chipped and dented but still okay. The men laughed at scents like Supreme Cream and Exotic Aromas, but took them from you anyway, to hide under their clothes or in their beds. Sometimes the parcels brought clothing: track pants all the same colour with sporting names on them. Your first winter in Paradise, dozens of men walked around wearing maroon pants with Junior Pro League printed down the side of one leg. Everyone fought over the Bondi Breakers baseball caps, though no one cared for the sport. You were happy to unpack and distribute these parcels to help the numbing boredom before it got to you like it seemed to have hollowed out so many of the men, including the shitters who stared at you as they crouched and smoked as if their life depended on it, and maybe it did.

But a week or so after the lawyers/officials departed, men were still walking around talking of their new life, as soon as they would leave. Even the shitters were seen talking in huddles, with a look of expectancy in their eyes. One of them almost smiled. Another charity box arrived and by now you knew that the AIDS guards were likely to keep these parcels from you as punishment or for fun, their fun. But this time you were called over to the guardhouse at the gate. The box was already ripped open and the contents tossed about, most of the items out of their packaging, but that was normal.

Toiletries, the guard said. You're the kid who likes shaving and that, aren't you?

Barber, sir. Third-year apprentice, you said.

You take this, then; see if you want any of this. I reckon no one else will be interested, not with your hairy lot.

There was more Lux, this time only Exotic Aromas, and tubes of Colgate toothpaste, and other products squashed and split and out of their boxes: shaving gel and foam cream, aftershave balm. Vaseline hair oil. Gillette and Palmolive and a brand you hadn't seen before – Fast, with a large signature across every tube. Fast Aloe Vera Shaving Gel, by Ross MacDowell, Master Shaver. Fast Shea Butter Face Balm, by Ross MacDowell, Master Shaver.

What is this master shaver? your uncle said when you showed him. He has some kind of award for it?

Don't laugh, uncle, you said.

Mr Kondappan had taken you on as a promise to your father, before he disappeared. He wore a pale blue buttoned tunic and had a red-and-white striped pole outside the shop. He favoured sticks of Palmolive shaving soap, and hair waxes that came in tins, ordered from America. Mr Kondappan, who could have been a master shaver if there were an award for it, was in his shop on the wrong day, along with tens of others when white vans with missing numberplates tore through the town. The soldiers trashed the barbershop, smashing the window with the red-and-white pole before dragging him out to the street and into the van. When you crept home, much later under cover of night, your mother opened up the box where she kept her valuables – wedding certificate, birth notices, your grandfather's silver cigarette case, and your grandmother's rings. Enough, she said, we have had enough, controlling her sobs in front of your wide-eyed little sister. This will be enough for three fares, she said, handing you a large sapphire ring, and when you reached out for it you realised you still held tight the badger-hair shaving brush.

Afterwards, you had an idea. The guard shrugged, though later you would wonder at his calculated indifference. You put up your sign, chalk on cardboard, propped at the doorway to your uncle's hut. The Master Shavers' Association of Paradise. Free Life Membership. Shaves and Haircuts. No appt. necessary. At the bottom of the box, under the litter of packaging from toothpaste tubes and plastic combs, was a torn pack of razors, Gillette Proglide, a six-pack, one razor overlooked. Gillette, the best a man can get. Overlooked, or ignored. You took this to your tent and hid it in the bottom of your bedroll, then took it out to the dark gap behind the step and the hut, and then put it into the pocket of your cargo pants. You would be responsible for this razor, and you had the right to it, of all the men in Paradise.

Mani and you were sitting at the doorway under your sign when your uncle appeared from mess hall duty, panting from having run across the quadrangle.

Are you crazy?

Maybe, you said, but at least I will not be bored.

Listen, he said, six men have just been taken away. It is said they had ropes, shaped as nooses, in their tents. There will be an inspection, he said, looking over his shoulder. Soon, before dark. Take down your sign.

No, you said. But you hid your razor, this time under the cement slab step.

The Master Shavers' Association flourished and you performed numerous excellent shaves and many beard trims until one morning your Gillette Proglide was missing, and later that very same day a man was carted off with bleeding wrists.

And now it is the last day in Paradise. Your uncle and Mani were taken away some weeks before, and in all that time none of the remaining men have spoken a word to you. At least the men in their stalls no longer stared at you. There has been a report, it is said, several reports. The guards are doubled, and the clients are diminished. Clients, you are now called. You have not read these reports, naturally, but representatives of Red Cross have returned to discuss developments with you, part of your basic rights, you are told. You are now called clients and the Red Cross representatives report details. The clients are termed problematic. The clients do not cooperate with security personnel. Clients refuse to formalise their concerns in writing. Clients continue to be involved in voluntary starvation protests. Clients are being monitored. Termination of client services is imminent.

You, one of the last clients, wait at the doorway of your hut until a whistle will blow, after which you will be transported through the gates onto a truck and thence to the landing strip further into the island. After all this time, during which your beard has finally grown to something respectable, and you have attained your full height, or so your uncle claimed, you will leave still not having sighted the waves on the beach that you hear as you sit beside your carryall and wait, your cardboard sign in your hands.

THE TRUE STORY OF MY FATHER
SUE WOOLFE

When he was very young, Dad impulsively did something that changed his life forever, and the lives of his children, on and on through the generations. Yet we never knew about it; in fact, he never dared tell a living soul in this country about it, except perhaps my mother, though even of that I'm not sure. If he did, it does at least explain in part their unlikely life-long collusion.

I also knew little about my mother's past, but on her deathbed she gave me an old daguerreotype of my grandmother's grandmother. In my astonished hand was my mother's face, but this was not my mother, this was a laughing Spanish coquette under a flamboyant confection of a bonnet. My mother explained that the picture was of the daughter of military might and great wealth. 'She eloped with the enemy's drummer boy,' my mother said. She could see I was charmed and her emaciated face glowed, revelling in her ancestors' fateful escapade. In her last few hours of life, she became that daring teenager. It was the closest I'd ever been to my mother.

It all unfolded like this. We were a large family, at first. I had four older brothers, and then there was me, the youngest and the only girl. My parents were an odd pair: my mother in turns removed and terrifyingly intense, my father amusing but easily horrified at his children's demands for new shoes, exercise books, pens. 'You'll put us in the workhouse,' he'd say.

'What's a workhouse?' I remember asking.

'A prison,' he said, the humour drained from his voice. From then on, I'd carefully temper my demands, using, for instance, the same toothbrush until the bristles were splayed out in horizontal lines. It still seems a luxury to me to have a toothbrush with vertical bristles.

But my mother would say:

'Don't tell them that sort of thing.'

As I look back, I ask myself: was there a warning in her voice of what she might divulge if he disobeyed? She had a way of commanding us all, as if she was born to it. And she so yearned for us to be a middle-class family. Perhaps he did too. But now I wonder if more was going on.

She'd say the same when we'd beg him for stories of his childhood – we were forbidden to ask my mother for stories because, my father told me one day when we were alone, she'd been brought up in an orphanage from the age of seven though she was not an orphan, and no stories were permitted about that orphanage.

But my father's London childhood sometimes spilled out, and we carefully constrained children delighted in glimpses of what seemed to us a scandalous, licentious life. For example, he'd gone without shoes, a glorious liberty we were only allowed on the beach. Once when I complained about soggy salad sandwiches in my brown bag school lunch, he said he'd have been lucky to have been given bread wrapped in a bit of newspaper.

'Newspaper,' I'd echoed enviously. And I longed to ask Mum – but didn't dare – to wrap our sandwiches in a sheet of newspaper, which I'd be able to smooth out and read at school, rustling it importantly like an adult on a bus.

When I complained about having to eat an apple every day, he said that he and his brother considered themselves lucky that they lived near the markets, because markets have big rubbish heaps of fruit if you get in early for the best bits.

'So eat your apple your mother has washed nicely for you.'

Once he told a story of how he'd seen ripe pears hanging from over a fence, and he'd climbed up and across a roof for them. I see them still, the golden pendulous pears glowing against the dark leaves like light globes. But the roof was a glass house and he'd fallen through —

'Don't tell them these things,' said my mother.

He was always hushed so easily.

'Did you get away?' my brother asked when my mother was out of the room.

'I was always lucky,' he said.

When my brothers wanted to deliver newspapers before school, he said that he'd got up at four in the morning himself and worked two jobs.

Unlike my brothers who didn't want to go to school, he'd been in the scholarship class, and planned to become an architect, but he'd had to leave at twelve.

'Why?' I asked in quick sympathy, because I was the bookworm of the family and hoped to be allowed to remain at school, even though I was only a girl.

'To support my family,' he answered.

In my imagination he was like my brothers, bicycling around the neighbourhood, importantly hurling rolled newspapers over trimmed hedges and into neat front gardens.

There were no photographs of his mother, his father or Florrie or John or Frederick or George or him – I can still recite their names, these children of such liberty who were allowed to be shoeless and rummage in rubbish heaps. Only a postcard showing a suspension bridge – in Pitlochry, Scotland, said the quaint, old-fashioned print.

'I'd walk that bridge wearing a kilt,' he said. 'The wind would blow ice up my legs.' He told us that he and his brothers and sister went for holidays to his mother's parents in Pitlochry, but suddenly that all ceased. Before Mum could stop him he managed to burst out in a thick Scottish brogue a few lines:

If they say it's a bright bright moonlit night,
That's all right, ye ken.

Instead of becoming an architect, he went to work in a munitions factory with his brother. He walked miles there with his brother every morning, and back again at night. There were often explosions, and they worked in small huts to prevent the explosions taking the entire place out. Their hut exploded.

'Was your brother all right?' I asked. (I managed not to ask him if he'd lived, which would've brought scorn from my brothers.)

'We were only singed,' he said. 'I was always lucky.'

It was then he decided to go to sea instead, to be what he called a 'navy'.

Anyway, he needed to run away from his mother —

'Don't,' commanded my mother.

By a peculiar quirk of fate, my parents shared the same birthday, 10th May, though they were born years apart. There seemed to be about a decade between my mother and Dad, 'seemed', because I grew up thinking he'd been born in 1901, one of my brothers thought 1903, and another brother thought 1905. We were all firm in the knowledge, however, that he'd been born in the world's cultural centre, the most civilised, the only sophisticated city in the world. He'd joined the navy   we never knew to ask if it was the navy or the merchant navy – his ship had been torpedoed but somehow he sailed on and eventually came to this cultural desert, Australia. He'd landed in Adelaide, he told me, he'd fallen in love with the light and had gone

bush and become a rabbito, he told me, a painter of bush schools, he'd
told my brothers. I still see my childhood picture of him: a boy in a
white and blue sailor suit – sailor-suit blouses were very fashionable
in my childhood, so I was on home ground there – stumbling down
a gangplank like the one at Circular Quay, tripping over the raised
boards meant to steady people's disembarking, but he was dazed by
light, his astounded eyes not on the unfamiliar city before him, but
fixed on the transparent heights above him.

We didn't think to ask him when this had happened. With the
immersion of children in the present, it was enough to know he'd
come to Australia and met our mother, the important events for us.
He was probably banking on that childish immersion. And he was
glad to get on to a more comfortable subject.

'The smell of Australia,' he said. A man who crept up shyly on
words, he tried for more accuracy. 'The perfume,' he managed. He'd
been up the mast, and for hours before he sighted land, he'd smelled
the spicy sweet eucalypts.

'I had to see those trees,' he said.

'What's a rabbito?' I asked.

'I was good at it, lucky, always lucky. Rabbits were everywhere,
food for the taking. I'd catch them, skin them and sell them to house-
wives, they'd be at their doors, ready with the money. '"Rabbito,"' I'd
call' – his voice high, remembering, laughing.

'Stop it,' warned my mother.

He was enjoying the telling. Satisfied she'd silenced his memory,
she left the room.

I knew the romantic story of their meeting at a dance. He'd taken
from his pocket some paper and a carpenter's pencil and drawn a
house – the house he'd build for her if she'd marry him. She'd asked
what the dots at the windows were, and he'd said simply:

'Our children.'

Now he told me what became until her deathbed my only
knowledge of my mother's past – that her mother, my Australian

grandmother, had no sooner been introduced to him at Central Station than she punched him on the nose.

'What did you do?' I asked.

'Fell over,' he said. 'On my back. There on the platform.'

'Why did she punch you?' I asked.

'She thought I was putting off marrying your mother, I suppose,' he said. 'She hated men. A man had stolen her fortune.'

'Fortune!' I gasped. It sounded like something out of a fairy tale.

'But I was only waiting for the fuss to die down. Your mother, she was the most beautiful creature ever.'

He paused, thinking, I was sure, of my mother's black cascading Spanish hair, blue-black in the shadows, and her huge, brown eyes, which, when she fixed them on you, however thin and prickly you were with indignation, you'd become like water and swim into her. I longed to belong to her, belong to her beauty, I longed to have it for myself, especially since I believed she'd accept me more if I looked like her.

'Beauty is a woman's passport,' she often said, to my despair.

But my looks stubbornly refused to comply with my wishes – which is probably why I remained Dad's child.

So I didn't ask, What fuss?

Instead I asked the question that intrigued me more.

'What fortune?'

Apparently my mother's mother had given away the fortune inherited from the wealthy Spanish eloping and deserting ancestors, to a man only known in the family by a photo – a doctor with a hat tipped on one side, to hide his scheming eyes.

Dad had two jobs. One we weren't allowed to tell kids at school about. As for the other, the proper one, he was a handyman. We were living in the Blue Mountains then, with bushfires raging, it seemed, every summer, when the water tanks were empty. There were always burnt-out, sadly abandoned houses, only a stone chimney still standing, and a blackened shell. You could buy them for next to nothing. We'd move into a blackened shell, and soon there'd be walls, floorboards, a roof, and when it looked like any ordinary house he'd sell it and we'd move to the next shell. Around us, many families lived in Nissen huts. The family in one street nearby, the Ormes, cooked on open fires, always, it seemed to me, on jolly holidays like we could never afford to have, camping like The Famous Five. But Mum ordered us to look the other way when we passed. We weren't allowed to play with them. When we misbehaved, she'd say: 'You're behaving like an Orme kid.'

But in my childish estimation, my parents behaved far worse than the Ormes, despite the hope of bringing us up to a middle-class life. They often screamed at each other, their fingers around each other's throats, her long smooth lovely olive-skinned neck, his red, crumpled one. Only in those moments, when I feared for my mother's life, was I my mother's daughter. The rest of the time, I was the child of Dad's soul.

Then one of my brothers died of meningitis, from a germ in the milk of a cow in next door's paddock. Another brother, wild, incoherent and unmanageable, probably autistic, but in the parlance of the day an imbecile, had to be taken away and put into a home, to die there. We were never to visit him. Grief rolled in our door.

My mother was blamed; in the family talk, he'd been 'a beautiful baby in his pram', and my mother had failed him.

But my father refused to sign the papers to send him away, refused to put his name to them. He had to be signed away under my mother's name.

'What a bastard,' my mother's relatives said. 'Fancy disowning your own child. He didn't want his name besmirched.'

One day I came upon Dad sobbing while he painted, and, transfixed at the door, knew he'd disowned no one.

Life's fragility continued to intrude. My parents more often than ever had their fingers on each other's throats, for my grief-stricken mother became ungovernably violent. In the night she shouted lies, the truth of which she believed steadfastly. I concluded that she wasn't lying, though what she said wasn't the truth, and learned to think of her lies as 'Mum's truth'. We were entirely unchurched but had heard in school scripture lessons about God and Satan – in fact I could recite the whole of John 3:16 on the thrilling trip in my brothers' billy-cart before it crashed into the heap of asbestos in the back yard:

'For God so loved the world that he gave his only begotten son that whosoever believeth in him should not perish but have everlasting life.'

I didn't allow myself to jump out to safety before I got to 'life'.

As unchurched children we argued, like a group of short theologians, that Mum might be Satan. The theory was even more thrilling than the billy-cart ride, that we'd been chosen for such celestial evil. One of my brothers finally disappointed us all by pointing out that Satan was a man.

'Your mother's got a nervous condition,' my father said. 'She has nerves.'

It never occurred to my father in those pre-Medicare days to take my mother to a doctor. He believed a dash of metho or turps would fix any ailment, sometimes both together. At the most we consulted the chemist, and about my mother's nerves the chemist had nothing to say.

The comfort for us all was my father's secret job. As soon as the houses had upright, painted walls, they were festooned with paintings, three deep, even in the outside dunnies. Usually he painted landscapes, always Australian landscapes – after all that was what he'd come for, the light – even though it was the age of modernism and abstraction. We all learned to despise modernism and abstraction. Occasionally, very occasionally, he'd sell his landscapes full of light at exhibitions in city stores. We were very proud when he was invited to exhibit in David Jones, especially when they sold. Not only because suddenly there were new uniforms and shoes, but also because I hugged to myself the thought of my dad's paintings hanging perhaps in a bed-room like those I'd examined in glossy magazines, a bedroom a girl of my age had all to herself. Perhaps I would meet her one day, introduce myself as Dad's daughter, and I'd be her friend.

In a wealthier family we might've had a shield over our many front doors: 'In Art We Trust.' I became a writer, still trusting in Art.

But even when his paintings sold, we still weren't allowed to tell the kids at school, although I ran home from school to watch him paint, dabbing a landscape into light. I assumed that he knew how to paint because he came from the cultural centre of the world, a land where giant golden pears were pendulous over fences, where there were art gal-leries gleaming with oils all along the street, why, you could pop into one and gaze at a Rembrandt whenever you were sent to the local shop for bones for the dog. He was entirely untutored, but that was easily expli-cable to me: anyone from that magic land would be good at painting.

I was a late reader and when I finally learned to make out his sig-nature on the lower right-hand corner, I discovered that the name wasn't the name I knew him by.

'You left out Arthur,' I objected.

'I don't like "Arthur",' he said. He could often turn a difficult moment into a joke. He was always joking. 'If you had a name like Arthur, wouldn't you leave it out?'

It didn't occur to me until much later that it had been a difficult moment.

I got my wish and stayed at school, largely because he and my mother were embroiled in murderous fury. He still resisted my education, but when I won what was then called a Commonwealth Scholarship, he relented.

'The Commonwealth means the queen, and if the queen wants you to study, who am I to disagree?' he said.

He'd always doffed his cap to what he called his betters, and taught us to be obsequious. It was hard to work out who our betters were in

Australia. As a young activist, I told him once, just as the young today blame baby boomers, that it was his generation and him who'd created the appalling world we young ones had to reform.

He was speechless with amazement at the picture I'd painted of his power.

It was only when I came home from university, after he and Mum had split up, and I was wiping up while he washed, that I realised I towered over him. I was five feet high. He'd always been toothless and thin, and now he'd lost one eye, though, after a few months, that hadn't stopped him painting. In Art We Trust.

When I wrote my first book, a textbook that unexpectedly sold well in schools, I bought Dad a ticket to fly back to London. He'd never been back; the family finances hadn't allowed it.

'To see your brother,' I said.

The ticket bore his full name. He wouldn't take it out of my hand.

'But your brother, your favourite brother,' I said.

I didn't dare mention his parents, the mother he'd run away from.

'I mightn't get back,' he said.

I thought he meant that the cultural centre of the world would be so alluring, he wouldn't be able to drag himself away.

Some time later, there was a great to-do while he wrapped up a painting to send overseas. The wrapping and the posting seemed to take days. He normally never went to such trouble. Months after, he held up a letter, happier than he'd ever been. The Royal Academy of Art, London, had accepted his painting for their summer exhibition.

'But you exhibit every year in Sydney,' I said. 'In David Jones.' I was struggling to understand his elation.

'This isn't like that,' he said.

He seemed to run out of words, he couldn't explain more.

I never checked what name he'd signed the painting with.

One of my brothers finally went to London and, insisting on reluctant directions from Dad, tracked down his older brother, now in his dotage, and found out enough to acquire Dad's birth certificate. I was still in my twenties – I tell myself that I never had time to ask the real questions, though that's not true, I had a whole long childhood – when Dad's luck finally petered out. He had a heart attack so minor that going to hospital in an ambulance embarrassed him. He should've walked there, he said. It was hard to tell if he was blushing, with all the instruments on him, all the beeping. I never wondered why he asked so little for himself.

'I've got to get out of here, I've got a painting to finish,' he whispered to me. He didn't want the nurses to know he was ungrateful; they were going to so much trouble for him.

But his luck ran out.

It took me a decade, and the birth of my daughter, to say his name again. When circumstances forced me to, I'd manage 'my father'. It was my daughter who brought me back to life. I'd died with Dad.

But suddenly she was five, and clamouring for grandparents to romp with her and spoil her. I knew Dad's parents must be dead by now, but there must be something to show her. I now knew Dad's father had been a gardener, and, given Dad's artistry, maybe he'd been a Capability Brown, maybe there were landscapes he'd created. Or maybe there was a house still standing, the family home. My brother found for me the address of Dad's brother's second wife, our Auntie May, now widowed, now in a hospice. He hadn't been able to trace anyone else. We went to London quickly, for it might be too late to ask the questions I'd never asked.

Auntie May was sitting up straight in her chair by her impeccably made bed, a shock of white hair, strong and wiry, leaping out of her fragility. It refused to be subdued when she ran trembling fingers through it.

'We weren't expecting you so early in the day,' she said. She was a sweet-faced old woman with the quick, grateful smile of the seldom visited. Every chance she got, she'd signal a passing nurse and say proudly:

'This is my niece from Australia. She's come especially to see me.'

One of them stopped and said to her:

'But we didn't get around to setting your hair!'

'It looks lovely,' I assured her. In fact, the shock of white was so perpendicular, it gave her the startled look of a cockatiel.

'Your brother showed me a photo of your mother,' she said enviously. 'She was very beautiful, wasn't she!'

Not inheriting my mother's beauty still rankled.

I asked if she had photos of Dad's family. She seemed taken aback.

'No, dear, of course not.'

Or, where were the gardens done by Dad's father?

She struggled to comprehend this question.

'Gardens? He was just a handyman, dear.'

And the house where they lived?

'Oh, the worst of the slums were cleared out in the thirties. There's good social services now but —'

She saw me taking this in.

'Your father spared you all this? Perhaps I should too.'

'No, please —'

She sighed, settled back in her chair.

'There was no house, not as such. They didn't have a house, they had a room.'

I laughed, disbelieving her.

'A room! What, for all those children – it must've been a big room – George and Frederick and —'

She interrupted me.

'Seven feet by eight.'

A nurse came with a cup of milky tea, and one for me, since I'd come all the way from Australia.

'But there wouldn't be enough space for all the beds —'

I was gulping my tea.

'There was only one bed, dear, for Walter and Hannah. The children slept under it, on the floor.'

I tried to make light of this.

'Such a squash, five kids under a bed. They probably had fun.'

'And there was a lodger, who worked night shifts, so he used the bed during the day.'

'A relative?'

'No, dear, people lived like that in those days, there was desperate, terrible overcrowding in the slums, and few jobs to go around.'

There seem to be no late Victorian or Edwardian novelists who cared to write, like Dickens, with sympathy about the poor of their times, but in 1883, a compassionate London journalist, Andrew Mearns, published a pamphlet that caused a sensation, though he was at pains to tell his readers that 'far from making the worst of our facts for the purpose of appealing to emotion, we have been compelled to tone down everything, and wholly omit what most needs to be known, or the ears and eyes of our readers would have been insufferably outraged'.[1]

Mearns described the plight of the poor, whose work helped turn the wheels of London's prosperous industries, but went almost unpaid, such was the competition for jobs in that time devoid of total de-regulation, devoid even of mercy – it was what Mearns called 'a grinding of the faces of the poor which could scarcely be paralleled in lands of slavery and of notorious oppression'.[2] Mearns gives many instances: for example, a man who explained that his master 'gets a pound for what he gives me 3 shillings for making' (there were 20 shillings in the pound).[3] It seems that the poor had little chance of earning their way out of poverty.

Mearns asked his readers: 'Have you pitied the poor creatures who sleep under railway arches, in carts or casks? They are to be envied, in comparison to London's outcasts.'⁴ Overcrowding, he explained, was an understatement: he instanced a London court 'eighteen yards long and nine yards wide. Here are 12 houses of three rooms each, and containing altogether 36 families.'⁵ He went on:

> To get into [such rooms] you have to penetrate courts reeking with poisonous and malodorous gases arising from accumulations of sewage and refuse scattered in all directions. You have to ascend rotten staircases, which threaten to give away beneath every step. You have to grope your way along dark and filthy passages swarming with vermin . . . Walls and ceilings are black with the accretions of filth which have gathered upon them through long years of neglect . . . it is running down the walls, it is everywhere. What goes by the name of a window is half of it stuffed with rags or covered by boards to keep out wind and rain; the rest is so begrimed and obscured that scarcely can light enter or anything be seen outside . . . As to furniture, you may perchance discover a broken chair, the tottering relics of an old bedstead, or the mere fragment of a table . . . or, more frequently still, nothing but rubbish and rags.⁶

The prices charged for these rooms were unmerciful. Journalism in those days was not given to offending the Victorian Establishment but another crusading journalist, W. T. Stead, wrote ironically of rent prices in the slums: 'These fever dens are said to be the best-paying property in London, and owners, who, if justice were to be done, would be on the treadmill, are drawing 50 to 60 per cent on investments in tenement property.'⁷

But this was twenty years before my father's birth. However, apart from church groups sending earnest missionaries to the slums to save souls, nothing had changed by the time Jack London, the US novelist, himself born into poverty and brought up roughly in America, travelled to London in 1903 and made believe he was one of the poor to observe London's shameful secret, the one and a quarter million people living in the way I was coming to understand Dad's family had lived:

> In such conditions, the outlook for children is hopeless. They die like flies . . . they have no home life. In the dens and lairs in which they live, they are exposed to all that is obscene and indecent. And as their minds are rotten, so are their bodies made rotten by bad sanitation, overcrowding and underfeeding, and sitting up [at night] to drive the rats away from the sleepers.[8]

Mearns had written of the 'stunted, misshapen . . . utterly neglected' children: 'Their bodies and rags are alive with vermin . . . many of them have never seen a green field, and do not know what it is to go beyond the streets immediately around them, and they often spend the whole day without a morsel of food.'[9]

Under my auntie's tutoring, I was painstakingly reconstructing my childhood image of Dad and his brother naughtily eating from the streets (I realised I'd always imagined the food they plundered as being contained in Sydney-style neat garbage bins) and replacing it with a new image of ragged, shoeless, starving children, arms plunged in a rubbish pile up to their elbows, devouring bits of mouldy food.

'So he was always hungry,' I said.

Auntie cried out so loudly a passing nurse came over to ask if all was well. 'He's told you nothing, has he? They were starving.'

The novelist Jack London wrote of two slum-dwellers he walked the streets all night with, who picked up from the 'slimy, spittle-drenched sidewalk . . . bits of orange peel, apple skin, and grape stems, and they were eating them . . . They picked up stray crumbs of bread the size of peas, apple cores so black and dirty one would not take them to be apple cores, and . . . chewed them . . . In the heart of the greatest, wealthiest and most powerful empire the world has ever seen.'[10]

Jack London walked the streets with them because well-to-do Londoners demanded of their police that the poor never be allowed to sleep in doorways or under bridges or in their carefully tended parks – for the poor must be kept out of sight, so as not to offend the delicate sensibilities of the wealthy.

He wrote that if the poor had two pence to spare, they could go to the workhouse, now converted into quaint, expensive apartments, with red geraniums nodding smilingly at sunlit windows. It was competitive to gain a bed, since there were so few, and the poor so multitudinous. Jack London described the scornful treatment he received from the managers, the hard labour he had to do to qualify for a place, the bath he was permitted whose water had been used by the twenty-four other men before him, the beds that were only narrow strips of suspended canvas, and then the breakfast:

> At eight o'clock we went down into a cellar under the infirmary where tea was brought to us and the hospital scraps. These were heaped high on a platter in an indescribable mess – pieces of bread, chunks of grease and fat pork, the burnt skin from the outside of roasted joints, bones, in short all the leavings from the fingers and mouths of the sick ones suffering from all manner of diseases. Into this mess the men plunged their hands, digging, pawing, turning over, examining, rejecting, and scrambling for. Pigs couldn't have done worse. But the poor devils were hungry, and they ate ravenously of the swill, and when they could eat no more, they bundled what was left into their handkerchiefs and thrust it inside their shirts.[11]

But still, as I sat with my auntie, I was aware there were still pieces of the puzzle missing.

'What was my grandmother like?'

Auntie made me jump by clanging the cup on the saucer.

'Alex didn't tell you anything, did he?'

She was exasperated that it all had been left to her.

'Hannah was a washerwoman. But most of the time —'

She looked over her shoulder, bent her old white head towards me so not even the ghost of my grandmother would hear.

'I don't like to speak ill of the dead, but – she was a drunk. That's why they hated her. She took any money there was, and drank it. And then – the stories George told me of what she got up to when she was drunk!'

She slumped in her chair, deciding to spare me the stories.

But I learned that Hannah had taken to drink early. She'd been brought up in Pitlochry, Scotland.

'Pitlochry!' I echoed. The place of holidays, the place of the only photograph, the suspension bridge.

Though her mother, like Hannah, had also been a washerwoman, she'd married well and her husband, Hannah's father, had been the caretaker of what Dad had called the Big House on the Hill, a job my great-grandfather was proud of but which he'd lose with a drunken daughter. So they'd sent her off to London, but had brought her back for the birth of every child, hoping she'd reform.

'But she always went back on the bottle. She always got worse, back there.'

Our eyes met, with a hundred questions neither of us could put words to.

My auntie said that my grandmother's parents had wanted to rescue George and Alex and the little children and bring them up in the clean air and comparatively good life of Pitlochry. But after a couple of holidays, it all stopped.

'George never knew why. Perhaps there was an argument.'

'Did Hannah love her children?'

'She loved the bottle more.'

Alarmed church groups and charities tried to help the poor, to little avail. Jack London wrote ironically of an exhibition of Japanese art that was shown to the poor of Whitechapel 'with the idea of elevating them, of begetting in them yearnings for the Beautiful and True and Good'. He added, 'Did destiny today bind me down to the life of an East End slave for the rest of my years, and did Destiny grant me but one wish, I am pretty confident that I should get drunk.'[12] He wrote: 'These people who try to help! They do not understand the simple sociology of Christ, yet they come to the miserable and the despised with the pomp of social redeemers . . . They come from a race of successful and predatory bipeds.'[13]

Auntie said: 'George and Alex went to work as soon as they could. Till the end of his life George was proud that the two of them had made life easier for the younger ones. They knew they could get killed in the munitions factory but anything was better than the family being thrown into the workhouse.'

'Then my dad disowned them all to go to sea,' I whispered sadly, because I so wanted to believe well of him.

'Never!' cried my auntie. 'Whenever his ship came to London, he'd get word to George, who'd come to meet him at the docks,' she said. 'He'd hand over most of his wages to George, never to Hannah. He helped support the family till he had troubles of his own. I know he had lots of troubles —'

Auntie May slumped in her chair.

A nurse came immediately.

'I know you've come a long way but perhaps another visit —'

As I leave, Auntie tells me to go to his school, and to Pitlochry – perhaps I'd understand more.

'Come back quickly,' whispered the nurse as I left. 'She's been holding out for you, like the very old can – but we may not have her with us much longer.'

I went to his school in Lewisham, and there, on the wall, in big bold brass letters freshly polished, is my father's name, his full name, no longer a secret, but just as he'd told us, and the dux of his school.

There must've been other names in a list, but my memory sees only one name in big shining letters; my father.

Then we hurried to Pitlochry, my daughter, my partner and me.

I saw a wild white river, I saw shadowy but quaint little cottages, ones which Dad and George would've filled with happy cries and laughter, suddenly well-fed, and housed. I saw the Big House on a hill, now occupied by the Forestry Commission. But the first thing I saw was the suspension bridge of the only photograph of my dad's past. I took a photograph of Dad's granddaughter running on it, warmly clad in a red tracksuit.

But all that sadness is now buried in the ground.

I hurried back to my auntie in her hospital room, too anxious about her to think of warning them of the exact hour of my arrival. This visit they'd set her hair, twisting it into tight pink rollers. She was embarrassed by the rollers and called for a nurse to take them out, but there was a crisis in the hospital – another old lady had fallen and there was much running and calling.

'You take after our side of the family,' said my auntie warmly, having no idea she was fingering an old wound. 'You look like George and Alex.'

I tell her that the only person from my father's past I encountered was an old man who called out to me from across the street, 'Tillie, Tillie.' His face worked in disappointment when he found I wasn't Tillie.

'That was the name of one of Hannah's sisters,' said Auntie May.

'So my face belongs!' I cried, to her confusion.

'George adored Alex,' said Auntie.

'Did George ever think of following Dad to Australia?' I asked.

My auntie shook her head no, but sighed again. I was exhausting her. I wished I'd come to London earlier and got to know this woman.

So she told me the last piece of the puzzle, the story that was always kept a secret.

'George didn't dare.'

'Dare?'

'It might've complicated things for Alex.'

She was preparing herself. I didn't realise this; I was in my own memories.

'I tried to send Dad back to see George,' I told her warmly, trying to emphasise that at least I knew of the love between the brothers.

So she had to say it.

'Your dad wouldn't have got back in,' she said.

'In? To England?'

'To Australia!'

She'd known I'd flounder.

'It's a wonder they didn't catch him,' she continued. 'His name would've turned up on official documents —'

'His name?'

'It'd have turned up somewhere. He must've lived in fear all his life,' she said. 'There would've been such a fuss.'

I remembered the word 'fuss', the word I'd never questioned.

'He didn't emigrate properly,' she said. 'George thought there were amnesties but your father probably wouldn't have trusted them, or even known about them with all your family's strife —'

My face was working, my face that belongs to my dad and his brother and my grandmother's sister.

And so she spelt it out.

'He jumped ship. He was in the navy and he jumped ship. That was a criminal offence.'

I said, hotly, but suddenly realising that what had been an explanation for us, would have been no explanation for the rest of the world:

'But he fell in love with the light!'

'He was an outcast here and an outcast there,' she said. 'In the old days, he'd have been shot, or at least court-martialled. He was used to the poor being pushed around. At least he'd have thought so, and that was the important thing, wasn't it, what he feared!'

The crisis in the hospital seemed over, and a nurse had time to come up and tell me I'd better go, I was exhausting my auntie, and she had a big event later today.

'But this is the big event,' Auntie cried out. 'This is my niece from Australia, and I'm still in my curlers!'

On the day of my return to Australia, a nurse rang to tell me my auntie had died. 'Right up till the last, she never stopped talking about George and Alex,' she said. 'We know George was her husband, but who was Alex?'

EXODUS
DOROTHY HEWETT

In such a time as this when multitudes
stream out abandoned bombed from ruined cities
grandmothers hobbling babies bicycles
luggage on carts and backs the crying children
there are no boundaries a private grief
shrinks to a pin-prick on this frontier
the ditches filled with blood and suitcases
lovers shot through the heart abandoned toys
dragging a severed limb
a three-legged dog limps off across the plain

this unmourned multitude who trudge
across earth's thunderous surface
Belgrade to Kosovo to Baghdad burning.

FROM *THE PEOPLE SMUGGLER*
ROBIN DE CRESPIGNY

The Kurdish militia seem disinterested when we are handed over in Sulaymaniyah. All they ask for is our names and then they let us go. I am ready to head back to Iran and my family as fast as I can, but Mustafa likes alcohol and wants to get as much drinking done as he can while he is here.

Then there is the problem of paying for a smuggler. I now know that while it is not difficult to get across the border into Iran, it remains impossible to get any further on your own. I had hidden fifty American dollars and some Iraqi dinars in my shoe, but it is hardly going to be enough to live on.

At first I remain patient but on the third night Mustafa staggers into our tiny hotel room singing. It is three o'clock in the morning, and he wakes me up to ask for money to keep drinking. His alcohol breath and maddening behaviour remind me of my wayward youth and I am unable to contain my fury. 'What are you doing? I hardly have enough left for us to eat!'

'No alcohol in Iran,' he says with a hiccup, 'so we have got to drink as much as possible before we leave.' He leers at me and I have to stop myself from hitting him.

'Are you out of your mind?' I yell, but as I watch him stagger around with a ridiculous smile on his face, I remember that complete aban-donment of any responsibility and the glorious sense of freedom that alcohol brings. For a moment I wish I could say, 'To hell with it all,' and join him. But instead I grab Mustafa and throw him on the bed.

I cover him with a blanket, but he flings it off and tries to strug-gle back onto his feet. I raise my fist to him and he slowly shrinks back down. Then I restore the blanket and command with one hand still clenched, 'Sleep!' and he quickly shuts his eyes. Within minutes he has fallen into a deep drunken slumber and snores so loudly that I give up on any chance of further rest and sit at the window waiting for the sun to rise over the city.

I must have dozed off because the call to prayer begins to waft mournfully out from the mosques and my eyes snap open to see Mustafa sitting, head hanging low, on the edge of the bed. I go to the bathroom and get him a glass of discoloured water from a rusty tap in our cheap hotel. He gulps it down and looks at me. He is not about to apologise but he is clearly full of remorse.

'Do you still have the US$50?'

I stare back at him, wishing I had never told him what was in my shoe.

'Yesterday, before I was too drunk,' he says sheepishly, 'I met a smuggler who can take us to Qom.'

'Even if we get ourselves across the border, US$50 will hardly get us around one checkpoint and there are at least five or six before we would be out of the woods,' I say sceptically.

'If we give him your US$50 up front, he is prepared to trust us to pay him US$150 when we get to Qom. I have someone there who will lend us the money for him when we arrive.'

I look at Mustafa, wondering what sort of smuggler would make that kind of risky deal. There is no way of knowing what condition Mustafa was actually in when he made it, so I am understandably uneasy. 'Is he any good? I mean, why would we trust him?'

Mustafa shrugs. 'Do we have any choice?'

I want to shout at him, 'If we had gone immediately, and not had to pay for three days of drinking, hotels and food, we may have had more options,' but I don't, because I know the price of blame, and I just want to get back to my family. Besides, I identify with Mustafa's need to salve the pain.

The smuggler, Fadi, is friendly enough. A tough, swarthy Kurdish Iranian in his forties. We meet him in a small village on the Iraq side of the border. Considering how Fadi came our way, I am slow to trust that he knows what he is doing and am already wary when he says, 'Tomorrow we go by car and then by bus.'

I had assumed we would be going the same way as when I finally escaped from the border camp in '97.

'Isn't it safer through the mountains?' I say, trying not to show my irritation.

'I always go on the road,' he replies casually.

'Great,' I say and glare at Mustafa. 'I appreciate your deal,' I tell Fadi, 'but it's worth nothing if you can't get us there.'

'Don't worry.' He waves his hands dismissively. 'You get there.'

I feel as vulnerable as I used to with the resistance, when they would organise our papers then leave it to us to get ourselves out of trouble.

Next day a car arrives to pick us up. As we approach the border Fadi turns to us in the back seat. 'When we get there you say nothing. Even if they ask you something you don't say anything. You ignore them.'

With the prospect of another jail term or deportation looming ahead of me, I join Mustafa in nodding compliantly.

A bull-headed guard leans into the car and looks us over. I am waiting to be dragged out, when he exchanges a few words I don't understand with Fadi and waves us on. I put my head back on the seat and breathe again. Despite my pounding heart, that certainly was easy.

At the first checkpoint the same thing happens and I begin to feel a little embarrassed that I doubted Fadi. He is smarter than I had given him credit for, and whatever deals he has in place with the authorities are being respected. My confidence in him has grown to such an extent that I settle into my seat and fall asleep.

I am woken with a jolt by Fadi issuing new instructions. 'We eat and sleep here in Marivan, then tomorrow we go by local bus.' I don't know what had tempted me into becoming so complacent; of course this dream ride couldn't last. Now the nightmare begins. Fadi sees my face and laughs reassuringly. 'No problem, you will get to Qom.'

But I doubt it.

Next morning, before we leave to catch the bus, Fadi says, 'We'll have to get off the bus to get around the checkpoints. The driver will find a way to let you off and on without the passengers knowing, or they might tell the police as we pass through.'

I stare at him, astounded. 'How?'

'Don't worry, we will work it out,' he says, again waving his hands.

I am now having serious qualms, but I am comforted by the fact that he said *we*, so at least we're not expected to work it out by ourselves.

When we get on the bus the driver takes no particular notice of us so I begin to worry that while Fadi shone on the previous leg, the deal with the driver may not have been as convincing. Mustafa and I sit together, with Fadi across the aisle. After a couple of hours we are approaching another checkpoint, and I become uneasy.

Then I notice the driver making a show of finding he has run out of cigarettes. He throws the empty packet on the floor and shortly after pulls over into a roadside cafe. As he gets out he calls down the bus, 'Anyone need cigarettes or anything else, you can get it here.'

Fadi gets up and we follow with a group of other passengers. Some go into the cafe, use the toilet or stand outside and smoke. It is not difficult for us to sidle off. Then it is a mad dash behind Fadi to get to the pick-up point faster than the bus. We run like maniacs along rough, stony donkey tracks until we see the road again, then sprint towards a bus stop where people are waiting to get on.

The bus is filling up, so it is easier not to be noticed when, later that day, it stops and the driver announces he thinks he has a problem with a tyre. As he gets off to check it, Fadi pushes us out ahead of him and when no one is looking we sneak off.

Fadi knows the fastest route around the checkpoint but we have to really run to keep up with him. The poor bus driver must have thought we wouldn't make it and have actually changed a tyre, because we end up waiting for him. But this gives him a reason to stop again, to check if the new one needs tightening.

And so it goes. Holes in the road, engine problems that require regular attention, and tyres that need checking. Nobody seems to be paying the slightest attention. They talk with each other, play with their kids, read and sleep. Despite myself, I begin to think this is a pretty professional setup.

It is night when we approach the city of Sanandaj. When the bus stops to let some passengers off Fadi nudges us. 'You go with him.' We are near the exit and we see an old man getting off. I now trust Fadi enough to do whatever he says, so we follow the order. But as soon as this guy hits the ground he takes off like a hare. I thought I was fast but he is something else.

'Wait, you motherfucker,' I swear, but he won't. Mustafa is close to passing out after his three days on the bottle. But when he yells, 'You're killing us, you crazy idiot,' the old man calls back over his shoulder, 'They have dinner in the city, then the bus will go. If we are not there they will leave without you.' I must admit, as I gasp for breath and clutch my chest, Fadi certainly has a dedicated team.

After several kilometres up and down uneven hilly country we make it into the city and to our relief the old man grabs a taxi to the restaurant. We collapse into the back seat and try to get our breath back. The old man is hardly panting. When we arrive he beams, 'We made it.' I look into the restaurant and indeed the other passengers are still eating. 'Thank God,' I sigh and pat his back gratefully.

We don't know when we will eat again so we are gulping down chicken and rice when Fadi joins us and whispers, 'Okay. Let's go.'

'Where?' I sigh incredulously.

'You must hurry,' he urges.

Mustafa looks as if he is going to faint.

We drag ourselves into another taxi and while Fadi directs the driver we try to psych ourselves up for another lap. On the edge of town we get out and Fadi points to the lights from a highway nearly a kilometre away. 'We have to get to that road before the bus does, so come on.'

For the fifth time we begin to run. Fortunately it is downhill but it is so dark we can see almost nothing. We are running full pelt when we plunge into a hedge with sharp thorns. Then as we tumble over it and into the dry soil on the other side the dust is salty so burns our cuts and we howl like beaten dogs.

When we finally get to the road, we don't know if our bus has gone or not. We wait and wait but there is no sign of it. So when a different bus comes, Fadi pushes us onto it. I am alarmed because I know there is another checkpoint, which is meant to be impassable, and Fadi has no deal with this new driver.

Everyone on this bus is asleep so we stand up the front, with Fadi hanging over the driver. I can't hear what he is saying but suddenly Fadi is pointing and making him go faster. I peer into the traffic and there ahead of us is our bus.

Our original driver must have been going slow and watching for us, because when he sees us, he pulls over and we get back onto our bus. Everyone is awake, even the kids, sitting up watching us with huge smiles on their faces, glad we have made it. So much for our subterfuge.

Mustafa and I nod and smile back. We are deeply touched that they are on our side. I feel their warm embrace, and for a moment that deep wound of loss for my country, my little city of Diwaniyah, my home, opens like a bleeding flower. They make room for us to sit, and exhausted, we both fall asleep until we reach the last checkpoint. It is as I had heard, up in the mountains with no other way around.

I have no idea what Fadi has planned but I have come to trust he has thought of everything. He passes Mustafa a container and says, 'When we stop, put this water in the radiator.'

Then he gives me a wet cloth and a bucket. 'And you can climb up on the front of the bus and clean the window.'

Knowing that not just the driver but the whole busload are with us makes everything easier. We do what Fadi says and as the police march around the bus, checking the passengers, not once do they even notice us. So miraculously we pass through with no problems, and this time as we get back on the bus and set off everyone claps us, and we are at last on our way to Qom.

When we arrive Mustafa gets the money we owe from his friend and we pay Fadi. I wish I had some more to give him extra. I had mis-judged him. He is wily, diligent, clever and professional. Getting us here seemed to matter to him more than the money.

'Thank you,' I say, shaking his hand with admiration and respect. 'You are some smuggler.'

He grins and goes on his way, but I won't forget him.

THE STRANGER
CHRISTOS TSIOLKAS

It was only after the third time we had sex that we exchanged names, but I am still, to this day, not convinced that he told me the truth. I don't believe I am doing him an injustice in thinking this; he never lied about the important things, never pretended, for example, that what passed between us would be anything more than vain and fleeting.

We had met in a basement porno cinema in the middle of the city. There were two entrances, one off the alley with a narrow stairwell that led to the shop and the video booths, and a neon-lit main entrance on Elizabeth Street for the cinema and for the peepshows. I had been out dancing with friends, Friday night had bled into Saturday morning, and I was on the wrong side of an ecstasy peak: nevertheless, I knew that I had a few more hours before sleep was even remotely possible. I had the taxi driver drop me off at Flinders Street Station and then walked resolutely around the corner, weaved past the drunk adolescents fortifying themselves on McDonalds, descended the dark stairs, paid my entry and slipped into a seat in the back row. I unzipped; blankly I watched the two women on screen gyrating breathlessly with one another.

I had been coming to this cinema since the tail end of high school and by now I knew the etiquette backwards. The last two or three rows of the cinema are where you place yourself if you're looking for sex. Those who came for the screenings sat in the front rows, keeping a clearly defined distance from the perversion occurring in the back. On Friday and Saturday nights, the screenings would be interrupted every hour or so by an exotic dancer who would acrobatically and disdainfully perform for five minutes to a song by Prince, AC/DC, Rhianna or the Rolling Stones. It was considered bad form for us deviants to continue our solitary or group activities while these women danced. We would zip up, move away from one another, pretend to be paying attention to their act, and clap lamely at the end. Then the house lights would be turned down, the video would resume, as would our fumbling in the dark. None of the rules were ever explained, you learnt from a combination of observation and fear. Very early on, I had witnessed a young man rise from the back row, watched him walk down the aisle and plonk himself down next to a good-looking older man in paint-splattered overalls. Within seconds the tradesman had flown up from his seat, had roared, What the fuck do you think you are doing you poofter shit, and proceeded to punch the young man hard three times in the face. I remember I cowered in my seat as the poor guy rushed out of the cinema, nursing his bleeding lip and nose. An old man behind me had hissed loudly, Serves you right, you dickhead.

But tonight, it was after midnight and the floorshows were finished for the evening. On the screen a man had formed a trip with the women and my cock stiffened in my fist.

Ecstasy imbues me with confidence but also accentuates my impatience. There was an elderly gentleman in my row that night, he seemed an octogenarian, and he was dressed in a tweed jacket, a white shirt and floral tie; he was naked from the waist down. In the seat in front of me there was a stocky, attractive married man (I caught the glint of his wedding ring when my eyes got accustomed to the darkness), and he too was masturbating: but his eyes would not move from the screen. I got up, indicated that I wanted to sit next to him, and he shifted his legs but without once returning my gaze. I sat down and caught the whiff of dried sweat, the yeasty, salty stench of beer and greasy chips. I stretched my legs and my knee touched his. He neither shifted his leg away nor looked away from the screen.

I was in no mood for seduction, I wanted to get my rocks off. I rose again, this time he threw a startled glance in my direction, and I made my way purposefully to the toilets.

It was at the urinal that we met.

The sex was astonishingly rapid and remarkably good. He wanted to kiss, and he wanted to kiss me hard. He came first, and I followed with a lowing long moan only seconds afterwards. He immediately placed his hand over my mouth, cautioning silence. But his eyes were gleaming, and he was smiling. He was cleaning himself up with toilet paper and I said, Man, that was good. Yes, he replied, and I couldn't pick his accent. He left; I could tell that with the cessation of the rush of orgasm he just wanted to make his escape from the rancid stink of piss and semen, shit and vomit.

It was a great fuck. I might never see him again but knew I would always remember the sex and that I would remember everything about him. The birthmark like a squashed purple grape on the side of his neck, disappearing into his beard; the unsettling opacity in his heavily lidded caramel eyes, and the lumpy heft over his hips and belly.

He had been one of the men sitting in the front rows. I had noticed him as I had stormed down the aisle, clocked the metallic blue of the taxi-driver work shirt he was wearing. But I hadn't thought I had a chance in hell of having sex with such a bloke.

I was whistling, I was cocky and unashamed as I ascended the stairs. A young girl, shivering in the cold, dressed in a miniskirt and a tank-top, was hiding inside her boyfriend's embrace. She gave me a curious half-smile as I came up into the street. I winked back and she turned away.

I had checked my phone while washing up in the toilet. It was two thirty-nine in the morning. At two in the morning the following Saturday I was back. I stood up against the back wall, and though this time there were more men in the back rows I didn't pay them any attention. I was peering out to the front of the cinema. He was there, in the third row, at the end of the aisle, watching the orgy unfolding on screen. I recognised the bullish slope of his shoulders, the shock of his blue-black beard. I hadn't been there even a minute but I walked down the aisle, to the toilets. In a beat he was next to me again.

If the first time we fucked he had surprised me with his tenderness, this time he scared me with his aggression. I had to stop him, I had to push him away, I felt the acid sting of the bile rising to my throat, coating my tongue; I was gagging, I had to spit into the cistern. Don't fucking hurt me, I said. *Okay, okay*. His accent, in speaking English, sounded faintly American, the ubiquitous inflection of Hollywood that infects us all, wherever we are in the world. *Okay, okay*, he repeated, then touched the back of my head; he was playing with my hair, letting it slip through his fingers. And this time, we came at the same moment, he in my mouth, and I all over the stinking floor, drops of semen splattered on his cheap acrylic sneakers.

I was back there the following Saturday morning.

This time, when we finished, when we were wiping ourselves off, I asked, Can you drive me home? I could tell this alarmed him, there was a suspicious caution in his eyes. I'll pay, I gushed, Don't worry, of course I will. The wariness was still there. *Where do you live?* Clifton Hill, I answered.

The fare was fifteen dollars and eighty cents but I gave him a twenty and said you can keep the change. Then I followed with, quickly, diffidently, Do you want to come in? He was peering through the windscreen, the lights illuminating the plum red bricks of the terrace, the spindly parched branches of the rose bushes. *You live on your own?* I shook my head: No, I share with two friends. His fingers were drumming on the wheel, I hadn't realised how hairy his hands and arms were, thick tufts of black hair, so thick in parts that it seemed as pelt. *And they know?* Know what, I countered. *That you get fucked by men.* Yes, of course they know. And that's when I told him my name and when I asked his. There was only the sound of the tattoo he was beating on the vinyl surface of the wheel. Then he turned off the ignition, switched off the headlights. And he told me his name.

It was that hesitation, just that bare sputter in time, that made me doubt him.

In bed, I touched the thin gold cross that had fallen against his bare chest. I thought you were Muslim. He said something then, in his language, expressed it with such fierce and guttural vehemence that I knew it could only be a curse; it was much too violent to be a mere obscenity. He breathed in deeply and said, *Me no Muslim, me a Kristian.* He was banging his chest, hard, almost savagely, as if through this action he could demonstrate the defiance he could not convey through words. *And you?* I don't believe in God.

He had been silent; even though he had not moved, I sensed his retreat from me. And then he surprised me with a rich sonorous laugh, and he dived under the duvet and grabbed my dick, stretched my foreskin till it hurt. He had it pinched between his fingers. *No, no, no,* he kept repeating, triumph and glee in his voice, *No no no, you Kristian, you Kristian.*

When the thin grey light of dawn was just visible through the slatted blinds, he got up from bed and started putting on his clothes. He was shy dressing, modestly he turned away from me. He kept anxiously checking and rechecking his phone. Is everything okay? *I'm late,* he spat out resentfully, he would not look at me, *The next driver is waiting.* I'm sorry. He swung around, amazed and disbelieving. *Why you sorry?* I think I must have grinned, I didn't understand his fury. *Why you sorry,* he demanded again. And then he said something in his language, under his breath, but harsh and unforgiving. This time I knew there was something of an obscenity in it.

He didn't say goodbye, he just picked up his shoes, walked softly out to the corridor. He walked out so quietly I didn't hear the front door shut.

I had given him my number, I didn't dare ask for his. After he left that morning, I lay back on the pillow, counselling myself, Don't fall in love, idiot, don't you bloody dare. I had been in love, it had prospered and then the bond had been severed and left both of us spent and broken. There is nothing more punishing than the death of love. Though possibly the man I had just been with would be able to argue from experience that, no, there were worse punishments and worse fates than a broken heart. If only we had a language, if we had a history, through which to speak to one another; something more fundamental and grounding than the loose pieces of skin at the end of our dicks. Don't you dare fall in love, idiot, don't you bloody dare.

Later, I discovered that he thought we Australians were too easy with the word *sorry*, that we used it without reverence, we used it thoughtlessly. I think he meant by this that we were sorry about the inconsequential and unimportant things and that we were unrepentant about the things that mattered. I know he thought us selfish; and because of our ignorance, cruel.

I am loath to divulge any more of what I discovered about him, I fear that would anoint our relationship with a gravity that it does not deserve. That first encounter in the toilet of the porno cinema occurred just before the Labour Day weekend in March. The last time I saw him was the end of August of that year. We did not date, we did not go out for dinner together, we did not have romantic holidays away. He never met any of my friends or my family. He would text me when he wanted to see me; most often it would be the middle of the night, at the tail end of his shift. There were weeks when I would see him three or four nights, there were weeks when I wouldn't see him at all. When he came over it was for sex, the hunger was ferocious, and I don't think

I figured as important in his desire at all. It was *his* need, it was *his* lust, it was *his* confusion that mattered. I learnt that it was impossible to refuse him, that if I did not want sex he did not care. And I shocked myself at how quickly I acquiesced to this, how there were nights when I rolled over on my stomach and just let him fuck me. I am still not clear as to why I so readily accepted this submissive role. For all of my adult sexual life I had prided myself on my masculine assertiveness. He was woefully bigoted about women and homosexuals, despised the camp guys that climbed into his cab, had only contempt for what he called the *drunk stupid Australian sluts* that were intimate with their partners in the back seat. We argued, but it was pointless and to no result. He did not understand my criticisms and he did not yet have a vocabulary that could express nuance or doubt. When we argued, we fought like children, cuss words and insults. Once, when he said something so appalling about a woman who had been in his cab, had contemptuously argued that she deserved to get raped, I had been driven to such inarticulate fury that I spat out, You're a fucking ignorant uneducated refugee. I was already ashamed of that outburst when he smacked me. It wasn't hard, it wasn't a punch, he backhanded me across the mouth, that's what he did; but I hadn't been hit since primary school and I just fell on him, started punching and hitting him. It was over quickly, we were laughing by the end of it, but I remain to this day confused by the exhilaration I felt in allowing violence to make my point. What terrifies me is how efficient and clean it felt, to resolve an argument in such a way.

He did not only come around for sex. Sometimes he would come with beers and cheap foul red wine, and he would sit in my room and proceed to drink until he passed out. Those would be the nights he did not have to work the next day. No matter how wasted he had been, he would never shower or use the kitchen in my house, did not want to encounter Nikos or Patricia, did not want anything to do with them at all. He even pissed in my room, in an empty mineral water bottle; he'd empty it out on the front lawn as he was leaving. Patricia would always complain about the bloody yobbos who pissed through the front fence at night. I wanted him to stay in my room as well, I didn't know how I could bear for my two worlds to collide.

We had a *Refugees Welcome Here* sticker on our refrigerator. I am grateful that he never saw that lie plastered across the shiny metal door.

I had asked him early on, of course, I had, where did he come from, where was home? He had been thumbing the books on my shelves – it was one of the reasons my calling him *uneducated* had so outraged him, he had completed three years of a secondary schooling, it was one of the truths of his life he did tell me, it was something of which he was proud and wished to share – and my question made him bristle, I saw his neck stiffen, his back arch. Then, a shiver, it danced down the length of his spine, and he answered, not looking at me, *I have no home, it is no longer there.* But where was it, I insisted. That's when he turned to me, that is when he said, unsmiling, *You cannot understand, there is no name, there is no border, there is no place, it does not exist no more.*

Somewhere where Europe, Africa and Asia collided, somewhere there, his homeland had been crushed; somewhere there, his home had gone up in smoke.

We fucked then. That's all I could offer.

That was the night he told me of his wife, of how he was working to bring her to Australia, of the children he wished to raise, of the house he wanted to buy them. I realise now that even in sharing this with me he was careful, that he did not let on where this dream home might be, I never discovered where he was living. So when he left my room there would be no trace of him. What is she like, your wife? He shrugged. *I have not met her.* Seeing my shock, he added, in a rush, *It is okay, it is okay, she is very beautiful, I have seen her on Skype.* And of course, I wanted to say, It is not her looks that I am concerned about, that isn't the question I have at all. How can you marry and spend a life with someone you have not yet met? How can you commit to that?

But did I want to commit to *him*? The distance between our worlds was too vast; love and its denouement had left me exhausted. Fucking. That was all I could offer.

The night I had to stop myself saying, I'm sorry. I'm sorry for my stupid questions.

We met just before Labour Day in March, and the beginning of that spring was the last time I saw him. I doubt his name, I don't know where he comes from and I don't know where he is. I did not fall in love, I am more careful with my heart now that I am older. But I remember everything about his body: his lopsided upper lip that made every smile quizzical; the light flush of black curls at the base of his spine that spread to a thick fur across his buttocks; the birthmark like a squashed purple grape on his neck, disappearing into the bristles of his beard; and the white thin scars, like two tiny lines of cocaine, across his left wrist. I recall his smell, and the gravel and hoarseness of his voice. I remember his body.

THE GARDEN
DENISE LEITH

The woman who came today – sometimes I can't remember their names – asked if I was lonely. I had no idea how to answer so I stared down at my hands resting on the picnic table between us until they were no longer resting but clapping in time to the music at my cousin's wedding. In this little memory movie I have stopped clapping and I'm taking my handkerchief out to wipe the sweat from my brow. Everyone, including Aasera, is on the dance floor laughing, moving to the rhythm. She's looking at me now smiling, summoning me to join her. 'Sa'eed, you are *my* dancer,' she's saying over the noise. 'No one dances more beautifully than you, my husband.' She's lying, of course, but with her smile and her beckoning hands she's pulling me onto the floor. As I begin to move she throws her head back and laughs at my jerking, wayward limbs before leaning in to whisper, 'I love you, Sa'eed.' The memory movie stops and I'm left alone in this place without Aasera.

The woman's hand reaches across the table toward mine but it stops, is pulled back, and I let out the breath I didn't know I was holding. Three years, two months and eight days since a woman has touched me. I've begun counting even the days. This thing that I no longer have in my life – this three years, two months and eight days – took something from me when it left and although I don't know how to name it its loss keeps going around in my head, torturing me more than the men with their fists ever could.

When the woman returns the following week I tell her that I am lonely. I've been practising this truth since her last visit, but now that it's out I'm embarrassed.

'We're all lonely,' she says, hand reaching out to cover mine this time. 'Do you want a piece of my orange?' Her hand is gone as she offers me a segment she has peeled. I thank her and wave her kindness away before picking my own orange from the bag she's brought me and begin peeling it even though I'm not hungry. The juice is running down her hand, and as I watch her tongue flicks out to lick it off before another piece disappears into her mouth. A new thought has come to me: Is this woman lonely too? Is that why she visits me?

When she leaves I walk over to the main office to ask the man working there what my visitor's name might be. 'Shivorn,' he says as he checks a list. 'S.I.O.B.H.A.N.' I don't understand. Is this her last name or her first? I'm also confused about the spelling. He notices this and adds, 'It's Irish, or Welsh . . . or something like that and it's pronounced different to the way it's spelt.' I still don't know if it's her first or last name but I keep repeating the name in my head until I've remembered it.

The question about why the women come to visit us has taken hold in my brain and I need to find the answer. It's always like this in this place – small ideas are unable to escape and begin to whirl around inside your head until they become big ideas that can make you crazy.

Raheem, who sleeps in the bed below mine, is in the TV room watching the screen as if the bright lives he sees are more real than his own. I want to ask him this new idea about the women but his eyes won't leave the screen. 'Raheem,' I say to get his attention, 'will you come outside with me for a second, my friend.' The others in the room are looking at us but Raheem has already turned back to the TV. He doesn't want to miss any important minutes of his life. I sigh and am getting up to leave when he stands too and follows me out to the picnic table under the big eucalyptus tree. At first, when I used to sit there in the rain, the guards would tell me I had to come inside, as if I was a child, but now they just let me sit. Perhaps they think I'm mad. Perhaps I am.

'Do you think these women are lonely, Raheem, and maybe that's why they come to visit us?' He stares down at the cigarette burning between his stained fingers without answering. Even though I've known him for three years I know little about Raheem's life, and although he seems like a simple man he can't be because he has left all that he loves and knows behind and that is not a simple thing to do. But I'm worried about him and I know the doctors are too because they keep asking me questions about how he sleeps, and what he says to me, and how long he sits in front of the TV.

'I don't know,' Raheem says finally, taking a deep drag on his cigarette before looking over to the huge metal fences and the dirt track between them that keep us from the world outside. 'Maybe it's good for them too.' Raheem is a man of few words.

When Shivorn comes the next week I notice that she doesn't have her usual bag of fruit for me and as soon as we sit down she begins digging around in her basket to pull out small packets of seeds that she places on the table between us. 'I've brought you parsley, zucchini, cucumbers and some chives,' she says, separating each packet. 'Oh, and my friend sent you these.' She searches in her basket again before pulling out a packet with a photo of brightly coloured flowers on the front. 'It's a mixed packet of seeds. Potluck.'

'Potluck. What's this pot luck?'

'It sort of means you don't know what you're going to get. Lots of different flowers.'

'I like this,' I say, smiling.

When Shivorn is leaving I thank her again and again until I think I'd better stop because she's laughing and telling me, 'Enough.' She leans in and kisses me on the cheek before turning to go and just for a second I can smell her hair and feel the touch of her soft woman's skin.

Colin is sitting drinking coffee in the staff room, which I notice is not much better than our rooms with their cold linoleum floors and faded lemon-coloured walls. 'I'm going to make a garden,' I tell him when he comes out into the hallway so I can talk to him, 'and I'm going to grow vegetables for everyone like my garden back home.'

'Hold on a second, mate. You're getting a little ahead of yourself here. First off, you've only got a few packets of seeds and secondly, you don't have any tools. Bit hard to make a garden with a few packets of seeds.'

'Oh, but I'm sure Shivorn will bring more seeds if I ask her and you can get me the tools.'

He's shaking his head. 'Sorry, Sa'eed, but you can't have spades and things like that in here.' At first I'm confused because I've seen the workmen with them, but then I understand. Colin, though, who has only seen my confusion, thinks he needs to explain. 'You might use them as weapons and hit me over the head with something.' He laughs and I laugh too but it's not funny.

My brain immediately begins chasing around in circles with this new problem that needs solving. 'I know. I can use a knife and spoon from the kitchen.'

Colin looks back into the room to the woman who has been smoking and watching us. She shrugs. 'S'pose that'd be okay.'

I spend the afternoon pulling up the brittle grass that creeps across the barren patch of dirt outside my window before beginning to dig with the spoon and knife. Soon I'm lost in the remembered feel of my hands working the earth and fail to hear Colin come up behind me. When I sit back on my heels to rest he holds out an empty plastic milk bottle. 'To water your seeds with, mate.'

At the end of that first day I stand and stretch out the ache in my back. Five neat rows of seeds with a jagged line of damp across the top where I've watered them in with Colin's milk bottle. I feel my heart expanding and know that I'm already impatient to see them grow.

'Look,' Raheem says a week later, holding the cigarette he's been smoking out the window. 'Look at your garden, Sa'eed.' He moves aside to let me look. Dozens of tiny green shoots are beginning to uncurl as they poke their heads up through the soil. 'It's a miracle,' I whisper.

'This miracle happens every day,' Raheem says, flicking his cigarette onto the ground beside my garden before lifting the sheet that hides his bed and climbing back in. Those like Raheem who have the lower bunks have begun hanging sheets around their beds to keep the world out, while those of us on top have nowhere to hide.

'Not here it doesn't, Raheem.'

When he talks to me it's often of returning to Iran but I tell him you can't look back. 'You mustn't think of what your life might've been like because your life isn't like that any more, Raheem. It's like this.'

I learnt this from one of the Australian doctors. 'It'll drive you mad,' he had said to me.

'I could go back. Your government wants me to go back.'

I'm always testing them, wanting to know if the Australians like me or not. Some, like the doctor, give nothing away, but others I can see more clearly. Colin likes me; Shivorn likes me; my lawyer . . . I don't know. Maybe. No matter how many times I tell myself that it's not important I know that it might be the one thing that decides whether I can stay in Australia or not. It's another one of those ideas that keep chasing around in my head.

When Shivorn returns I let her know how much I like potluck, but especially how much I like the vegetables. She smiles and hands me more packets of seeds. 'Broccoli, carrots, lettuce and daisies. You need flowers too, Sa'eed.' She then gives me a cutting wrapped in wet newspaper. 'This's called "never-ending" basil.'

'Basil that never ends? I've never seen this before.' Aasera, who especially loves basil, would love this plant.

When Shivorn leaves I dig up more ground further out from my window to plant my new seeds and my 'never-ending' basil in fresh new rows, thinking all the time of Aasera and what she'll say when I tell her about 'never-ending' basil.

'That's one bloody huge garden you've got there, Sa'eed,' Colin says as he stands over my bent figure. My garden has begun to attract all manner of things, not just insects. I smile up with pride before leaning over to break off a piece of the parsley, its scent filling the air and lingering on my fingers as I hold it up to him. 'It's good for cleaning teeth.'

'Are you saying I've got bad breath?' It takes me a couple of seconds to understand that Colin's making a joke and I laugh a little too but I'll never understand these things that Australians find funny.

'Got any peas yet?' calls out Farooq from under the tree where he and Samad are sitting smoking. They have taken to watching me work: the idleness of old men claiming their days as they wait and worry.

'Soon,' I tell him, turning back to dig again. 'Soon.'

My lawyer has arrived. He only ever brings bad news, which he tries to disguise as good news. I tell him that the Australian government is trying to break us to send a message that it's not worth coming to Australia. He doesn't agree with this, but he doesn't disagree either. He's very careful about many things: good at not speaking the truth and very good at not telling lies.

'These people in your government won't listen to what I tell them.' I'm leaning forward now across the formica table in the visitors' room, my words rising in the air. When I notice people beginning to stare I force myself to sit back down again. I am ashamed. I no longer recognise this man I have become.

'I know, Sa'eed. I know.' He's rubbing his forehead and I see for the first time how tired he is. My lawyer has too many cases; too much worry. 'They'll eventually give you a visa. You know that, don't you?'

I'm stunned and suddenly all the things that have been racing around in my head come crashing to a stop, piling up and banging into each other. 'Relax, Sa'eed,' he is saying. But I can't relax and the thoughts have all righted themselves and begun zooming around again even faster and then he is gone. Nothing has been resolved. He'll be back next month unless there's a decision in the meantime.

When I return to my garden I try to still my mind by searching out the grubs that have begun to eat my broccoli, but there is a memory going around in my head that will not let me be.

'You must leave,' Abbas is saying as he sits on the cushion across the floor from me, each of us smoking. The ashtray is full and the hummus and bread are all gone and I'm wondering why Aasera has not come to take the mess away. 'Next time they'll kill you.' I know it's true but I'm finding it hard to speak after being held for so long in the dark – who would have thought that darkness could steal your words away? 'Take your family, Sa'eed, and go to Syria.' I look up to see Aasera busy in the kitchen preparing our evening meal and although she isn't looking I know she's listening. And then I know why she hasn't come in. She wants Abbas to say these things to me.

'You'll not come back next time,' she cries that night in our bed. 'And what will we do then, Sa'eed? Tell me . . . when I have no husband and your children have no father, what we will do? You must go to Syria.'

'Shh,' I whisper, holding her close in the dark. Can she not see that I am unable to make such decisions? Sometimes this memory is different and I am crying and Aasera is the strong one but I no longer know which is the real memory and there's no one now to tell me.

Raheem wants to have a smoke but he also wants to meet Shivorn because I've been talking about her too much. She's another thought chasing around in my head. He also wants to hear the answer to what I'm going to ask her.

'Shivorn,' I say, my heart thumping like a stupid schoolboy's, 'why do you come here?' I have practised saying this because I wanted it to be a nice question but I think it's come out all wrong. Raheem also thinks it's come out all wrong because he's decided that he really does need a smoke after all and gets up from the table. We watch as he moves away to the high wire fence from where you can see the Australian houses.

'I come because I think that what my government's doing to you is wrong and perhaps to give you some comfort. Are you married, Sa'eed?'

'Yes.'

'Me too.' I'm relieved to hear this, but strangely I'm also a little disappointed.

'I wish I could show you a photo of my wife, Aasera, but she's only in my head.' I smile and tap my head as if pointing to the place where memories are saved. What I don't tell Shivorn is that the photos in my head have faded so much that even if I could get them out to show to her she might not be able to see Aasera. I decide I don't want to think about these things so I take Shivorn to my garden, watching her closely as we round the corner and it comes into view.

'Sa'eed,' is all she can say as she stands looking out over my garden, which is now heavy with fruit and the bright flowers of potluck that frame its boundaries. Leaning down she runs her hand through the herbs that tumble out across the ground at her feet and as their scent fills the air she breathes in deeply and sighs, 'You have created a thing of beauty in this place, Sa'eed.' I smile. 'But how . . .?'

As I tell her about the other Australian women who have also been bringing me seeds, a white moth, soft and light and as perfect as snow, lands on a cabbage. I know it's laying its eggs and that when they hatch they'll start to eat the cabbage, but for now it is a thing of beauty. We walk around the garden as Shivorn points out what she loves most until she asks about my children and the smile leaves my heart.

'I had seven children,' I tell her, 'but one of my daughters died and a son was killed fighting in the uprising.' It's hard for me to talk about this but I also know that it's hard for people to hear because they're too afraid to even begin imagining what it must be like to lose two children. I need to change the subject again and as we walk back to the table I tell her about the new soap we were given that morning. What

I don't tell Shivorn is that when I lathered this soap and held my hands to my face my breath flew out of my body. The soap held the scent of Aasera's hair just after it's been washed. But it's always the same: the good memories lead to the bad. They will not be left behind. As I talk about this soap I feel the tears beginning to well and push them back. I don't want my new friend to think I'm crying over soap.

I told the doctor about the soap in our meeting that afternoon because I wanted to know why feelings that came from smells were more powerful than those from pictures but all he said was that I shouldn't torture myself with the soap. This young doctor has no idea. The soap isn't torture. This soap brings me Aasera better than any photo ever could.

At breakfast Farooq insists that the peas are ready to be harvested. Even though I don't agree I promise to check them again but when I'm about to go out to the garden the manager of the centre comes to my room.

'You'd better sit down, Sa'eed. I've got some bad news for you.'

The government has rejected my final application. This is the thing I fear the most in the whole world. I sit back on Raheem's bed waiting for this terrible news.

'I'm sorry, Sa'eed, really, really sorry but we've just heard that one of your sons has been killed.'

I'm not understanding this. 'One of my sons has been killed? But which son has been killed?'

'We don't know. We'll try to find out for you as soon as we can. Sorry, mate.' He puts his hand on my shoulder and squeezes it before leaving me alone.

I climb back up onto my own bed and turn to face the wall but I don't know which son to grieve for. I can see my little Ziad, when he is five years old. No, perhaps he is younger. I can't remember these things well but my wife will know. 'Aasera, how old was Ziad when we gave him that little red truck he loved so much?'

'Sa'eed, why do you not remember these things?' She has turned from the stove, the spoon she has been stirring the beans with is in her hand, which is now resting on her hip. As I lie on my bed watching her I can tell that she's pretending to be angry with me and I shrug for I know she'll remember. She always does. 'It was his third birthday and he was dressed in the little blue suit Mr Faiz made for him. Surely you can remember that, Sa'eed?'

'Yes, yes, I can remember it now.' Aasera turns back to the beans on the stove. I think she secretly likes being the memory keeper.

We had a photo from that day. I asked Ziad to smile and he gave me what he thought was a smile and Aasera laughed at his silly screwed-up face. He looked over at his mother then and started laughing too, even though he had no idea why she was laughing. That's when I took the photo of Ziad, but I can't properly find it in my head any more and I can't make the sound of Aasera's laughter either. When I don't try to hold these things they're there, but when I try to look more closely they slip away.

I cry for my little Ziad and for my wife's lost laugh until I remember that perhaps it's not Ziad who's dead. Perhaps it's Hussein and I pull up a memory of my older son. He's having trouble with a bigger boy at school – at least that's what I think is happening – and he's sitting on Aasera's knee – I remember thinking at the time that he was nearly too big to do that any more – and she's holding him, wrapping her mother's love around him until he folds into her and his tears all dry up.

This thin bed facing the lemon-coloured wall is not my bed. My bed is strong and was made from the cedars of Lebanon by my great-great-grandfather, and there is a window next to my bed that has lace curtains. It is summer and the curtains are drifting in the soft breeze, shadows playing up the wall. Aasera, heavy with our child, is lying on the bed with one hand resting on her thickening belly and the other on the windowsill, watching the curtains dust over her skin. 'They are the fingers of God,' she says as I lie down beside her. 'Listen, Sa'eed, and you will hear Him whispering. He's telling me that He will keep our child safe.'

One of my sons is dead. They still can't tell me which one and so I've decided that it's a bad mistake and climb down from my bunk and return to my garden.

'Ah, Sa'eed,' Raheem says, when he notices me. Getting up he dusts the dirt from his knees and the seat of his pants before pulling some packets of seeds out of his pockets. 'The women brought you these, and that woman, Shivorn, she's been asking about you.' He hesitates, looking worried as I take the seeds from him. 'I picked the peas for Farooq. I hope you don't mind. They were ready and I didn't know how long . . .' His voice trails off with uncertainty. There is a plastic bucket in the middle of one of the flowerbeds. 'It's for the birds,' Raheem says when he sees me looking at it, 'for when they're thirsty.' This is a new, more talkative Raheem who hasn't been watching so much TV. He bends and lays the knife he's been working with back on the ground.

'It's okay, Raheem. Everything's okay.'

There is something Raheem wants to say but he's hesitating. He looks over to the wire fence before looking back at me. 'Sa'eed, you know it's not good for you to think of what you've lost. It'll drive you crazy in this place.'

'Yes, Raheem, you're right.'

I have learnt that it's best to work the garden in the morning shade, but as Raheem and I bend to our tasks it's already late and I can feel the sun beginning to burn through my shirt. I must not think of this thing that I cannot even begin to hold in my heart and so I decide that I will think only of the sun on my back and of the life it gives to this beautiful garden. That is all I must think about today.

This story was inspired by the poem written by former refugee Hassan Sabbagh and the garden he built while in Villawood Immigration Detention Centre.

Hassan was released after four years and three months. At the time he had no idea if his family was alive. His wife and his four surviving children, two sons and twin daughters, joined him in Australia two years after his release.

Have you ever seen someone who loves his
torturer?
Have you ever heard about someone loved in his
fifties?
I am that one
When she is coming
I start shaking
My heart dancing
Embarrassing
Like a teenager meeting his girl for the first time
She is as gentle as the breeze of a spring morning
The rose in first blooming
A butterfly
She is a balsam on the wound
She is so gorgeous
When I see her
I forget my suffering, my torture and my
deprivation,
She makes me happy.
Who is she?
She is the old woman who comes from faraway.
She is the little girl who heard of asylum seekers,
She is young and middle-aged Australian women.

OBLIGATION TO NEED
RAIMOND GAITA

Some Australians are deeply saddened by the hostility that many of their fellow Australians have shown towards asylum seekers. Confronted with the aggressive nationalism that such hostility often expresses, some people never again want to hear talk of love of country. Even if there can be such love, not corrupted by what Ghassan Hage calls 'paranoid nationalism', they believe it is so rare and its distortions which are all too often murderous so many, that it should be discouraged.

Others are ashamed of the hostility shown by their fellow countrymen and women to asylum seekers, but their shame presupposes that their identities have been formed by their attachment to the country. They voice that identity when they use 'we' to express national fellowship rather than merely to record the fact that they belong with other Australians to a national group. Paul Keating's Redfern speech is one of the most powerful and well-known expressions of it: 'We brought the diseases and the alcohol. We committed the murders. We took the children from their mothers. We practised discrimination and exclusion.' Many people were moved to agree even though they were not even alive at the time when most of those things were done. That sense of fellowship goes deeper than the pride or shame that people can feel collectively considered only as citizens, in part because it is historically deeper than citizenship sometimes is, and because it involves attachment to, sometimes love of, aspects of the country in which even the most dutiful citizens need have no interest – the countryside, the light, the literature and the songs, for example.

Often people who oppose the cruelty inflicted upon asylum seekers try to bring their fellow citizens to a compassionate understanding of what it means to suffer such cruelties and the humiliations that are generally inseparable from them. They try to awaken an acknowledgement that we share a common humanity with asylum seekers and their families and to make such an acknowledgement inseparable from the 'we' of 'national fellowship'. They hope that most Australians will embrace rather than resist the fact that Australia belongs to a community of nations, constituted as such by international law. Admittedly, the sense in which such a community exists is still rather thin, and so, therefore, is the sense in which derogation of one's international obligations as defined in international law is an offence against humankind. It is not meaningless, however. The concept of a crime against humanity, for example, expresses the belief that those who commit this crime offend against the moral constitution of humanity itself – considered not only as a constituency of human beings, but of human beings who are citizens of the plurality of nations that comprise the community of nations.

The dispute (one cannot call it a debate) between the two major political parties about asylum-seeker policy has become what Kevin Rudd feared it would when he refused to join a 'race to the bottom'. In the short term our politicians have given us choices between bad and worse policies. We have little reason to think things will get better. Deepening political instability in many regions of the earth, inflamed by the shameful gap between the rich and the poor nations, aggravated by the effects of climate change, will almost certainly cause even more people to be uprooted than were last century. Strong nations are likely to protect themselves in ways that become increasingly brutal, testing the relevance and authority of international law. Angry and bitter, the dispossessed will ask: 'Why merely because some people are fortunate to be born in a particular location on this earth, should they enjoy the fruits of the earth and be able, in the name of sovereignty, to deny it to others who, merely because they are born elsewhere, suffer the miseries of the damned?' The way we now think about these matters – as finding the right balance between the rights of sovereign states and the human rights of those who seek refuge – will not take us far towards an answer. But if we are to share with the dispossessed even the vestiges of a common humanity, we must face the question truthfully and with the right conceptual resources. That will determine what we think should go on the scales.

No one, of course, can sensibly believe that anyone should expect to live wherever they want to. But if we rise to the question's simple moral force, we will, I believe, rethink the relative importance we attach to rights, on the one hand, and to our obligation to need, on the other. To explain why, I shall reflect on some of the last writings of the French philosopher Simone Weil.

In 1942 the leaders of the Free French in London asked Weil to contribute towards a new Declaration of Rights for the Fourth French Republic, as they hoped it would be formed after the liberation of France. Weil wrote instead *Draft for a Statement of Human Obligations*. It was published (unfinished) in France in 1949 as *L'Enracinement*, six years after her death. An English translation, *The Need for Roots*, was published in 1952 with the subtitle *Prelude to a Declaration of Duties towards Mankind*. In the same year that she worked on her *Draft*, she wrote an essay published posthumously in French as *La Personne et le Sacré* and in English (misleadingly) as *Human Personality*. It is one of the most beautiful works on human affliction, its nature and how we should think about it morally and politically that I have read.

Early in the essay Weil asks, 'What is it that is sacred in every human being?' On the way to her answer she enumerates and rejects a number of facts about us. Her list is not exhaustive, but its rhetorical point is that no list could enable us fully to understand what it means to wrong someone, especially when that wrong constitutes a violation of them, as rape and torture do, for example. She writes:

> At the bottom of the heart of every human being, from earliest infancy until the tomb, there is something that goes on indomitably expecting, in the teeth of all experience of crimes committed, suffered and witnessed, that good and not evil will be done to him. It is this above all that is sacred in every human being . . . Every time there arises from the depths of a human heart the childish cry which even Christ could not restrain, 'Why am I being hurt?', then there is certainly injustice. Many people do not hear it. For it is a silent cry which sounds only in the secret heart.[14]

Although Weil writes about what 'is sacred' in every human being, the moral work of that passage does not depend on reference to the sacred or to any religious concepts. She could have asked: What is precious in every human being? Or, What gives us even so much as the idea that some wrongs and crimes constitute a violation because they violate something precious? She writes of what is sacred *in* every human being, but she is asking why we think human beings are sacred. In the same spirit we might ask, 'Why do we think that every human being is infinitely precious?' The important point is that Weil invites us to think about this in a conceptual space in which it is natural for us to think of love and tenderness rather than of nobility or heroism. Had she asked what is noble and inspiring in humanity, to which we owe (perhaps unconditional) respect, her answer would have been quite different.

Later in the essay she is critical of the importance we attach to the concept of rights when we try to explain what it means to wrong someone, or when we try to protect people from wrongs.

> If you say to someone who has ears to hear: 'What you are doing to me is not just', you may touch and waken at its source the spirit of

attention and love. But it is not the same with words like 'I have the right . . .' or 'you have no right to . . .' They evoke a latent war and awaken the spirit of contention. To place the notion of rights at the centre of social conflicts is to inhibit any possible impulse of charity on both sides. Relying almost exclusively on this notion, it becomes impossible to keep one's eyes on the real problem. If someone tries to browbeat a farmer to sell his eggs at a moderate price, the farmer can say: 'I have the right to keep my eggs if I don't get a good enough price.' But if a young girl is being forced into a brothel she will not talk about her rights. In such a situation the word would sound ludicrously inadequate.[15]

The reason Weil says it would be ludicrously inadequate for the girl to protest that her rights had been violated is not because it would be pointless to do so. It is because the concept of rights is radically inadequate to the moral awfulness of what the girl is suffering. That is one reason why Weil says the concept of rights is a 'mediocre' one. The moral force of an appeal to rights depends upon elaborations of the kind to which we gesture when we say, incredulously, 'Don't you understand what it means to suffer this kind of humiliation?', or which a person who is seriously remorseful would seek in order to understand fully what he did. Imagine though if, at the moment of bitter remorse, the perpetrator of the evil against the girl were to say, 'My God! What have I done! I've violated the girl's human rights.'

It is characteristic of Weil as a writer that she should be able to convey so powerfully, in only a few words, the pitilessness of the assault on the girl and her powerlessness in the face of it. She presents neither a physical nor a moral obstacle to the man who seeks to enslave her. About those who 'have suffered too many blows' Weil says, 'that place in the heart from which the infliction of evil evokes a cry of surprise may seem dead. But it is never quite dead; it is simply unable to cry out anymore. It has sunk into a state of dumb and ceaseless lamentation.' The same is true of some asylum seekers, even before they reach our shores to spend years in detention or processing centres. We call it depression. That can distract from the fact that their affliction is marked through and through by the kind of incredulity at the evil done to them that Weil expresses so beautifully and which, distinct from the psychological and physical harm they suffer, is an irreducible source of a torment whose only expression is a 'dumb and ceaseless lamentation'.

Weil died in 1943 at the age of thirty-four. Her understanding of war and the almost limitless potential of human cruelty shows in much of her writing, perhaps most beautifully in *The Iliad, or The Poem of Force*. World War II gave the world urgent reasons to develop international conventions and laws to limit state sovereignty. For that reason a resurgence of interest in human rights developed as an important basis for international law. At the same time that Weil was working on her *Draft for a Statement of Human Obligations*, others in France, notably René Cassin, were working towards a Declaration of Human Rights. In his speech of acceptance for the Nobel Prize, awarded to him for his work in gaining international agreement in 1948 to the Universal Declaration of Human Rights, Cassin makes clear that he and others were driven by their outrage at the humiliations suffered by veterans of World War I when they returned to their native lands and by the failure of international institutions to constrain the aggressive ambitions of nation states. Against the imperious arrogance of states, he sought protections for the institutions of civil society and for individuals to invoke their rights rather than being reliant on charity, which is unreliable and demeaning.

The preamble to the Universal Declaration of Human Rights speaks of 'the inherent dignity . . . of all members of the human family' and of 'the dignity and worth of the human person'. Reference to 'human dignity' and 'inalienable dignity' occurs in many of the preambles to important instruments of international criminal law. Its place in those preambles suggests that the idea of the dignity of humanity, of a dignity that one possesses simply by virtue of being human, underpins the concept of an inalienable right and is fundamental to the elaboration of what it means ethically to violate such a right. The morally terrible character of crimes against humanity is often rendered as an offence against the human dignity of those who suffer them. This is the realisation of Cassin's noble vision. Weil believes it rests on an illusion. Talk of dignity was not as common when she wrote as it is today, but she heard the tone in which we now speak of it in the work of Cassin and his colleagues in France and elsewhere in the Declaration of the Rights of Man and of the Citizen of 1789. It is that tone to which she objects. 'I don't need your pity . . . I don't need your charity . . . I stand on my rights and the Dignity you cannot touch.' That, she thought, was the tone in 1789.

If we are to understand the ethical character of affliction when it is the result of evil done to those who suffer it, if we are soberly to understand what it means for their humanity to have been violated, we must, Weil says, keep a distance from words like rights and Dignity (when it takes a capital D) that move us because they are in a heroic register. In humanity's struggle against oppression, cruelty and the crimes of war, she believes, we have developed an ethical language that cannot enable us to speak truthfully about or to affliction. In the key of the heroic and the noble, the language of rights and Dignity has made it almost impossible to hear the cry of the afflicted, 'Why am I being hurt?' That is why she says it is often a silent cry.

Another example might make her point more persuasive. I hope that it will also explain why I said earlier that Weil invites us to reflect on oppression and affliction in a conceptual space in which concepts of love and tenderness are central.

In *If This Is a Man*, Primo Levi tells the story of when he and a friend, Charles, lived in barracks in Auschwitz with fellow prisoners who had typhus. They could hear the Russian artillery only a few miles away. One of the prisoners, a young Dutchman called Ladmaker, had dysentery. He fell from the bed he had soiled onto the floor, where he lay in his vomit and faeces. Levi writes:

Charles climbed down from his bed and dressed in silence. While I held the lamp, he cut all the dirty patches from the straw mattress and the blankets with a knife. He lifted Ladmaker from the ground with the tenderness of a mother, cleaned him as best as possible with straw taken from the mattress and lifted him into the remade bed in the only position in which the unfortunate fellow could lie. He scraped the floor with a scrap of tin plate, diluted a little chloramine and finally spread disinfectant over everything, including himself.[16]

Charles' behaviour is something to wonder at, but it can elicit two kinds of wonder. The first is directed towards him and his virtues: it is inspired by the fact that for the sake of a man who would almost certainly die within a day or two, he risked his life after years in Auschwitz, with freedom probably only weeks away. From the perspective of that kind of wonder one might call his behaviour supererogatory because it was above and beyond the call of duty. The second kind of wonder is quite different. It is inspired by the fact that Charles responded 'with the tenderness of a mother' and it focuses our attention more on Ladmaker than on him. From its perspective, the wonder of what Charles did is that he responded fully to Ladmaker's degradation, saw fully the depth of it, and was at the same time able to affirm that Ladmaker was inalienably precious – for that, I believe, is what his tenderness revealed. For that reason, I suggest that we do what comes naturally and call the acknowledgement of Ladmaker's humanity, as it showed in Charles' tenderness, a form of love. From the second perspective our wonder is a response to the *goodness* of such love and its capacity to reveal the full humanity of those whose affliction made their humanity at best only partially visible.

To return now to the point I made earlier: a religious person might say that Charles responded to Ladmaker as to someone who is sacred. Certainly his love is an example of the kind that has been shown by saints and could serve as an example of what religion has taught about

what it means to love one's neighbour. But one needn't be religious –
I am not – to respond to Charles' affirmation of the preciousness of
the wretched Ladmaker. Goodness, wonder, purity, love – those concepts take us to a perspective different from the one whose salient
conceptual features incline us to be struck most of all by the thought
that Charles' behaviour was supererogatory.

Supererogatory acts tell us what people are capable of. They are,
to exaggerate only a little, moral *feats* that leave us awestruck. Heroic
deeds are their paradigm. Many people speak of saints and heroes in
the same breath, but the works of saintly love do not leave us awestruck at the capacities of saints to do what they do. Instead, they
illuminate the world for us, and in the case of deeds like Charles',
they reveal to us or remind us that even people who are radically and
incurably afflicted and who are unrepentant evildoers are, in a sense
that is beyond what is natural or reasonable to believe, infinitely precious. But if that is true, then to say that when Charles responded to
Ladmaker 'with the tenderness of a mother' he responded to his inalienable dignity, is to speak in the wrong key – the heroic and noble
key in which talk of inalienable dignity so often moves us.

I would not wish to give the impression that the compassion
Charles showed should play the same sentimental role as love did in
the sixties. Nor would I suggest that we try to banish talk of human
rights. But I think that Weil was right to insist that if we are to respond
truthfully to affliction, it is imperative that we disengage the way
we talk of human rights from the illusion that even the most radically afflicted – those who, as Weil puts it, have been 'struck one of
those blows that leaves a human being writhing on the ground like
a half-crushed worm' – retain a Dignity that their degradation cannot take from them. Only saints can see, and their love reveal to us,
the full humanity of such people. That is why Weil said that compassion for the afflicted is 'a more astounding miracle than walking on
water, healing the sick or raising the dead'. When the concept of rights
is underpinned by a heroically inflected conception of inalienable

dignity, it tends to make us deaf to the cry of the afflicted and blind to what the love of saints would otherwise enable us to see.

Earlier when I tried to explain why the concept of rights could not of itself awaken us to a full understanding of the wrong done to the girl taken into sexual slavery, I said that when we speak of a right violated, we rely, even if only implicitly, on further elaborations of its moral significance. Such elaborations are made and understood against the background of a common understanding. But, of course, though we speak naturally in the singular of *a* common understanding, anything that counts as such is made up of many and sometimes conflicting traditions. In one, the idea of a violation is at its deepest the violation of human dignity. That idea of dignity is partnered in ways congenial to it by ideals of autonomy, integrity and nobility. Another has goodness, love and purity at its centre. In that tradition, they are the primary ethical concepts that transform, rather than replace, our understanding of virtues – integrity, autonomy, rights and dignity, among others – as they appear from a heroic perspective.

Weil's most important and hardheaded insight is that it is, at best, whistling in the dark to posit an inalienable dignity that no degree of degradation can destroy. At worst, that illusion degrades the only language in which the afflicted can give voice to the cry, 'Why am I being hurt?' and, perhaps paradoxically, makes us less respectful than we should be of dignity that is intrinsically alienable. No one should be so alienated from their ordinary, alienable dignity that only a saint can see them as fully human.

Weil believed that attraction to the heroic and the grand, which undermines our capacity to respond truthfully to the reality of affliction, also corrupts love of country. In *The Need for Roots* she describes being rooted in a national culture as 'food for the soul', and a country as a 'vital medium'. She also points out that in unusual circumstances it can be poison for the soul. (Think of Nazi Germany, when true patriots fought in the resistance against Germany as an expression of their love for it, for what it was and for what it might again become.)

Many intellectuals are sceptical of the prospects for and moral worth of the nation state. Most peoples in the world, however, depend on it for the protection of those distinctive institutions and ways of life that make them a people. For them, the fear that they might otherwise live under foreign occupation, be denied the right to speak their language, to honour their national institutions, fully to remember their past and to pass on its treasures to future generations, is only too real. In such circumstances people realise that responsible love of country seeks protection for what is loved and is owed to future generations. Protection is sought not just for the institutions of citizenship, the rule of law, democracy and so on – as these might be relatively interchangeable between different countries – but for those institutions as they are infused by the spirit of a particular people. In modern times the means of protection is almost always the nation state, for it alone has the necessary military power (even if only in alliance with other nation states). Weil's acknowledgement of our need for roots and the military force required to protect that need expressed the reluctant abandonment of her earlier pacifism.

Yet in *The Need for Roots* her hostility to our tendency to be inspired by grandeur and the heroic is not diminished in the slightest. Love of country, she argues, is nourished by appreciation of what is beautiful and vulnerable in one's country and its history rather than by what is grand and noble. True to her newly formed rejection of pacifism, she believed, in 1942, that when it is properly focused, such love of country can provide the energy needed for soldiers to fight as fiercely as German soldiers who were inspired by dreams of heroic grandeur that had been celebrated in European history since the time of the Roman Empire. The task, she says, is to turn away from the spirit of that celebration and to turn towards ways of thinking that would inspire soldiers to fight well and bravely while at the same time reducing the likelihood that they would, if justice were done, stand before an international criminal court, accused of war crimes or worse.

If we grant that there can be such a thing as love of country that is worthy of respect and deserves to be nourished, then we must distinguish, as with all forms of love, real love from its counterfeits – real love of country from the kind of aggressive nationalism that we call jingoism and which pollutes everything that comes into contact with it. Real love of country can be identified by at least two markers: the desire to love truthfully and the desire to love without the shame that would be the only truthful response to the wrongs done on behalf of the nation by our leaders or, in time of war, by our soldiers. Because it fastens onto something that is inevitably a mixture of good and evil, love of country is always a mixture of gratitude, pain, joy, sorrow, pride, shame and sometimes guilt. In the circumstances that make them appropriate, each can be a *form* of love of country, just as severe criticism of one's country can be a form of loyalty to it, and the desire to love without shame and without lies a form of concern for its welfare.

It is a truism that the international laws that constitute the nations of the earth as a community of nations express values that are in some sense universal. It is natural and common to think that the universal values expressed in those laws are principles that can be abstracted from the cultures of the nations that are answerable to those principles. Those values, this thought continues, could be – and ideally should be – expressed in a language that consciously disengages from the local, historically conditioned associations and resonances of natural languages.

But there is another way to think of universality. We see it if we reflect on the fact that understanding of what it means to commit and to suffer the crimes prohibited by international law is often deepened by art – when a film, a painting, a play, a novel or a poem, for example, moves us. Art provides a different model for universality than does science or a political or moral philosophy that seeks universal principles abstracted from the concrete circumstances for peoples who are intellectually and spiritually nourished by the way they have been rooted in this or that culture.

'Every writer needs an address,' said Isaac Bashevis Singer, 'even if it is more than one.' That is a fine way of putting the point I have been trying to make. Great literature potentially speaks to all the peoples of the earth (that is one of the reasons we call it 'great'), but only as translated from one natural language to another. That is not because we have been unable to develop a single universal language, as some hoped to do with Esperanto. It is because that is the kind of universality that is appropriate to the content of literature – content which often cannot be separated from its form and whose form cannot be separated from the contingencies that have nourished particular cultures, particular forms of living and particular natural languages – 'vital mediums', as Weil calls them. Only in such 'mediums', in the natural languages distinctive to them, can we elaborate what it means ethically to violate someone's rights, to commit crimes against humanity or against the laws of war.

Weil writes:

> We owe a cornfield respect, not because of itself, but because it is food for human beings. In the same way we owe respect to a collectivity – country, family or any other – not for itself but because it is food for a certain number of human souls . . . One sack of corn can always be substituted by another sack of corn. The food that a collectivity supplies for the souls of those who form part of it has no equivalent in the entire universe.[17]

Those words and others that I have discussed direct us to the concepts we need to discuss – what we owe asylum seekers, what we owe to ourselves and our descendants as citizens of a particular nation and what asylum seekers owe to us if we accept them into our communities and polity.

THE OCEAN
GAIL JONES

That year they grew further and further apart. That year the world was already strained and thin, as if stretched over a screen, like drying sheets, and this sorry quality to things was reversing her feelings for him. He looked at her with a kind of vague disappointment, and she at him as though he were a substituted husband, hired to sit before her, mute, as she placed a cup of trembling tea between his large false hands. His posture sagged. He detached himself. She watched as he lifted the cup to his lips and sucked with a tiny noise that had once seemed endearing and was now immature, even infantile, a boyish wrinkling of the mouth. They would never have children. They would never move beyond this complacent pattern of tea and routine and the way he wiped his mouth after the first sip with the back of his hand. She remembered when they weren't bored, when they undressed without hesitation, and smiling, his arm already around her waist.

On the telly they saw a shipload of foreign people. Four hundred and thirty-eight, the newsreader said, plucked from the ocean, from a sinking wooden boat. People smugglers, she heard, Indonesia, she heard, Hazara, Afghanistan, fleeing the Taliban. An aerial shot circled the container ship, like God assessing. The angle made it appear tilted, listing to the water, its human cargo a sliding, precarious load. In the foreshortened perspective the Afghans were indistinct and collective, a mere pattern of men, for some reason sitting on the deck, in rows, apparently quiet and obedient. The distance made them seem paltry and inconsequential. One man waved to the helicopter, his image flying up, a flung gesture sent skywards in affirmation from the Indian Ocean, then rushed in lit particles through the television screen. Her husband shifted uneasily in his armchair. She watched the little man with the spontaneous wave veer away. The newsreader returned, a blonde woman in a silk shirt, and then the news shifted to local politics and talk of the election; men's faces, then more men's faces, bubbling with empty words.

Later, as she listened to the radio in bed to help her sleep, she heard there were women there, and children, on that vast container ship. This intrigued her, somehow, this anomalous information. She tossed and turned in her bed. She felt the weight of her own body. She felt an imprecise grief burning inside her. And when at last she relaxed she thought not of these undescribed people, a mass, a collective out there on the ocean, but of herself as a child, struggling under the suffocation of an asthma attack.

They had all imagined their deaths. Of the rescued, there was not one single adult who had not imagined death.

Amina sat in a container, emptied to shelter the women and children and a few of the wounded and unconscious. Rust red, the colour of alarm, it had a severe metallic smell, like chains, or iron pots too long on the flames, or the burn of a body falling face forward, skin gone, after shelling and explosions. The walls were hot to the touch and she guarded the little ones. The air was still and putrid. The two pregnant women among them were weak with vomiting and the effort to sustain an extra life. Alongside, the next container was being used as a latrine; it was full of buckets and plastic bags, awash in their waste and sour with the stench of human bodies, ill and evacuating.

On the deck were others unconscious, another dozen or so, and rows of seated men. They were neatly arranged, as in a school, in lines equidistant and parallel. This detail struck Amina as particularly absurd. The chaos of their situation was not expressed in the usual configuration of crowds: random clusters, comings and goings, the hub-hub of a market, or a meeting, or a political rally. The lines reminded her – heretically – of men in the mosque, the series, the unanimity, the rising and falling in prayer. She thought of her father before dawn, his back curled, his supplication, and the gentle murmur of the Quran; she thought of his prostration, thrice, as he glorified Allah and his prophet Mohammed. When he rose his gaze had a faraway look. Devotion transported him, he was a man made holy.

They spoke in hushed tones or fell silent, eyes closing against the sun. Many were sick with conditions of the body or mind. Many envied the unconscious. Their faces were thin with exhaustion; the terrible nights of the journey had sucked away substance, so that their brown eyes were huge and their mouths appeared loose and enlarged. Her own husband, Ahmed, looked almost foreign to her. An engineer, he had stayed in the belly of the *Palapa* throughout the night, trying with no tools to restart the engine, banging with no hammer the nails popping loose in the deck, helping stuff plastic bags into holes or holding his thin hands over leaks, as if that might save them.

During the storm in the night they were all terrified. The name of Allah and his prophet were screamed into the wind. The boat pitched and plunged. Sea water swamped the sides. Their ears filled with a fierce, inhuman roar. With doom dripping over them, they tied their children to their bodies and were banged against the rough wood of the damaged boat. Their skin was grazed and blood and vomit formed a swill at their feet. They watched the ocean slowly enter the *Palapa* as fear of death might enter a man. It unloosed the shape and integrity of things; it distorted and bloated the sound of the elements; it made the darkness shiny, as if it had its own power. So small, the human will against the will of the ocean, and of the boat, which was animated, groaning in the cause of its own destruction. Ahmed said that in the Quran it was written that death always comes at the right time. That a man in a castle, walled up, will not be safe if it is his time. That any day, the prophet said, is a good day to die. Amina did not believe this teaching. She held her son Hussein against her wet body and felt the solidity of his existence against all that was disintegrating. His fine hair. His tiny hands. His interest in stories of the stars and the impossible deeds of heroes. When he had cried out she held him close, as if there was no other meaning.

The storm ceased at dawn. Those not sleeping were weeping, or caught in the spell of a sorrowful, distant stare. Men, for most were men, showed their dignity or distress in a silent closing down. The boat was still taking water and many were preparing for the next world, looking past the rising sun to the drowned future ahead. Amina had never seen men weep in this way before, nor seen how they too were undone, how they too might cling on to Life against Fate; and how the love of modest things – the glimpse of a silver sea-bird, the shred of a tender memory, the faint print of a manuscript tucked near the heart or a whispered endearment to or from a child – might be enough to make them wish to stay alive and endure their terrible suffering.

A man who seemed a simpleton, carrying an air of bewilderment, asked her: *On the ocean, where is Mecca?*

Another, who in the night-time had pulled a plastic bag over his head, furious at its failure, was this morning breathing full breaths as his last and noting their sweetness.

A third, older than the others, was praying in almost sing-song tones, the better for Allah to attend to his voice.

A fourth was writing something on a scrap of paper. He formed each letter with exquisite care.

It occurred to Amina that she would also like something written; that she did not want to disappear under water with no sign of her self left behind. She considered the mysterious persistence of words. Then she considered her own name, dissolving, or floating away in a bottle. So much depended on what was written on paper.

When the container ship loomed towards them they were crazy with joy. It was a kind of vision. They were the saved, *Insha'Allah*, they were not the drowned. In the Quran the prophet Noah is saved from drowning; Amina's father had told her this story when she was a child. She had never before seen an ocean or a vast body of water, and it was hard to believe that liquid shadows might be the ending of all life. Noah was saved, her father said, because he was beloved and righteous. He was buoyed up, he floated, his vessel was sustained.

It was like a mountain before them, as it steered alongside. An aluminium ladder lowered and sailors appeared. They wore crisp dry clothes. They expressed concern. The children were carried up the side of the ship, and each of the adults climbed slowly, hardly believing their own rescue. Amina's heart snagged as she watched Hussein hoisted up in the arms of a burly sailor, and she had paused, tired with climbing, and leant her cheek against the acid smelling wall of the great ship, as if to a mother. For just a moment it was like peace there, on the ladder, in the wind, her face pressed at the shuddering expanse of metal. The waves below looked small, and almost beautiful. The ocean was expansive, the darkest blue, then gleaming at the far horizon like sunlight on a mirror.

On the deck she discovered that sailors were throwing all their objects – bags, documents, clothes, even their holy books – back onto the sinking boat. Amina thought this an inexplicable cruelty from those who had just pulled them to the light. Now they had only their bodies. Now they were almost nothing. Now there was no written page to prove her nation or who she was. But she opened her arms and Hussein was returned to her embrace, and she praised Allah, and kissed her son, and for the first time, she wept.

In their quiet house, she was mending a frayed blouse. She listened for her husband's return from work. The meal was already prepared: when he entered the house he would wash, then they would take their dinner together, sitting in silence before the television news. She would read, or listen to the radio, and go to bed before he did. The fabric between her fingers was old; she wondered why she bothered to sew when she might buy something new, but she understood that the garment had a nostalgic attachment. She wore this blouse when she first met him, so it was a blurred symbol to her, a sign; and it was something that needed repair.

How long ago was it? They had met on the jetty and sat together, legs dangling, looking over the edge. The water was ruffled and agitated with a slight breeze; rings of light distended, opened, then closed up again below them. He had gently rested his hand on her thigh. She had looked away, towards the horizon, and never before felt so happy.

On the news there were more shots of the container ship in the middle of the ocean. *Tampa*, it was called. They were refugees. *Hazara*. She was not sure what this meant, but noted that the news item elicited from her husband an annoyed grunt of disapproval. Again there were no close-ups, just this lonesome drifting ship filmed from high above, like something stranded and fictitious; so she could not see the women and children, or imagine details of their lives. There was no man sending out an excited wave. No movement, nothing happening. They were all passive, waiting, sitting in tidy lines. Still, it struck her somewhere, this 438 people, all saved from drowning, all wanting to come to Australia. They had hope, these people. They had no cement in the soul.

But they don't realise, she suddenly said aloud to her husband, that nobody wants them.

It was Christmas Island they were heading for. *Christmas Island*.

Amina knew enough from her father's teaching to know that this was an island named for a holy day, for the birth of a prophet. It was an auspicious name. She was bruised and sore from the boat, she was uncertain of their future and worn down by anxiety, but she was also filled with a spirit of gratitude that lightened and exalted her. She closed her eyes and tried to think of all that was sacred. She thought of her father praying, his warm deep voice, and the rustling of his robes as he rose up with his faraway look. The muezzin, calling. The shape of the mosque against twilight. Then she thought more simply: of the sound of the *danbura*, its strings seeming to know human feeling; of the scent of tomato leaves lingering on her fingers; of the warmth of the red earth under the palm of her hand; of making bread, and the moment she sprinkled caraway seeds in the hollow at the centre. Then she thought of her husband, now sitting in a row with the other men, and of her son, asleep, folded into the promise a new life. And of that time, a few years ago, when her own body opened, oceanic, and a baby washed out, breathing.

IMMIGRANT VOYAGE
LES MURRAY

My wife came out on the *Goya*
in the mid-year of our century.

In the fogs of that winter
many hundred ships were sounding;
the DP camps were being washed at sea.

The bombsites and the ghettoes
were edging out to Israel,
to Brazil, to Africa, America.

The separating ships were bound away
to the cities of refuge
built for the age of progress.

Hull-down and pouring light
the tithe-barns, the cathedrals
were bearing the old castes away.

—

Pattern-bombed out of babyhood,
Hungarians-become-Swiss,
the children heard their parents:
Argentina? Or Australia?
Less politics, in Australia . . .

Dark Germany, iron frost
and the waiting many weeks
then a small converted warship
under the moon, turning south.

Way beyond the first star
and beyond Cape Finisterre
the fishes and the birds
did eat of their heave-offerings.

—

The *Goya* was a barracks:
mess-queue, spotlights, tower,
crossing the Middle Sea.

In the haunted blue light
that burned nightlong in the sleeping-decks
the tiered bunks were restless
with coughing, demons, territory.

On the Sea of Sweat, the Red Sea,
the flat heat melted even
dulled deference of the injured.
Nordics and Slavonics
paid salt-tax day and night, being
absolved of Europe

but by the Gate of Tears
the barrack was a village
with accordions and dancing
(Fraulein, kennen Sie meinen Rhythmus?)
approaching the southern stars.

—

Those who said Europe
has fallen to the Proles
and the many who said
we are going for the children,

the nouveau poor
and the cheerful shirtsleeve Proles,
the children, who thought
No Smoking signs meant men
mustn't dress for dinner,

those who had hopes
and those who knew that they
were giving up their lives

were becoming the people
who would say, and sometimes urge,
in the English-speaking years:
we came out on the *Goya*.

—

At last, a low coastline,
old horror of Dutch sail-captains.

Behind it, still unknown,
sunburnt farms, strange trees, family jokes
and all the classes of equality.

As it fell away northwards
there was one last week for songs,
for dreaming at the rail,
for beloved meaningless words.

Standing in to Port Phillip
in the salt-grey summer light
the village dissolved
into strained shapes holding luggage;

now they, like the dour
Australians below them, were facing
encounter with the Foreign
where all subtlety fails.

–

Those who, with effort,
with concealment, with silence, had resisted
the collapsed star Death,
who had clawed their families from it,
those crippled by that gravity

were suddenly, shockingly
being loaded aboard lorries:
They say, another camp –
One did not come for this –

As all the refitted

ships stood, oiling, in the Bay,
spectres, furious and feeble,
accompanied the trucks through Melbourne,

resignation, understandings
that cheerful speed dispelled at length.

That first day, rolling north
across the bright savanna,
not yet people, but numbers.
Population. Forebears.

–

Bonegilla, Nelson Bay,
the dry-land barbed wire ships
from which some would never land.

In these, as their parents
learned the Fresh Start music:
physicians nailing crates,
attorneys cleaning trams,
the children had one last
ambiguous summer holiday.

Ahead of them lay
the Deep End of the schoolyard,
tribal testing, tribal soft-drinks,
and learning English fast,
the Wang-Wang language.

Ahead of them, refinements:
thumbs hooked down hard under belts

to repress gesticulation;

ahead of them, epithets:
wog, reffo, Commo Nazi,
things which can be forgotten
but must first be told.

And farther ahead
in the years of the Coffee Revolution
and the Smallgoods Renaissance,
the early funerals:

the misemployed, the unadaptable,
those marked by the Abyss,

friends who came on the *Goya*
in the mid-year of our century.

ZAHRA'S LULLABY
ARNOLD ZABLE

He cannot sleep. He paces the living room late at night. He watches television into the early hours, yet cannot sit still. He descends the stairs from his second-floor flat. And walks. Allows the beat of his steps to still his thoughts. He walks the streets of the neighbourhood, the gravel paths of Princes Park. Walks further afield to Sydney Road seeking the comfort of night-lights.

When at last he does sleep, it is in short bursts – from nine till noon, from noon till three, from four until the fall of night. Even then there is no respite. He dreams – of the boat going under, of his wife Layla, his daughter, Zahra. They come to him as he last saw them. They are floundering in the ocean. His daughter's hand is in his. She slips from his grasp. He follows her, but she is like melting butter, appearing, disappearing. Vanishing.

Years later, in a one-bedroom flat in Melbourne, he sings to her as he sleeps. A lullaby, in Arabic, the same lullaby night after night. It is Majida, his wife of three years, who hears it. She listens to Faris Shohani mouthing the words. It is Majida who has become his witness, his saving grace.

They sit, Faris and Majida, in the living room of the flat. 'With Faris I am lucky,' she says. 'I tell him he looks like my dad. He says the things my dad said, and like him he is patient.' Turning to Faris, she says, 'I am lucky to be with you. We suffer the same fate.'

'I am like the wind,' says Faris, distracted, 'one hour good, the next hour bad. I feel hot all the time.' No matter how often she has heard the tale, Majida follows every word. She is with him as his spirit rises, and with him when it falls.

'Faris,' she repeats. 'We suffer the same fate. Our great-grandfathers were Kurds who came to Iraq from Iran, but settled apart. We were both born in Iraq, you in Wasit, I in Baghdad – I in 1967, you in 1968. I lost my mother at thirteen. You lost your father at the same age. I looked after my younger brothers and sisters, and you looked after yours. Our families were deported from Iraq back to Iran, but you lived in Yazd, and I, in Teheran. We came from Indonesia by boat – I in 2000, you in 2001. I settled in Sydney, you in Melbourne. And after all that time we met. Faris – that is why I understand you. That is why when you are sleeping in the daytime, I don't wake you.'

'Why, my brother, why?' Faris asks, turning to me, a tone of urgency in his voice. The question can rear up any time. 'Why did the boats leave us? Why?' In the twelfth year since the sinking the question still plagues him, as it plagues many of the forty-five survivors, scattered over many lands – Sweden, Norway, Canada and New Zealand, Finland. And the seven who settled in Australia of whom at least one has since died.

In the early years Faris would ring survivors living abroad. They shared a common bond. He no longer calls. 'I am tired. They are tired. I have no answers. They have no answers. What can I say to them? It is the first question they ask: "Why, Faris, why? Why did the boats leave us?" I saw the boats. They saw the boats – two bigger boats, and one smaller boat; but they left us, and still we don't know why. This question makes us sick.'

Faris was about 400 metres distant when he first saw them. The waves pushed him closer, and with him other survivors, clinging to debris, pieces of timber, to this and that. One was carried so close he hammered his fists against the hull.

'There were many people in the water. The people on the boats saw us. They put on the searchlights. The lights were very strong. They entered our eyes. They turned night into day.'

'I am a witness,' he says, over and again. It imposes a duty. It is his curse. He leans back on the sofa – possessed by the haunted look I have come to know well. It rarely leaves him. He relives the tragedy at any time. The images rear up, unbidden, day and night. 'I am sorry,' he says. 'I don't want to think about it, but it happened. It is like a tattoo. I can never wash it off.'

His anguish is evident even as we eat. Whenever I visit there is food on the coffee table – bowls of almonds, pistachios, cashew nuts, Majida's walnut and date scones, her home-baked cakes. The flat is clean and neat, the living-room floor of polished wood. The kitchen is covered in linoleum, patterned in alternating squares of light and dark blue. Our shoes are shelved by the front door. We walk barefoot. The floors are cool to the touch. From the living-room sofa I have a view of the kitchen window. It looks out on a canopy of leaves. They rustle in the breeze. Mid afternoon, behind closed windows, can be heard the distant murmur of voices, the hum of cars. Inside, all is still.

'My brother, this is my home.' Faris says, with a wave of his hand. 'This is my palace, my everything.' Glancing downwards, with a tap of his foot, 'This is my soil, my earth.' And gesturing outside at the neighbouring apartment blocks, 'This is my country now. Thank God. Iran and Iraq are finished for me. Finished.' He flicks his hand in a dismissive gesture.

'He cannot be away for long,' says Majida. 'Only in these rooms he feels safe. When he visits his mother, Fadilha, and his son, Ali, he cannot stay still.'

They live nearby, a twenty-minute drive. Within half an hour of arrival Faris is anxious. 'Majida, we must go home,' he says. 'Why?' asks his mother. 'You have just come.' 'No, I must leave,' he replies. He is on the edge of panic. He must return to his trusted retreat.

'Would you risk the voyage again?' I ask. 'Of course!' Faris replies.

He is emphatic. 'For many years I was nothing. No one. My brain became hard, my heart thick as rock. Nothing could frighten me. Too much they pushed me in Iran and Iraq. In Iraq we have a saying: "If someone is wet, he is not afraid of the rain."'

Faris's ordeal began in 1980. He was twelve years old. He was at school that day. His family lived in the city of Wasit, two hours southeast of Baghdad. His great-grandfather was a Kurdish Shia who lived in Iran, in the mountainous regions near the border with Iraq. He set out a century ago, from the city of Ilam in search of a better life. He made his way to the Iraqi town of Badra and journeyed on through the mountains towards Baghdad. He finally settled in Wasit.

With the outbreak of the Iranian–Iraqi war, his people were placed under suspicion. To be both Kurdish and Shia was perceived as a threat in the paranoid regime of Saddam Hussein. Or was it simply an opportunity to grab homes and possessions, a chance to steal and loot?

The police entered the classroom. Faris was ordered out. The teacher saw the colour drain from his face. The headmaster, Mr Omran, protested on his behalf, but was ignored. Faris was escorted to the police station. His entire family had been herded there – his three brothers, four sisters, his mother and father, his cousins, uncle and aunts. They were stripped of their identity papers, robbed of citizenship. Rendered stateless. Interrogated for two days, they were driven by army vehicles to the Iranian border and left to fend for themselves.

They had no possessions bar the clothes they wore. They crossed the border and spent eight months in a refugee camp living in a grass-floored tent, and a further two years in tents in a second camp. They were moved to yet another camp where they lived for five years in one room. Throughout their twenty-one years in Iran they remained stateless.

Faris shakes his head in wonder: 'In Iraq they said you are from Iran, you are not one of us. And in Iran they said you are from Iraq, you are not one of us. The Kurdish people in the north of Iraq were Sunni. At school my children were called bad names. They were "Arabi" not Persian. We did not belong anywhere.'

His son Ali was nine, and his daughter Zahra seven, when the family pooled their last resources to purchase passports and tickets. They were flown to Kuala Lumpur and bussed to the east coast. The adults waded out with their children and possessions on their shoulders, to the boat that conveyed them to Indonesia. Faris sought out the smugglers in Jakarta and in the markets of Cisarua. He was told to look out for the man driving a Mercedes.

The smuggler said he was only able to take four members of the family. He would accept payment once the boat arrived in Australia. He offered to take Ali for free. Ali left in mid-August with his grandmother Fadilha, Faris's sister, Mina, and brother, Mohamed. The boat made landfall at Ashmore Reef, well short of the Australian mainland. Another sister set out with her husband and children on a second boat and made it safely to Christmas Island.

Faris continued to search for a way out. He made contact with Egyptian-born smuggler Abu Quassey. He was suspicious of his grand promises, his claims of a spacious, well-equipped boat. Abu Quassey charmed the children. They were drawn to his extravagant boasts. Zahra called him uncle. She was overjoyed she would soon be reunited with her brother. Faris, running short on money, was to pay him in gold jewellery.

On 18 October 2001, Faris, his wife Layla, and Zahra, were three of the 421 asylum seekers bussed from a school building in Sumatra in the dead of night. They were offloaded on a beach on the southern tip of the island in the pre-dawn dark. Smaller boats ferried them to a boat moored offshore. The women and children were taken out first, since they would offer less resistance. They were sickened by what they saw. Nineteen metres in length, four metres wide, the ageing fishing vessel bore no resemblance to the boat they had been promised.

On the living-room bookshelf stands a model of a schooner,

carved in wood. Faris had brought it back in 2008 after a return journey to Indonesia, seven years after the tragedy. 'My heart told me to go,' he says. He visited his old haunts. He went back to the markets of Cisarua, to the Villa Amelia, the hostel where he had stayed with fellow asylum seekers while they awaited the boats. He searched for the fishermen who had saved him. 'I wanted to take them presents. Flowers. A cake. To say thank you, but I could not find them. No one could help me. It was like a big secret.' He returned home none the wiser, and with nothing to show bar the wooden sailing boat.

He lifts it from the shelf and holds it aloft. It helps him depict the conditions on the boat that was to become known as SIEV X. The women and children were crammed on the lower and upper decks. The men sat up front, on the cabin roof, or stood clinging to the rails.

Despite the dangers, Faris remained resolute. 'I sat in the boat like this,' he says. He folds his arms, sits back, and puts on a blank face. 'What did I care? What did I have? I am suffering for what? To die was much better.' He continued to sit, unmoved, even as, later that morning, twenty-four Mandaean Christians, fearing for their safety, disembarked near a group of islands south of the Sunda Strait.

At night the boat rose and fell into deepening troughs. The children were screaming. A collective prayer rose from the ocean, 'God please save us. Please save us.' Zahra clung to her father. In the morning the children saw dolphins. The captain announced they had entered international waters. They were just six hours from Christmas Island, the captain informed them. Zahra was overjoyed. 'Are we going to soon see Ali?' she asked. 'Yes, God willing,' replied her father.

In the early afternoon the boat floundered. The engine was sick. The captain called for mechanics among the passengers to help fix the pump. The back-up machinery was corroded. The sound of a plane above them lifted their spirits. They dragged out t-shirts, jeans, blouses and shirts from their bags, and set them alight. The smoke signals rose, but the skies were clouded. The plane disappeared. The engine stopped. The men worked frantically to revive it. The boat was taking water. Luggage was thrown into the ocean to lighten the burden.

Zahra wept as she saw the presents she had planned to give Ali cast overboard. Then the men began to jump. Faris reassured his daughter. He held hands with Layla on one side, and Zahra on the other, wondering whether to leap or stay on board.

A mountainous wave settled it. It hit the boat side on, with full force. The SIEV X went down at 3.10 p.m.; many watches stopped at this time. The women and children were trapped below decks. Others were catapulted into the ocean. People were screaming, 'God help us. God help us.' Layla and Zahra clung to Faris.

Zahra lost her grip. Faris saw her slip from his grasp. Layla screamed, 'Don't come to me. Go to Zahra.' Faris followed his daughter like a fish. She was wearing a life jacket, but she was elusive. Like melting butter. Appearing, disappearing. Vanishing.

Faris returned to Layla and found her floating. She was dead. Faris was supported by a worn life jacket. He stands up to show me. There were three pieces of foam. 'One here,' he says, pointing to the right side on the lower back, 'one here'; and he points to the left. 'And one under my head.' Debris floated by, suitcases, water bottles, fruit and timber, oil slicks from the sunken boat. Rain was incessantly falling.

At nightfall the horizons vanished. Hours later the boats appeared – two larger boats, and a smaller boat. Faris paddled frantically towards them. There were many others in the ocean. They held onto debris, floating corpses, with one hand, and with the other, they rode the waves to edge closer. They screamed, 'Help, help, please save us.' Searchlights probed the waters. The small boat darted between the larger boats. Then all three boats vanished.

The thought of seeing his son Ali had kept him going, but when the boats abandoned him Faris was finally broken. He leans back on the sofa, but he is no longer with us. His eyes are focused elsewhere. The living room has vanished. He is on the ocean.

Awakening from his trance, his gaze returns to the living room. He stands up to show me. 'My brother, I did not care any more. I lost all my feeling.' He lies down on the floor. 'I lay on my back. Like this. I rested my head on the life jacket.' He folds his arms on his chest. 'I closed my eyes and fell asleep.'

He awoke in the dark, to lightning and rain. Faris screamed: 'Where are the people? Where are the people?' 'No one is answering. Everyone is gone. I am alone. I am with the winds. I am with three bodies – a boy and girl, and a younger boy, four or five years old. The bodies stuck to me. They did not leave my side.'

He turned back over, folded his arms, returned to sleep, and awoke, hours later, to a rising sun. The three bodies were still by his side. In the distance he made out a fishing boat. He did not believe it. He no longer trusted. He was weary. He was hungry. Thirsty. He saw a black plastic bag floating by. He swam over and grabbed it. Inside there were three red apples, two packets of biscuits, and one bottle of water.

'I started with the water, and drank all of it. Then I ate the three apples. The biscuits I kept for later. I put them in my pockets. I now had energy for another twenty-four hours. The water and apples gave me hope. A seagull sat on my head. I saw a whale. I was scared. "Faris, you are finished now," I said to myself. I prayed. The animal dived under and I did not see it again.'

Faris headed for the fishing boats. As he drew near, the three bod-ies left him. 'My brother, I never told you this before. What happened was amazing. As soon as I came near the boats, the bodies went one way, and I went the other.

'The fishermen threw down a rope and pulled me out of the water. I was the first one saved. They gave me a shower. They gave me tea. They hugged me. They were sitting beside me. They put their arms around me. I showed them a photo of my wife and daughter. I told them I want to go to Christmas Island.

'I said, "Please take me." They said, "We can't." The captain said, "We are going back to Jakarta." I said, "No, you must look." The fish-ermen told me they only saw dead bodies and baggage. I told them,

"There are fifty people, somewhere." They had good boats. Timber boats and a satellite. The captain was a good man. He said, "Okay, we will look."'

Faris saw each survivor being hauled on board. He assisted in the rescues. There were forty-four in all. They came on board, weeping. Looking for their children, wives and fathers, uncles and aunts, mothers and sisters. For a moment they were frantic with relief, but relief quickly gave way to panic. They pleaded for their loved ones, begged the captain to search for them.

'My brother, why?' Faris asks. 'Why did Abu Quassey put us on this boat? He knew it wasn't safe. He knew the weather was no good. He knew the engine was old. And in the night, why did the boats leave us? My Zahra, why did she vanish?'

All that remains of her, somewhere in this flat, are two possessions, a doll and a handbag. She had left them behind in Indonesia. Faris retrieved them in Jakarta, after the sinking.

And there is the lullaby. Again he sings it to her in his sleep, and again it is Majida who hears the words, and Majida who has learnt it. She recites the lyrics in Arabic and translates. 'Don't cry, your mum is coming back soon. She's bringing you toys, a bag full of toys. One of the toys is a duck, and it goes quack, quack, quack.'

Faris lights up at the memory. 'Zahra learnt this song from an Egyptian man, when we waited for the boat in Jakarta, in the Villa Amelia. His name was Ibrahim. He had a daughter, Sara. She was four. She played with my daughter. The Egyptian man told Zahra, "I will teach you a song." Zahra sang the lullaby to me. She tickled me in the stomach whenever she said "quack, quack, quack".' Faris laughs. Then the light drains from his face. 'Ibrahim and Sara were on the boat with us. They disappeared when it sank.'

Faris leans forward, buries his face in his hands. Hidden in the flat are the shirt and trousers he wore in the ocean. He cannot throw them out. He cannot find respite. The anguish is writ upon his face.

And yet . . . dare I say it? Do I have the right to say it? And yet . . . there are saving graces that keep Faris afloat – there is his surviving son, Ali. They were reunited in mid 2002. Ali continues to live with his grandmother, Fadilha. Faris sees him often.

And there is Majida. Her story mirrors his. She too is an Iraqi Kurd whose ancestors migrated from Iran. Majida was fourteen when in 1982 Saddam's police came for her family in Baghdad. They were ordered out of their home at night. They were detained in a hall crowded with over one hundred Kurdish people. In the morning they were taken by busses and left at night near the Iranian border.

They set out at first light in mountainous terrain, and walked until they came upon a patrol of Iranian soldiers, late at night. Two of Majida's brothers, aged sixteen and twenty-two, had been imprisoned in Baghdad. Her father did not care about the loss of his home and possessions, his truck-hire business. In Iran he worried only for the two sons. It was after the fall of Saddam Hussein, in 2005, that he learnt of their fate. They had been killed in jail in 1990. When he heard the news, he had a heart attack. He died a year later, a broken man.

Tired of their decades of statelessness in Iran, of being called names and sworn at in the streets, Majida, a brother and two sisters left for Indonesia in 2000. They embarked in Sumatra for the final leg of the journey. They sighted a plane with a kangaroo insignia and were elated. Their boat made it to Darwin. The sisters spent four months in Port Hedland detention centre before finally settling in Sydney.

'I knew about the people who drowned on SIEV X, and about Faris, before I met him. When he came to me in Sydney he told me everything. He told me he was always sick and worried. He showed me his tablets. He told me he can't sleep at night, and he told me that sometimes he did not want to talk to anyone. I told him, no worries, I want to be with you. I could see he was a kind and honest man. I told him, I will marry you.'

Now, after many visits, over the years, to the one-bedroom flat,

I see it. After many welcomes, intimate conversations, shared meals, I am beginning to understand it. This is a story of profound loss and tragedy. It will always be that. It cannot be otherwise. The tattoo will never be washed off. To expect so, is an insult. And yet . . . it is also a tale of profound love.

It can be seen in Majida's calm demeanour, in the concerned expression on her face. It can be deduced from her ease in Faris's presence. It can be seen in the intent way she listens to his words. It can be inferred from the manner in which she allows his stories to rise from, and return to the tormented silence from which they arose.

Majida and Faris walk each afternoon in Princes Park, a vast space in the inner city. On a clear day, in the distance, beyond the cemetery, can be glimpsed the mountains of the Great Divide. On the western flank, the park runs adjacent to elegant, tree-lined Royal Parade. The crescent curves to the south are lined with eucalypts and pines. On the playing fields, cricketers and footballers are training for the weekend round. Around the two-mile circumference, walkers and joggers move by. The beat of their feet upon gravel rises and fades as they pass.

Majida and Faris sit on a bench as evening falls. Children play in the miniature playground nearby. For a moment, all is calm, the mind stilled. All that can be heard is the twitter of birds, the laughter of children.

And yet . . . Faris sags back in his seat. He feels hot; his haunted expression returns. Zahra, Layla, Ibrahim, Sara, 353 men, women and children, all gone. And the boats abandoned him. 'Why, my brother? Why?'

CAMP AHITERERIA, NEW ZEALAND
STEPHANIE JOHNSON

At the camp gate Rena lifted her eye to the camera, blinked once, twice, until her iris implant complied with the sensor, and drove through. Despite yesterday's riot there was the usual group of wide-eyed children pressed up against the inner fence, their fingers hooked through the wire. Behind them Rena could see the devastation, clear in the early morning light, row upon row of cabins charred and fallen. A smashed toilet gleamed pearly white in the maw of the burnt amenities block. Blackened clothes and books lay about, some of them raked into heaps against the massive gum, which had been planted years ago to make the residents feel at home. Now it keeled over on its side, showing a mat of twisted, shallow roots, somehow obscene.

The children were mostly of European extraction, their parents being the ones who could afford the outrageous sums asked by the traffickers. Rena could pick out the most privileged recent arrivals among them, the ones with nice hair and teeth, the children who had arrived on pleasure craft owned by their families. It was surprising how many boats were capable of crossing the dangerous stretch of sea without mishap, either because they could carry the requisite fuel, or because they were skippered by sailors who had sailed here before.

A recent adult arrival had tried to evade her query, 'How did you know how to get across the Hokianga bar?'

'I'm a New Zealander! I went away twenty years ago.'

She hadn't believed him. Neither obviously had the local, who had heard his accent and reported him to the authorities. There was too much ill feeling, a national rivalry gone septic even before the current crisis. The local's rationale would have been this: for generations thousands of us flocked west, drawn by the money and job opportunities. Many prospered, but too many were treated badly, made to feel like second-class citizens. *The Mexicans of Australia*. A phrase that had come into play in the early 2010s. For some, it was payback time.

On the other side a smaller gaggle of dark-skinned children were kicking a soccer ball against an improvised net made of blackened webbing. Waving at them, Rena drove through. Distrustful – and why wouldn't they be? – they didn't wave back, except for Jimmy. He came from an outback mob, from a place with an unpronounceable name, which had become uninhabitable. Two degrees made all the difference, if it was two degrees, which was the official line. Greenie bloggers put it more at four, as high as six. If it wasn't fire, it was flood, if it wasn't flood it was drought, sometimes one following hard on the heels of the other. *Ahitereria*, Australia, either a conflagration or under water.

Outside her building, a low concrete bunker with '*Processing: Women and Children*' skew-whiff above the door, Rena parked and waited for security to escort her inside. Management wasn't taking any chances, not after yesterday. Nearby, leaning against the inner fence were some Muslim girls, their white veils segmented by the wire and smutty from the fires. They had grazes and scrapes on the little that was visible of their robed bodies – their hands and wrists – from where they'd got too close to the action. Studious, they sat among a group of children with Asiatic faces, salvaged books open on their laps. Rena watched them, thinking how there was no telling how long their families had been in Australia, or even if they'd been here before, passing through on their way to the sunburnt country. *Gummies*, another Oz name for Kiwis, short for gumboots, traditionally kept by the back door.

At 120 kilos Galahad formed a kind of solid barrier, blocking her view of any assailant game enough to climb the double fence. The revolver bouncing against his giant hip might not be so much of a deterrent as hoped – Australian police had always carried arms, inuring the nation to the public display of arms. He left her on the front steps, or what was left of them, and she took one last glance at the already blazing early morning sky. Emergency meeting then a double shift – she wouldn't leave until after nightfall.

Aircon had chilled the reception area to near freezing. Shivering at the desk was a runty, blond man with enormous spectacles. She recognised him from a popular website, watched by the general populace with as much attention as news broadcasts had been in the old days of public television. Rena's grandmother still talked about it, how in past centuries families would gather around a single screen and watch the day's current affairs, how companionable it was, how they trusted it. This guy went by some silly name. *News of the Apocalypse* was it. Something like that. Rumour had it he had the ear of the Prime Minister and influence in high places. He was Australian, one of the early migrants, when it was still legal. Before the worst of the fires, the worst of the floods. Before the exodus of New Zealanders turned and came back the other way, bringing thousands of Australians in their wake.

'Who let you in?'

'In your interests, isn't it? People want to know what's going on here. The whole of Auckland could see the smoke.'

'We'll make an announcement later today.'

'I could do that for you, Rena. Get it out there, professional job.'

He'd read her name off her nametag and was mispronouncing it, giving it a long e, but she'd given up correcting them. It's Maori, she used to say, not Reena. Rena.

'No. I don't think so.'

She pushed past him to her office, where the curtains lifted and fell in the hot breeze from the broken window. Shards lay at her feet – in the last budget the cleaner had been let go and the task handed on to one of the seekers. Many of them were so willing to ingratiate themselves in the hope of early release that they jumped at the chance. No pay of course, but an opportunity to be of use, to have an occupation to fill some empty hours. And instant coffee available in the staff kitchen. But the chosen one wouldn't be in today, the latest riot looming large in everyone's minds.

Prisms played around the sharp edges of her view. On the other side of the fence the adult residents were assembled, sitting cross-legged in two blocks, divided male and female. Half a dozen guards patrolled the perimeters of the yard, while Matrix was up the front with the microphone, giving it heaps. Beside him stood his mate Awesome, nodding and agreeing. They were speaking English at least. Yesterday they'd harangued the residents in Te Reo for four hours, just before the riots erupted.

News of the Apocalypse was waiting quietly. She could see him partially reflected in one of the jagged remnants, his mop of gleaming fair hair, angling his head in an odd way, blinking oddly. Long short, short short long. He was controlling a recording device.

'Take your glasses off.'

Some of his cool deserted him. Nervously, his pale reflection lifted a hand to his face and dropped it again. Rena shifted her gaze to the crew working on the burnt accommodation sheds, dragging away lumps of charred wooden framing and heaving plastic roofing sheets melted to fungal shapes.

It was a shame the seekers couldn't be recruited to tidy up their own mess, but they weren't to be trusted with mallets and bulldozers. She almost said it aloud – it was all she thought about, how to make the budget stretch to feed all of them, how to keep the medical staff and schoolteachers on, how to avoid disaster. How to recover from this mess.

'I really haven't got time today, mate.' She went to her desk – the jumble of overlying papers and gleaming screen, all of it fuzzed with a fine layer of ash.

'There was a story about beer.'

'I said to take your glasses off.'

'Let me talk to you. You're head of this department, aren't you? Women and Children? I thought the media would be here breaking the door down.'

'No one's interested. Old story. More of the same.'

'I want to do a story on how the conditions here compare to Christmas Island. Historical overview. You're doing a better job. Why aren't the children at school?'

'It's burnt to the ground.'

'What do you know about what went on in the men's camp?'

Rena shook her head, opened her portal and squinted at the screen.

'The home brew?'

Rena said nothing.

'It was tipped away, tipped out on the ground in front of them. Would've been a good move to let them keep it, don't you reckon? Mother's milk and good PR. Nation of inebriates.'

There was a message from the Prime Minister's office urging her to call at her earliest convenience to arrange his visit. He meant to show his concern, his willingness to do something about the situation. Let me guess, thought Rena. Ask Australia for more money? There were still reserves, though depleted, an indication of just how wealthy the country had been. Before tipping point, before bush fires summer and winter, dry seasons gone to deluge, before the desert encroached on the tropical north.

'Don't you think, Reena?'

'We can't let them have alcohol. Use your brain. Please leave.' She took out her phone and punched in a number.

He sat down companionably.

'Just the guards drinking, eh? Often pissed on the job so I hear. Numbs the pain.'

In the seconds while she waited to be put through, News of the Apocalypse smiled at her, and she had a hint of his charm and wit, an inkling of how he had earned his popularity. He had very piercing blue eyes, magnified by his glasses, and was about her age, mid-thirties. Invercargill accent, deepest South. Old Pakeha[*] perhaps, family here for generations. They were as resistant to the influx as sections of the Tangata Whenua[†]. Called it an *invasion*.

The automated voice asked her name and business.

'Rena Lazelle. Ahitereria Detention Centre 3. Prime Minister's office, please.' Then she had to repeat the last part without the 'please', which had confused the answering system, since it hadn't been enabled for manners.

A secretary made a time for later in the day – they would fly the PM up from Wellington. While the arrangements were being made, Newsboy picked up a pen and paper and wrote something down. He pushed it towards her when she got off the phone.

'*If you wish to put off all worry, assume that what you fear may happen is certainly going to happen.*'

'Seneca,' he said. 'Roman philosopher, early Christian era. He was sent into exile too.' He gestured towards the crowd outside, still sitting, heads bowed, some of them dressed in issued polythene orange onesies, their own clothes having burnt along with the sheds.

Sweltering, thought Rena, but she said, 'They weren't "sent into exile". They came of their own volition.'

'For Seneca it was Caligula, who was so jealous of his prowess in the senate that he had Seneca sent away. For them it was the climate. Just as unpredictable and psychotic.'

Rena answered several messages and flicked through some images of the riots, already in cybersphere. A guard having his head kicked in,

---

[*]   Pakeha: New Zealanders of European descent

[†]   Tangata Whenua: The people of the land, i.e. Maori

a child running with his hair on fire, a seeker felled by beanbag bullets, the little pillows of lead shot pioneered at Christmas Island.

Newsboy tapped the piece of paper. 'A good maxim to live by, don't you think?'

She had a crisis meeting in the main building in fifteen minutes. It would take ten to get there and only if Galahad was ready and waiting to escort her.

'Everyone should,' he said.

'Sounds like an inspirational motto for pessimists.'

'Quite the opposite. What's your worst imagining, Reena?'

He had a flirtatious tone, and Rena felt herself open up to him, a treacherous softening in her belly, a tension in the air. It was a long time since a man had flirted with her. You wouldn't want to have anything to do with the men here, the sort of guys attracted to this job.

'Same as most people's I suppose. Illness and death.'

'How many?'

'How many what?'

'Died. Yesterday.'

'Look.' Rena stood. 'I'm not telling you anything.'

'The world needs to know.'

'The world has its own problems. There are millions of people washing around the globe with nowhere to go. The worst predictions have come true.'

He raised his eyebrows, a triumphant grin creasing his freckled face. She had played right into his hands. Or Seneca's.

'And is it as bad as they said? Or worse? I think it's better.'

Outside in the yard Awesome got the asylum seekers to their feet, perhaps a thousand of them – one of the skills learned on the job was the rapid assessment of crowd size – and started them on an old song. Eyes closed, loving lips close to the microphone, his face cast on the massive screen behind him, he crooned, '*Sheryl Moana Marie, back home she's waiting for me . . .*' The captive audience comprised those who knew it from long exposure, and those who hadn't been here long enough to learn the words. Ex-Gold Coasters, some of them insistent they were Maori but couldn't prove it, formed a rowdy harmonising choir, even those fresh off the last boat from Queensland. The guards stood with their backs against the fence, one every metre, some of them joining in although it was against the rules. The centre was a big employer and discipline increasingly hard to enforce.

'Why did you pick me?' Rena turned her attention back to the blogger. 'You could've talked to anyone.'

'I've wanted to meet you for years. Ever since they put in Ahitereria-cam – I often log on. Watch you going about, handing out books and sedatives, tea and sympathy. You look like a nice person. The Human Face. That's what we'll call you.'

He typed rapidly on his left forearm, the faint glow of a touch-screen under the skin.

'No one died.'

'No one?'

'There's a man in bad shape in medical. But that was because a burning roof fell in on him. They're not sure if he'll pull through.'

'You're minimalising. There must be more than that. How many injured?'

'I don't have the figures. Come on. I have a meeting to get to.'

She went to the door, ushering him ahead of her. Soft as a caress he asked as he approached, 'Where are you from?'

'Here.'

'Where, here?'

'Up north. I'm not giving you my whakapapa‡.'

'Let me come to the meeting with you.'

She shook her head.

'I think you should let me come to the meeting.' He put his shoulder against the door and looked at her intently.

'Step away.'

'It would be in your best interests to let me come to the meeting.'

‡   Whakapapa: Record of ancestry

Rena wondered why was it that men of every colour believed that it improved their case to repeat themselves over and over.

'Reena. Rena. Please. It's best you let me come.'

'Why?'

'You'll see.' He seemed sad suddenly, sad for her as well as for himself, and she felt it as genuine, real empathy, even though he was still blocking her path.

'What do you know?'

'You'll see.'

Galahad was waiting. As they walked past the groups of children, Jimmy came running up to the wire. He had a smile for her – and a cast on his arm, new since this morning. Medical was slowly working its way through the injured children.

'Kiaora!' he sang out, in his high reedy voice, and Rena made a game of it, calling hello to him all the way up the internal road, while he ran along the fence-line answering her each time. She wondered if his arm hurt him, as it bumped along. He held it close to his tatty t-shirt with a faded image of the Sydney Harbour Bridge, and only passed out of view when they reached the entrance of the main building. It was crawling with police and armed personnel.

The manager scowled at her across the windowless boardroom.

'You're late.'

He was wearing a red baseball cap and t-shirt with the white logo of a popular soft drink, manufactured by an international conglomerate. It was the centre's major sponsor.

'Sorry, Mr Wang.'

'Who's that?'

'My new assistant. He started today.'

She didn't know she was going to lie until the words came out of her mouth. Keep it simple. Nobody even looked at her, though some did at Newsboy. He never wore his glasses onscreen, so they formed an effective disguise in the outside world.

There were two empty chairs at the board table beside Jingo, the official historian. While more latecomers found their seats and the meeting settled down, Newsboy involved Jingo in a discussion. The old man had achieved a kind of fame pertinent to the moment, being a specialist in previous camps from the Boer War to the Great, from the Second World War to the latest conflicts raging in Asia. Controversially, the government had seconded him to advise on previous experience and outcomes.

'How many of Ahitereria's inmates are descended from the original boat people?' asked News of the Apocalypse.

'I'd say . . . 15 per cent.'

'Was it them that started the riot, do you think?'

Jingo shrugged. 'Could be. They proclaim their ancestry as proudly as the original convict stock.'

Newsboy blinked away, making sure he was getting it all down.

'But I'm not guessing who it was. We're all fighting a losing battle. There won't be any winners.'

A look passed between them then, over the top of Rena, which she failed to interpret, but it seemed to her that the old historian startled a little, as if he'd inferred some communication from Newsboy that alarmed him.

Wang clapped his hands and drew the meeting's attention to the first item on the agenda – how the protagonists of yesterday's riots could be identified, and which methods of interrogation were allowable by the United Nations High Commissioner for Refugees.

'Ancient toothless tiger,' said Wang. 'We can do what we like.'

Waterboarding? Sensory deprivation and torture? Electric shocks? What had Seneca said? How to put off all worry? Rena decided that he must have lived in a more stable world, even though he'd had to share it with Caligula, the cruellest of the emperors. She would ask Newsboy more about Seneca's life, whether Caligula died before he did, how the philosopher had reached his conclusions about anxiety.

But the climate was more depraved than Caligula ever was or ever could have been; it was all-powerful, merciless, inhuman, an angry beast shaking mankind off its back and all creation with it. The sooner the better, perhaps.

No. You're not interpreting it correctly, Rena told herself. Imagine the worst so that you're not surprised when it happens, not so that you feel nothing but sick panic until it does.

The console above Wang's head came to life, a multiple feed from the yard. The asylum seekers were up on their feet, singing another old song, this time more upbeat – 'Poi E', from the 1980s, the Patea Maori Club. You could tell who was genuine in their claim of a place here – the ones whose eyes had misted up. Lots just stood, staring at Awesome, Matrix and the twenty or so others they'd brought in for the harmonies and moves. Close-ups of the seekers showed bewilderment. How did I get here? What happened to my life? Why are they singing?

'No wonder people think this is a holiday camp,' said Wang. 'It's not just the beer and the tea and sympathy. It's all that nonsense, music and dancing and better food than what real New Zealanders are getting on the outside.'

'Shades of Trial Bay Gaol, New South Wales, 1916,' said Jingo. 'That's where they put German civilians resident in Australia during the First World War. Had a whale of a time. Caused widespread resentment.'

'It's our way.' This came from the only other woman at the table, Mereana Harawira, descended from a staunch separatist and activist. The same grit and determination, but a heart of gold. 'They're guests, even though they're unwelcome. Even unwelcome guests must be fed and entertained. It's the Maori way.'

'It didn't do you any good the first time,' said Jingo. 'In the colonial era village after village buckled under the weight of having to feed numberless arrivals.'

The console flickered again, the song cut off, and the picture showed a Qantas jet standing on the airport tarmac. Men with guns spilled out of it, firing towards the building. One by one the security cameras were shot away, went blank. There was the sound of scream- ing, the roar of another jet, and then another and another, coming in to land.

Beside her, News of the Apocalypse exhaled noisily, and Rena turned to look at him. This is what he'd known. He'd known they were on their way. Blinking fast at the screen, he was sending the images out to his vis-tweet followers. He gave her a small, distant smile and took her hand, urging her to return her attention to the console.

Deprived of visuals, the system was searching for another chan- nel – the port this time, and a view of a line of frigates and aircraft carriers, great grey beasts following nose to tail like migrating ele- phants. Miss Harawira jumped to her feet, her lips white, horrified.

'But why would they . . .?'

'Because we're a pain in the arse,' said Jingo. 'This is the swift solu- tion.'

Personnel were loading onto troop carriers and speeding for the shore, hundreds of them.

'Canberra's been pissed off with paying us reparations for ages,' Jingo went on. 'At least we siphoned some of the money off to Christchurch.'

'It's over.'

Wang rose slowly to his feet. Some of the staff were already head- ing for the door, pushing at one another, wanting to get home.

'It's all over.'

Wang was motionless, still staring at the console, which was searching again for another location. This time it found sections of Queen Street, soldiers jogging up the hill in their hard hats, tanks roll- ing beside them.

'This is where you need an airforce to stop them in their tracks,' said the historian, 'but the fools got rid of it in the twenty-first cen- tury.'

Rena knew what she had to do. She hurried outside, Newsboy

coming after her, dodging the staff cars racing to reach families and loved ones.

'I hope they make it,' she said to him, 'It won't be safe anywhere.'

He ran beside her to the main gates, and she wondered whose side he was on, how he managed to remain in the role of objective observer. Was he her enemy?

Up ahead they could see Awesome and Matrix on either side of the gates, which they'd opened. They had the same idea as she did – to let them all go. The inner fence had been disarmed and one of the demolition bulldozers commandeered to break down the wires. *Now is the hour, when we must say goodbye*, sang Awesome and Matrix with their guitars, serenading the fleeing captives. As they ran they grabbed up their children, the last of their precious possessions, and disappeared in a flood towards their avenging countrymen. Newsboy went after them, not wanting to miss anything even if it cost him his life, and not pausing to say goodbye.

Slowly Rena returned to her office. There was no point in trying to get home. It would be chaos out there. Feet up on the desk, she gazed out the broken window. The camp was quietening, emptying. Imagine the worst.

The worst would be for the fighter jets now flying overhead to drop incendiary devices and blow her to smithereens, but the camp would be marked for them as a small piece of Australia. *Ahitereria*. They would know where we were keeping them.

As the jets withdrew, zigzagging down the Auckland isthmus, a small sob and choke came from under the desk. Little Jimmy, his slender legs cut from where he had climbed through the broken window. She drew him onto her lap, his plaster cast hard against her stomach.

'Imagine the best,' she whispered to him. 'Imagine that a time will come when no one will believe how we behaved, how we fought over what we've got left, our narrowing resources. A time will come when we live in peace and welcome one another to our shores.'

The child snuggled in, his face tipped up to her and she could see from his dreaming eyes that he was doing just as she'd asked. With his smoke-smelling hair, broken arm and stinging legs, he was imagining the best.

A FANTASY OF
SAND AND SEA
KIM SCOTT

I can only imagine what it's like to sail over a watery horizon heading for Australia's shores. On TV I've seen thin people, near the end of such a journey, rise apprehensively to their feet to greet the uniforms and the sharp and shiny craft that lowers itself in the water even as its bow wave rushes toward them.

Why wouldn't they be apprehensive after so long on a crowded, leaking boat, so long imagining a moment like this? They might have thought the approaching craft was just another mirage and, sick of the leaking boat and the ever-shifting sea, preferred their own fantasy in which one:

> . . . rowed always slower, looking over his shoulder, choosing a way among channels or shoals and shallows that he alone could see. The boat shuddered as the keel dragged . . . Ged drew the oars up rattling in their locks, and that noise was terrible, for there was no other sound. All sounds of water, wind, wood, sail were gone, lost in a huge profound silence that might have been unbroken forever. The boat lay motionless. No breath of wind moved. The sea had turned to sand, shadowy,

unstirred. Nothing moved in the dark sky or on the dry unreal ground
that went on and on into gathering darkness all around the boat as far
as eyes could see.

Ged stood up . . . and lightly stepped over the side of the boat. Vetch
thought to see him fall and sink down in the sea, the sea that surely was
there behind this dry, dim veil that hid away water, sky, and light. But
there was no sea any more. Ged walked away from the boat. The dark
sand showed his footprints . . . and whispered a little under his step.[18]

Actually, this passage is from a fantasy novel but to judge by a *Sydney
Morning Herald* news report, the asylum seekers arriving at the north
Western Australian coast in 2001 might almost have been following
the still-whispering footprints of Ged (above) because they were:

> . . . dressed in their best suits to be ready for prospective job inter-
> views, but had their trouser legs rolled up and shoes slung across their
> shoulders to wade through the waves. When one group came across
> a telephone linesman, they asked him for directions to the bus. The
> linesman stopped to fill their near-empty cans with water before leav-
> ing to telephone the police.[19]

Suvendi Perera, in drawing my attention to this incident, pointed out
the 'casual, serviceable brutality' of the linesman who told the asylum seekers 'there is a bus coming to meet them' before reaching for a
phone to summon the 'cop's bus'.

People of the Australian continent have not always been so brusque
in their treatment of newcomers wading through the shallows and up
into the dunes. Books like *Dancing with Strangers*, or *Shaking Hands
on the Fringe* show Aboriginal people – First Australians – greeting
new arrivals with curiosity and empathy and genuine attempts to
communicate across a vast cultural space. Instances when this attempt
was not successful can be instructive, as this account from an 1849
expedition journal reveals:

> While traversing that part of this dreary waste which borders on
> the sea-coast, we came suddenly upon the skeleton of a human
> being . . . Our native immediately explained they were the remains of
> one of three seamen who had quitted a Hobart Town whaler some 18
> months ago . . . for the purpose of walking to Albany . . .
>
> The natives seemed to have been fully aware of the death . . . and
> ascribe it to actual starvation and exhaustion, disclaiming most
> strongly having used any personal violence but on the contrary, hav-
> ing endeavoured to assist the only one of them they saw before his
> death, he had, however, through fear or distrust invariably pointed
> his gun when any of the natives offered to approach him . . .[20]

Sad that the nineteenth-century seaman was so frightened he was
unable to accept help. Sad, too, that the Tamil asylum seekers had
no Aboriginal people to meet and help them, rather than the unsympathetic linesman. It could've been worse: they might have met the
armed fear and mistrust of a runaway sailor who'd found himself a
home of sorts. Perhaps, in a way, they did.

I have offered these few random examples of encounters on the
continent's edge and, in a way, confused the issue, not so much because
the incidents are separated by many years, but because the identity of
hosts and refugees – who are the Australians and who the non-Australians? – shifts and turns about. In the older account, it is Aboriginal
people – the First Australians – who are the hosts, and a (presumably
white) colonist is the refugee. In the other incident, Tamil people are
the refugees, and newer, less accommodating Australians are in the
position of hosts.

Such is the nature of contemporary Australia's reaction to the
arrival of refugees on boats that sometimes it almost seems as if the
dead nineteenth-century runaway has risen zombie-like from the
blowing sands and clumped his way to the very heart of the modern
Australian metropolis. Aggressive when threatened, and easily threatened because fearful, he's the sort that might insist that he is the one

who will decide who comes to this country and the circumstances in which they come.

I think I've seen him, or one of his relatives, at my local shopping centre this morning. The stickers on his car argued his case: 'Fuck off we're full' and 'I grew here, you flew here'.

Although it seems that Australia is not nearly as upset by airline arrivals – even though a much higher number of illegal immigrants arrive that way – as by those who come by boat. I'm tempted to identify some neurosis, something deep in the psyche to do with the First Fleet and land theft, as the cause. Or do we worry less about those who come by air because they're rich? Tony Birch suggests it's simply racism:

> Approximately 20 per cent of arrivals to Australia who overstay their visas are British. There is no mention of Britain in the blacklisted countries. Nor do we see the fair skin of the back-packer behind the barbed-wire of the detention camp.[21]

The rifle-wielding sailor was both fearful of and threatened by Aboriginal people. It's been argued that such attitudes remain characteristic of Australian identity, and that the 'othering' of Aboriginal people so that they are not only 'reduced to silence and then fetishised and controlled, becoming an endlessly fascinating object of discourse' but also, by such opposition and exclusion, serve to bind the scattered fragments of a British heritage together, is integral to Australian society.[22] Other arguments identify a similarly racist, 'orientalist' attitude in regard to Asia:

> . . . fear of Asia is integral to a white Australian identity in which particular white Australian collective memories of Asia are externalised and objectified, forming a stabilizing element of identity.[23]

But, despite its continuing influence on our social infrastructure and institutions a white, predominantly Anglo-Australian identity may itself be under threat. A greater proportion of our population is from something else than British descent. If the exclusion of both Aboriginal people and 'non-white' immigrants is indeed fundamental to Australian identity, then that exclusion can also serve as a means of linking those excluded. Birch links Aboriginal and Torres Strait Islander people, along with immigrants from non-English speaking countries, as playing an important, perverse role in defining Australian identity:

> Aboriginal people continue to be abused as a result of crimes committed by white Australia both in the past and contemporary society. The abusive treatment of refugees is similar to the treatment of Aboriginal people in this country in that they pose a threat which, more than being based on any material manifestation, either real or imagined, is a threat to a way of life erected on xenophobia, selfishness and a fear of difference.[24]

He is not alone in grouping Aboriginal and Torres Strait Islander people together with refugees because of relationships with a 'mainstream' Australia. Let me offer yet another shoreline encounter, this time from an altogether different part of Australia – Melville Island – where, in 2003, an asylum seekers' boat ran aground. As in the fantasy novel, it must have seemed as if water had suddenly become solid, because observers noted that the boat came toward the beach across a series of shallow bars until, eventually, its keel struck the sand.

Police and customs officers arrived. Soon, the Tiwi Islands had been effectively excised from Australia! This is no fantasy. An 'exclusion' zone was created around the boat itself, and planes were prohibited from flying over it so that any asylum seekers were denied access to the Australian legal system and any communication. This changing of the national boundary, and therefore of who was and who wasn't Australian, was intended to preserve Australian sovereignty and security. The islands were restored to nationhood only after the Australian navy had towed the boat back to Indonesian waters. One Islander, among the many offended at being so perfunctorily excluded from Australia, said, 'We know what it means to be non-Australians. If that boat comes back, we'll welcome them and give them food and water. You know why? Because we're all one group – non-Australians.'[25]

In this instance, it is First Australians articulating an alliance between themselves and refugees based upon a shared sense of being excluded by a dominant Australian group identity and also, I suggest, because their hospitality and responsibility as hosts has been aroused. To me, it provides an exemplar. After all, there are many historical instances of First Australians behaving with such courtesy and compassion: Noongar people, for example, tried to help the blunderbuss-wielding runaway.

This alliance is what an alternative Australia, founded upon the heritage of First Australian communities, those responsible for first developing society on this continent[26], might allow. Together, First Australians form a contemporary community that, arguably, has good reason to search for some other Australia, some un-Australia that can sustain and nurture all its people. The heritage of many coastal First Australians includes an older idea of the ocean as something that connects rather than divides. The point has been well argued that in Northern Australia social connections were maintained across the ocean. In south-western Australia, Noongar people also saw the sea as a means of communication, eagerly using ships as a means of 'extending kin networks and enhancing geographic knowledge and perspectives of country'.[27]

At times in Noongar history the boundary of land and sea changed at a rate of hundreds of metres a year, which makes for wide, constantly moving border country, and footprints constantly being added and washed away again. No point in drawing a line in the sand in such times. Instead they thought of family and friends, lost beneath the waters, and their connections.

We might need just such a non-Australia, an un-Australia, if we are ever to have First Australians – many of whom have themselves learned fear and mistrust from Australia's history and would be wary of repeating past mistakes – in a position to rebuild and continue traditions of compassion and hospitality. Such an un-Australia would be founded upon various Aboriginal traditions, with waves of immigrants – beginning with the British – grafting themselves (rather than assimilating) to deep and ancient regional roots and growing an increasingly dynamic sense of place. In this way a young and shimmering nation state might anchor itself to the oldest continent on earth.

For now, those denied entry, those excised and excluded – along with friends and allies – exist either in this as yet undefined and sandy borderland of un-Australia, or on a shifting sea, trying to reach shallows, a shoreline, an edge of a nation they might join. At the same time, a great many of the Australian population are either immigrants or descended from immigrants, with ancestral homes far beyond the ocean's horizon and, even if never having fled persecution, can also never return to their home as they remember it. This even applies to those whose identity and heritage are at the core of our nation state, and yet it is this core that is so defensive about asylum seekers on boats, and which is prepared to pull back its borders, to shrink, and which uses the power it carries in its hands against new arrivals who seek only to join and strengthen it.

Instead, it might be helpful for more of us – not exclusively those of us in un-Australia – to think of ourselves as refugees rather than as nationalists. As has been argued, admittedly in a different context:

> . . . the refugee is perhaps the only thinkable figure for the people of our time and the only category in which one may see . . . the forms and limits of a coming political community. It is even possible that, if we want to be equal to the absolutely new tasks ahead, we will have to . . . build our political philosophy anew starting from the one and only figure of the refugee.[28]

It might help us reconsider our attitudes to anyone who has arrived at our shoreline, felt the sand between their toes and, believing they are no longer at the mercy of the sea, suddenly finds that:

> . . . the sand sank under his feet, and he struggled in it as in quicksand, as through a heavy flow of water: until with a roar of noise and a glory of daylight, and the bitter cold of winter, and the bitter taste of salt . . . he floundered in the sudden, true, and living sea.
>
> . . . he struggled as best he could to the boat, and pulled himself up into her. Coughing and trying to wipe away the water that streamed from his hair, he looked about desperately, not knowing now which way to look. And at last he made out something dark among the waves a long way off across what had been sand and now was wild water. Then he leapt to the oars and rowed mightily to his friend, and catching Ged's arms helped and hauled him up over the side . . .[29]

The above is an extract from the novel with which I began this essay. Land has transformed back to sea, and one character saves first himself, then another. Having hoped to make the case for some grounded brotherhood of humanity, and some deep shared heritage, I'm afraid I conclude almost exactly as I began: all at sea, and in fantasy land. But of course their journey, and ours, is not yet complete.

FROM *HALF A LIFETIME*
JUDITH WRIGHT

My mother used to say that it wasn't so much things she had done
that dogged her conscience as things she hadn't. One of her bitterest
memories was of the episode described here, which she wrote of
in her autobiography *Half a Lifetime*. It was for her a haunting
moral failure, and she would surely have raged against this same
moral failure writ large in the sorry story of Australia's treatment
of refugees today if she had lived to see it. She would have heartily
approved of the present anthology and its aims.

Meredith McKinney

Cecily had an itinerary drawn up for her by a friend who had many
contacts in Europe willing to host and instruct tourists, so we set out
disregarding threats and rumours of war. In Holland we stayed with a
charming young couple whose Amsterdam house was beside a canal.
Thereafter we were to lose track entirely of Dieneke and her husband,
and with Holland invaded within a couple of years of our visit, no
good news was forthcoming afterwards. In Germany we stayed with
a somewhat run-down baronial family, at Unkel am Rhein, where we
were introduced to the Nazi faiths and the worst of German sausage.

Escaping to Austria, we found apprehension everywhere for the harvest in Germany was rumoured to be bad, and there was much marching and menacing at the border.

Hungary was equally in fear. There we were entertained by a couple of young students desperate to escape to the 'New World', one of whom had Jewish blood and was therefore more menaced. America was their hope, but if not there then anywhere beyond the immediate reach of the European threat. One of them had qualified as a doctor and being tall and handsome was Cecily's choice, the other, Andrei, stouter and unhandsome, was allocated to me. He was to be a thorn in my conscience forever after, for his grandmother was Jewish and he feared the threatening purge that would eliminate all Jewish people to the tenth generation – only those of 'pure Aryan strain' would be spared when Hitler's legions took over Hungary.

When we met in Budapest I was a young girl (for though I was just past twenty-one that did not mean much in terms of maturity), he a young chemistry student. In that early summer, the trees along the Buda streets sprouted new green plumes and feathers and there was a smell of peach brandy, the scent of American female tourists and the damp odour of the dark brown river. Andrei, in a new stiff Panama hat, was timid and bemused, his English unfamiliar like a new language but adequate. He was ugly, comically not strikingly, small, square with a face like a dog, a shy dog anxious to please, who if encouraged would probably jump and tear your stockings.

We had three days in Budapest before the train left. Andrei gambolled – we went to the museum, to the cafes, to the galleries, we boated down the Danube, we drank curious drinks on terraces above the river where the little cafe tables glittered under their canvas umbrellas. Andrei talked of his Jewish grandmother. 'My brother and I, we loved her. But now, we are afraid. Is it not cruel that my grandmother, so kind, should be a fear to me? Hungaria, poor Hungaria,' he cried with a note in his voice I had heard when he translated the posters I saw everywhere on cafe walls in shops and hostels. 'She is a nutshell in the jaws of the – tool, what you call it, if not one then the other will get her . . . But how be free? Your country there is free?'

After a time in Europe, my country looked to me like a far-off heaven of freedom.

That night, Andrei announced, he would take me to an island in the Danube, to the nightclubs. 'Tonight you taste peach brandy, tomorrow you will forget me.'

'Of course not.'

'You will not?' Andrei was extravagant. Whatever one said either cast him down into some private hell of humiliation or raised him to quite unnecessary exuberance. He had no sense of the conventions of conversation. The smooth words that I had been taught to use did not fall into place with him as understood phrases. He picked each up enthusiastically, polished it, admired it and put it away as a cherished piece of personal communication. 'You will in truth not forget me?' He had read Shakespeare and his remarks were often teasingly familiar to the memory, Shakespeare translated into twentieth-century Hungarian English.

'Then,' he continued as he paid the bill at the counter with a very unBritish ostentation, 'I may tell you what otherwise I would have secreted to myself. I shall never forget you. Let us correspond, let us always remember June in Budapest 1937. Let us make a vow to meet again, in your lovely Australia.' And like a rubber ball he bounced beside me down the river bank and over the long bridge to my pension, talking with his entire person.

'Andrei,' I interrupted at last, 'I want to pay some of these bills. I should like to entertain you too.' I was accustomed to independence in my entertainments and I knew his money was running short. The contours of his face were suddenly rearranged from joyful Sealyham to the melancholy of the bulldog as he insisted, 'In Hungary women would not do such a thing.'

I had been accustomed to the insensitive Australian view of life, in which money ruled personal relationships and kisses were a secondary method of payment for such bills as the male took upon himself. The following night, at two in the morning, I was not surprised and certainly not alarmed when on one last moonlit walk through the island's miniature wood, almost at the end of the path back to the bridge, Andrei asked for a kiss. I complied as I usually did, with no particular interest, as one might kiss the affectionate and amiable dog he still reminded me of.

Next morning in the train out of Budapest, I thought Hungarians to be curiously emotional in these matters. Moreover, the flowers which Andrei, almost speechless and looking most unattractive at 6am, had stuffed into my arms were most inconvenient, and inappropriate for the Vienna express.

The harvest was drawing near in that sombre summer of Europe in 1937 as Cecily and I turned back to England through a flower-bedecked landscape. My conscience was sore, knowing that Andrei regarded me as his last hope of escape. I did not think to plead, untruthfully, that I was already engaged – indeed John, the medical friend of my student days, and I had agreed not to write to each other, to test out our mutual feelings. (Cecily, on the other hand, was indeed engaged and was very shortly to meet her fiancé and marry him in London.)

Back in London, I was soon to leave England and a Europe that remained as a threat, as materialised horror and a lifelong warning rather than the source of all learning and respect. If Australia could do no better than the parent country and Europe, then what, I thought, would be the point of those thousands of years of religion and civilisation – and of wars supposedly intended to defend the right and colonise the world with the good.

It was not until I reached Australia that Andrei's letters began to catch up with me. I found them a pleasant reminder of a few summer days. Their schoolroom English was always good for a laugh, the foreign stamps were impressive. I answered them, although it was often hard to think of anything to say. Our worlds did not touch.

I found myself using his own stilted phrases but the warmth of his confidences, the length of his letters and his pleas for more pleased and flattered me.

I learned that Cecily's friend reached New York but I was never to see Andrei again, and the last of his pleading letters and gifts – one of them a length of handmade lace intended as a wedding dress – have vanished now. It would have cost me only the fifty pounds demanded as a surety by the Australian government of the time, to ensure that an immigrant did not become a burden on the state, to help him escape, though fifty pounds in those days was a sum to frighten a young woman without a job. But I could not see myself as a fiancée or wife to Andrei, and I failed the test of self sacrifice. Though my father advised strongly against bringing a Hungarian migrant into the dairy industry (Andrei was by then an industrial chemist working in that industry) and did not welcome the idea of his immigration on my guarantee, I could, if I had been enterprising enough, have raised the money somehow. That I did not try was always to be on my conscience: sure enough, once Hungary was taken, Andrei's letters ceased abruptly.

The sins we commit in ignorance taste bitterer to the tongue than those we intend. For intentional sins there is always an excuse, a justification, thought out beforehand and made to cover ugliness, like a tombstone under which the thought is buried. I meant no harm to Andrei. That is why he haunts me. More deliberate cruelties I have forgotten.

THE COMPANY OF LOVERS
JUDITH WRIGHT

We meet and part now over all the world;
we, the lost company,
take hands together in the night, forget
the night in our brief happiness, silently.
We, who sought many things, throw all away
for this one thing, one only,
remembering that in the narrow grave
we shall be lonely.

Death marshals up his armies round us now.
Their footsteps crowd too near.
Lock your warm hand above the chilling heart
and for a time I live without my fear.
Grope in the night to find me and embrace,
for the dark preludes of the drums begin,
and round us, round the company of lovers,
Death draws his cordons in.

TENDER MERCIES
ROSIE SCOTT

It was a short paragraph on page 4 in the *Sydney Morning Herald*.

'A detainee suspected of terrorist links was found dead in his cell in Villawood yesterday. It is believed he took an overdose. Officials are investigating.'

The office she was ushered into was completely impersonal. Just bare grey walls, rows and rows of steel-grey files, a desk and two chairs. The view of the city with the blue harbour glinting beyond was extravagantly flamboyant in contrast.

'We'll keep this brief if that's all right with you. I've got a meeting in a minute,' the unsmiling man said to her. 'I have to tell you, I'm very familiar with this case, so I hope we're not just wasting our time here.'

'You read the appeal, Mr Smith? I can summarise – Mohammed's been in Villawood for four years. He's a teacher. He belonged to an organisation campaigning for democracy – so he had to leave the country. If he goes back to his country he could be jailed. Or executed.'

'That's what you say.' (She would have to remind herself later that that was truly what he said.)

The man was leaning back importantly, so far back she thought his chair could go right over. She began to pray for him to tip arse over head.

'The authorities think differently, I can tell you that for free.'

'Yes, well, the authorities,' she said carefully, knowing she had to choose her words, 'have been wrong in lots of cases. They seem to assume people are terrorists before they even begin the hearings. A lot of refugees they said were terrorists or liars are now on permanent visas. They all turned out to be legitimate asylum seekers.'

'That's not really the point, is it? We have to consider each case on its merits and this man has lied to the RRT and other authorities.'

'They're interviewed by officials the day they arrive. They're terrified and exhausted after their ordeal. They don't understand English. Evidence like that wouldn't stand up in a court of law.'

'That's what you say,' he said again.

'That's not just what *I* say,' she said, trying to control herself. 'International organisations have vouched for the truth of Mohammed's evidence. And legal experts. I've sent the department all the documents.'

'What international groups? Haven't they mostly got a hidden agenda, these groups? PEN, Amnesty International, Journalists without Borders? Who are they run by? They don't have any authority for Australians. They're a big zero as far as we're concerned.'

'What about the UN? You don't think that has any authority either?'

'The UN? Good example. It's well known they're weak on terrorism. We're not going to go soft on terrorism because of a few suits in Geneva. They can say what they like – they don't have to defend our country.'

'But they're innocent, most of them. What about the children in jail? Do we have to defend ourselves against them?' (Her temper was rising and she knew urgently that she had to calm down, mentally lie back and think of England, or she'd begin shouting and ruin any chances she had.)

'That's a bit strong, isn't it?' he said weightily. She realised mentioning the children was a mistake; she could see by his body language that he was dismissing her. 'Deporting this man is what's been decided on by the correct authorities and I can't intervene at this late stage on such flimsy evidence.'

'But Mr Smith, it's very solid evidence. Deporting him will mean he's in great danger if he goes back.'

'That's his lookout,' he said with a brief flash of teeth. 'We didn't ask him to come here. Have you ever thought of that?'

She had a fleeting fantasy of springing across the desk and taking him by the throat, squidging his cheeks and twisting them till he squeaked with pain and fear. Or rising gracefully with some eloquent speech that would destroy him:

'You and your kind will get your comeuppance one day. And it'll be sooner than you think. The bell's tolling for you, you little creep. You'll be held responsible for your crimes in a way you didn't expect.'

Exiting gracefully and leaving him stuttering and growing pale as intimations of mortality paralysed him.

But none of these pleasurable fantasies could exorcise the feeling of impotent rage she had at that moment, facing him across the desk. She was powerless because she had Mohammed's fate in her hands. She couldn't afford the self-indulgence of abusing the man who held all the levers, even if she'd been brave enough.

As it was, she stood up and said, stuttering, 'Mohammed's an innocent man – he's a legitimate asylum seeker. Deporting him is — it's injustice. We'll do everything to stop it.'

She couldn't bring herself to shake hands. Outside in the corridor she stood trembling. She felt like a horse that'd been ridden too hard, waves of fear and sorrow washing over her. What was she to do now? She thought of Mohammed's vivid dark face, his courtly manner, the despair in his eyes when she'd last seen him. He was so different in every way from the man who was sending him to his death – he was small and gentle and kindly and cultured and had a disarmingly boy-ish giggle when amused.

In the early days he was amused by everything. When she sat beside him on the plastic chairs at the Villawood visitors' compound he always held her hand. The gesture reminded her of her children when they were small, the same tender trustfulness.

'I'll go and see them,' she'd promised him. 'Don't worry, love. We'll get you out. What does Helen say?'

Helen, the lawyer struggling under an impossible load of refugees' cases. Each case equally urgent and heartbreaking – all of them lost in the labyrinth of immigration law.

'She put the appeal in. We have to wait. You know how long I wait? Three months already. This appeal. How many other appeals have I waited for? That are nothing? Like smoke?'

'I'll talk to her,' she said. She could see by the sudden clouding over of his eyes that he no longer believed her. Despair and depression emanated from him like a fever.

'I have done nothing,' he said. 'Why are they torturing me? Four years in this fucking hell hole. Excuse me, Louise, but I have to say it. For nothing.'

'I know, I know. I'll do my best. They can't do anything while there's an appeal on.'

She knew as soon as she said it that sometimes they did deport people anyway. She'd heard of armed guards crowding into their cells and taking them handcuffed to the plane, with no one to hear their cries.

He wasn't listening to her.

'A terrorist. Can you think of that? How funny is that description? Of me? But I cannot laugh.'

She laid the plastic carry bags in front of him like an offering – the usual phone cards, apples, oranges, sweets, medications, car magazines – but she could see how useless they were in the face of his despair.

Recovering his usual politeness with an obvious effort he stood up to escort her to the gate. He was trying to smile, but she saw his eyes were glittering with stress.

She hugged him, felt his small bony body unyielding.

'We won't let them do it. Hang in there, Mohammed, you've got a lot of friends outside. You're a brave man. You're the nicest man I know.'

She felt herself on the edge of tears; it was as if she were saying goodbye.

'See you next week,' she ploughed on. 'I'll ring every day. I'll let you know what's happening as soon as I hear. I'll put a rocket under them.'

He stood there silently, watching her go.

The hollowness of her words hit her once she was outside the gate. She was trembling with the strain of trying to appear optimistic and encouraging for Mohammed.

She was a fool, mouthing platitudes. How could that help him?

And now after the fruitless meeting with this man Smith she felt the same hollowness and feeling of failure. She should have let fly, shouted at him, demanded to see his superior.

Outside in the street she rang Amy on her mobile.

'He was ghastly,' she said. 'An android. No hope at all from there.'

'Was that Peter Smith?'

'Yes.'

'That explains it. You'll never get anything human out of him.'

'Amy, I'm feeling desperate. Mohammed's in a bad way. Can you come round? We have to organise something.'

'Oh dear,' Amy said. 'Are you okay?'

'I know. I'm sorry, I'm losing it a bit. I'll talk to you later, love.'

All the way home on the bus she obsessed about the man Smith. What kind of man could say those things, think those things, be responsible for such misery? It was as if the drive to power burnt out everything human in him. Pity, humour, despair, the vulnerabilities of love. He reminded her irresistibly of certain boys she used to know at university when she was a student – cold-eyed, short-haired, sporty woman-haters, conformists, with those unreadable faces that were all tight surface, no give anywhere. They went around as if they owned the place, exuding certainty, righteousness.

The funny thing is he and his kind wouldn't even have been considered by her and her laughing long-haired girlfriends, the in-group in those days. Sexually he wasn't even in the race. He had to make do with his own type – churchy, mousy, bitter girls who had their own axes to grind. She and her friends knew instinctively, in the way women do when they're considering mates, that there was something potentially pathological about a cold clenched soul so young.

To be so frozen, pinched, cut off, such a conformist at nineteen, what would he be like when he was a man? But people like that never doubted themselves for a minute, they made it clear they would get revenge one day, exacted drop by drop over a lifetime if necessary.

And here she was all these years later with Smith and men like him running the country. Rubbing it in was a joy for them – they had been a generation of dull kids, nerds, and they were getting back at the style and exuberance of the sixties. Theirs was the triumph of the grey ones, the nay-sayers, the haters, and their revenge was sweet.

Mohammed was nothing to them, a pawn in the political game of fear-mongering; whether he was innocent or not didn't worry them. They all used the same language about people like him, weak on terrorism, queue jumpers, the final solution of deportation.

She had a sudden image of Mohammed, going mad in his little cell, his eyes turned stony with fear, his face to the wall.

Walking home from the bus stop she wondered if she was cracking up herself. She felt such an uncontrollable storm of grief and rage. She went into the corner shop to buy some cigarettes.

'I thought you'd given up,' the Indian shopkeeper said. 'I've half a mind not to sell them to you.' He wagged his finger. 'Bad, bad, bad for your health.'

'I know,' she said, 'but it's either that or scream and set fire to something.'

He smiled sympathetically. 'Okay, okay. Smoke them all at once then and it'll put you off. You will learn then that they are only a false comfort.'

'The point is I could see he genuinely didn't give a stuff,' she told Amy. They were sitting on the balcony in the afternoon light. It was like being in an eyrie high among the trees, the leaves motionless with heat.

'I know it's too soon for wine but I need a drink,' she said, pouring herself a glass and motioning to Amy to help herself. 'It was genuine, that was the unsettling part. He wasn't being an apologist or covering up for something he knew was indefensible. I saw the indifference in his eyes. If Mohammed turned up dead in Iran he wouldn't turn a hair. One less terrorist.'

'I know. I come away from phone calls with those dweebs shaking with rage. Shaking with rage. And on the whole I'm a pretty placid soul. It takes a lot to rile me.'

'You can get quite fierce sometimes.'

'Only when I have to.'

They were both silent for a minute, gazing out onto the soft view, unseeing.

'So there it is – our last port of call, a dweeb. No one else in authority we can appeal to. Publicity . . . it comes down to publicity every time.'

'So you think we could get some?'

'Mohammed's not keen on it is he? It's hard at the moment. Even the decent journos are talking about compassion fatigue. But it might be the only way out. Helen says she's not that optimistic about the appeal – there really isn't enough new evidence.'

'Except he's going mad,' she said, with a little sob. 'And he's completely innocent. But hey what relevance is that? You can't let the facts get in the way of an execution.'

'Hey,' Amy said, leaning over to give her a little pat.

'I know. I'm sorry. It's just so frustrating. We've got such a dwindling repertoire of ways to save him.'

They both sighed simultaneously.

After a while Amy said absent-mindedly, 'Dweeb. God, I haven't used that word for years. I don't know where it comes from. Strange isn't it. It sounds Russian. It just popped into my head.'

'It used to be a teenage word for beyond ghastly.'

'So what comes next?'

'We're just waiting for the 417. I've organised masses of letters of support. Unions offering him jobs, people confirming his evidence, experts saying he's in danger if he goes back. And Helen's on the case.'

'I forgot to tell you. Bad news about Helen. She told me the other day she's in burn-out. She doesn't know whether she can go on.'

'Oh Christ. The poor woman. What a disaster.'

'We might have to find another lawyer.'

'The thing is, he's strong. And sane. He's always helping other inmates with their appeals and translating for them. But I've noticed he's beginning to rant a bit. You know how they start to rant? He was such a gentle person. Now he's starting to shout. Even at me.'

'You're really fond of him, aren't you?'

'He used to call me mum. He doesn't any more. It's as if he's turning against me.'

'Don't cry, love,' Amy said, coming over to put her arm around her. 'We just have to keep at it. I'll go home and ring a few journos. Can you ring Helen and see if she can continue with this case? It might come better from you.'

'Yes,' she said, 'yes, I'll do that. Of course.'

That night she dreamt of Mohammed. They were sitting together peacefully somewhere and then the dream changed, it had become dark and still. She was trying to find him. In the distance she could hear his voice calling to her from the darkness, but she couldn't reach him.

THE INDIANA JONES STORY
BELLA VENDRAMINI

I was seventeen years old when I got locked up in a Spanish jail. I like saying that sentence. Though to be fair, it wasn't the drippy-walled kind with manacles and screams resounding into the night; it was a sort of halfway house really, for beggars and nimble-fingered pickpockets or the occasional thick-necked prisoner waiting on the court's pleasure. The jail itself was made of sandy stones and set high on a hill so you could see the woods below like a great pad of buoyant green, then beyond that the encroaching city of San Sebastian spread out like a basking lizard in the heat.

But the story begins at the ripe and responsible ages of eighteen and seventeen, when Luke, my sandy-haired, violet-eyed boyfriend, came into some inheritance money and wanted nothing more than to quit school and see the Europe of his dog-eared picture books. And he needed a sidekick. So just a few months before our HSC, we horrified my parents by stuffing our bags with Indiana Jones comics and lustful imaginings of B-grade-movie-style adventures and jumping on a plane bound for Europe. We bought two motorbikes in England, drove them down to Dover, hopped on a ship to Calais then made our way through the tumbling countryside of France to arrive breathlessly on the sunburnt shores of Spain.

It was there that we crashed our motorbikes into each other. Though the gods who protect small children and animals smiled down upon us and we were miraculously saved from snapped spinal columns and future stutters. But, when the police turned up – and with them their big thumping black boots and waddings of bulletproof vests and blusterings of testosterone – they demanded paperwork; the sort we didn't have. At seventeen I was sure bribing police officers was wrong (admittedly, as was driving without a licence) so we called their bluff and they called ours and they won out; they ordered a bus to take us to jail.

I have to admit here that we didn't really think they would take us to jail; maybe they'd scare us a little and drop us off at the train station or embassy. But then I'll also have to admit that I wasn't a normal sort of person; I got a surge of Indiana delight at being herded into a rickety old bus and through the then increasingly stormy night with whips of leaves and brambles scratching at the windows as Luke and I were taken up a mountainous road on the outskirts of the city. Our very own adventure movie! A shrine to the invincibility of youth! Up and up and round and round into the sky we went until we arrived at the foot of a set of dark iron gates which opened for us hardened criminals then promptly clanged shut behind us.

'Unbelievably cool,' Luke whispered as I nodded violently in agreement.

Once inside, though, I got separated from Luke and was marched off to the women's section as my adolescent invincibility wore paper thin and floated off. I entered the cell and turned to watch the sunken-breasted warden pull the door shut behind me. I found myself in a small dark room with a whipping milky light coming from a barred window perched near the ceiling. I hoped it was only the storm that had churned up the chalky dust from the courtyard, blowing its thickness into the cell and creating the white ghostly air swirls. I mean, I didn't really believe in ghosts. Not really.

I looked around and saw that there were three other bunks, all empty . . . except, I realised, for one.

It's true what they say about necks bristling. Mine went from normal to pig-haired in a second flat. It was the noise that did it; a painful-sounding keening was coming from the huddle of blankets, it sounded like a bird was in pain, but muffled somehow; a pillow over its beak? Listening closer, I realised the sobs came from too painful a place to be truly scary; they were sore and small and scared and cracking. Maybe the person was sick? Or was she in intense emotional pain? Perhaps, though, she was a brick short of a load and would cut me into pieces and feed me to a small ferocious prison mouse she kept as a pet?

'If you're an ah . . . everyday woman, I'm very sorry that you're upset . . . But if you're not . . . very everyday, or if you happen to have a pet mouse, or be a ghost or something, then it's okay, and I'll just sort of . . . sit here quietly.'

Then I heard the lump of blankets giggle.

Her name was Amina and (after I'd convinced her that I wasn't an axe murderer, or a ghost) she unfolded her story to me. She was a Somalian refugee (around thirty years old I thought) and she was vastly and completely beautiful. She had the kind of face a painter would hopelessly try to capture then place in rooms with giant vases and dangly vines. She had flawless skin and huge, gold-flecked black eyes – though strangely haunted-looking too – which somehow only managed to make her look even more appealing. She'd lived through years of brutal warfare in Mogadishu, hammered by American and Pakistani bombings as well as inter-clan territorial warfare. There had been mass starvation too when Red Cross supply routes were corrupted. Her husband Dalmar, a GP, and her brother, a writer, had contributed anonymously to a newspaper article condemning General Aidid for using civilians to shield his troops. But they'd been identified and the very next week her brother had been killed under suspicious circumstances. To her, it seemed likely that her husband would be next.

Driven to it, Amina and Dalmar packed up their sparse belongings, sent messages to their families and, with the gods on their side, managed to escape over the sea between Africa and Europe, to southern Spain and safety. There, they'd wended their way as far as San Sebastian and attempted to cross the border into France, after which they'd hoped to make it to Switzerland where they could apply as asylum seekers. But they'd been caught at the border and were hauled to the jail, which was why she was there, alone, crying and sobbing into the darkness on a single bunk.

I'd watched her when her sobs stopped; and as her story came out; then I watched her as she finished and her eyes lidded down and all that was left was an eerie empty look on her face.

'Bloody hell,' I said at last.

I noticed that Amina's eyes were feathered in a million black lashes, and when she replied, 'It's okay, we'll survive,' her downcast eyes made them point to her feet.

But it was too simple the way she said that, and the way she looked down; too resigned. Why wasn't she shouting her story from the rooftops? Or yelling blue murder for justice? Or at least getting a movie made about her life.

The next day in the yard, I nearly burst waiting for Luke to arrive so I could recount Amina's amazing story. When I finally did, his eyes grew wide and he let out a low whistle.

'Holy shit.'

'Yep.'

He stared off into the distance. 'Fuck, that's cool.'

'God, you're immature. It's not *cool*, it's, like, serious.'

'Yeah I know, but it's still kind of cool! Escaping a murderous general and rowing across the ocean on a raft to Spain, it's just like a movie.'

'Yeah, that is pretty cool.'

We both stared off into the distance.

But the night before, as Amina and I sat on her bunk with the swirly ghosts all around us, she'd told me that the Spanish authorities were going to send her and Dalmar back to Somalia.

'But if they send you back, won't you be in danger?'

She nodded.

'But, you must tell them that! They won't make you go back. Just tell them about your brother and the general and the raft. You'll probably get a medal.'

She looked at me with a smile. But it was the sort you'd give a kitten trying to gnaw through a thigh bone of a large mammal.

'They wouldn't. Would they?' I asked her.

She gave me the kitten/thigh bone look again.

Luke was an Aboriginal man and he reckoned he knew what it was like to be persecuted.

'It doesn't matter how white my skin is, I can feel it,' he'd once said, stabbing at his chest.

'Feel what?'

'Black deaths in custody.'

We came to call it his BDC look and when we sat on the hot sandstone of the jail's courtyard, he was wearing it with gusto.

'We've got to bloody well do something.'

I turned to watch a guard pucker his lips over a styrofoam cup, then pause mid-way to yell something at an inmate.

'What would Indiana Jones do?' Luke mumbled, scratching a pattern in the dust at his feet.

'Befriend a monkey, crack a whip and break them outta here.'

'That's helpful.'

'You got a better idea?'

'I do not think there are very many monkeys around here,' offered a voice nearby.

I hadn't noticed the well-dressed man sitting in the dust with his back stretched up against the wall. His face was gentle and quite beautiful but the bones of his wrists were smooth, big, round bolts from which dangled his impossibly thin fingers. His knees, folded to his chest, were the same: wide, flat bone caps that his skinny legs clung to.

I told him he looked like Blair Underwood.

'Because he is the only black man you know?'

'Possibly, maybe. You're Dalmar, right?'

'I'm Dalmar,' he agreed, as if we were positioned around a laden dinner table with the polite tinkling of glasses drifting around us.

Luke plugged his cigarette butt into the ground in a very cool way and sized him up. I copied Luke.

'Dalmar, I'm Luke and this is Bella —'

'— It's good to meet—'

'— and I have no bloody idea how we're going to do it. But —' began Luke.

'— we're like totally gonna get you out of here,' I broke in.

Dalmar looked back and forth between us, his expression unreadable. Perhaps it was amusement around his mouth, perhaps fear? Most probably it was incredulity. Luke kept squinting and staring forebodingly off into the distance a la Indiana, his chest inflating that little bit extra until both Dalmar and I stood fascinated, watching his chest blow upward and upward with each breath, his eyes growing wild with the effort. We were just waiting for the blue tinges of his lips to pop out and explode in a Monty-Python-wafer-thin moment. But I wasn't much better; I began nodding vigorously – in what I thought to be a supportive way, but which only managed to make me look like a wind-up toy with mental issues – while simultaneously trying to copy Luke's cool squint. Being Indiana is a hell of a lot harder than it seems.

In our lives it was the small things that were big. The first time Luke and I wagged school – and got caught – that was huge. When we egged each other on to eat a foot-long block of blue cheese and ended up chundering all over the kitchen of a friend's house, the details of who broke first were examined over and over again. The first time Luke's faltering fingers undid my bra; those were big things. Violence and bloodshed and life and death were small things, on the small screen. They weren't real; they were just the stuff of movies. Everyday filmic flickerings of corruption, hideous regimes and dark monsters who snatched innocent people away – and of Indiana Jones and Bruce

Willis ready to defend us. The monsters weren't real – but the heroes, we figured, most definitely were.

THE PLAN

We discovered that the jail was nothing like what we imagined an Australian one to be. Forgotten in a muddle of bureaucracy and content to spend our days in the courtyard hidden from the heat and chewing over escape plans that didn't involve grappling hooks or large-sized women's clothing, it was almost two weeks by the time we worked out a do-able plan.

We quickly learnt that the culture of the jail was exceedingly permissive. If you slipped some money into a guard's open hand you could have anything you wanted, including getting a 'pass' to a local swimming hole buried in bush about 200 metres away on the other side of the fence. Perfectly positioned right next to a local bus stop. The locals got away with it and they diligently returned by nightfall with conveniently wet hair and back-slapping smiles.

On a dry run to test the waterfall plan we slipped Alonzo some peseta (and a re-enactment of the death scene in *Star Wars* equipped with whooshing sound effects and a borrowed guards hat) and watched his chuckle – and his hand shoot out obligingly palm upward. Hiding near the waterhole until we could jump onto the rambling bus into San Sebastian, we spent the afternoon scoping out the train to the border and trying to mime out the phrase 'do you sell night-vision binoculars' to bemused local storekeepers.

Alonzo trusted our upbeat smiling white-people faces and got a giggle out of the antics we performed to make him laugh but when we tried the same deal the next day with Amina and Dalmar, he wasn't quite so forthcoming. He was mistrustful of Dalmar's serious ebony skin and Amina's suspicious-looking head coverings. But in firm possession of our Australian passports (we indignantly told him that

Amina's and Dalmar's passports had been stolen by nefarious-looking Spanish prisoners) he again, with a graceful bend to his neck, let us go swimming.

THE ESCAPE

All four of us took a bus from the compound, barely speaking, hushed and skittery with expectation. Alighting, we made our way across a large square bursting with tourists and buskers and shoppers until we got to the train station that would take us across the country and on to the border with France. From our earlier reconnaissance mission (which admittedly we'd suited up entirely in black for, only at the last minute deciding not to smear black shoe polish on our faces) we knew that passports were checked intermittently on the train by ferocious-looking police with snarling and straining German shepherds – but if we managed to make it to the turnstiles of the border there was no passport check, just a bored-looking pimply guard reading a magazine.

We split up in case anything went wrong. Luke took Dalmar to the front of the train as I ushered Amina to the middle section. I sat across from her as the train slid to life and studied her trembling hands. She stood out, no doubt about it, especially her head covering. What if the passport police recognised her from their first escape attempt?

She spied me worrying about her head and reading my mind, she nodded, then with delicate fingers she carefully peeled back the fabric to take it off – it was a horrible sight. Her scalp was splotched with scabs that mushroomed in bald spaces as wiry patches of thick black hair sprouted out chaotically like trees in a gnarled forest.

Maybe she'd worn the covering for so many years it had rubbed the hair off? Maybe the lack of sun had made her hair die off? Or was she herself sick and dying? I watched her sitting there with such high-chinned dignity, her beautiful delicate features staring straight ahead. Then I watched as a single tear rolled out of her. It was beautiful and violent in its simplicity – her impassive face betraying nothing. She'd lost everything – her brother, her family, her freedom – and now she was losing her religion and dignity too. Too much in one lifetime, I figured. There was nothing for it but to motion her to put it back on.

She answered with one of her Mona Lisa smiles, then used those delicate fingers again to put it back on. There was a bubble in that moment; the past and the future didn't exist any more. It was subversive, and for that moment we were both enjoyably and wilfully defiant like new kids in a dangerous playground, unwilling to bend; tipping over an edge and freefalling into whatever would come.

But, the bubble did its glistening and then it was made to pop . . . as the first group of big border police with their big snapping dogs got on at the next stop. They entered at the back of the train and formed a dark wall; glowering and intimidating locals and tourists alike; making their way through, studying passports and the faces they belonged to. They wore thick bulletproof vests and dressed in black fatigues; a pair of oversized mirrored aviators completed the movie-perfect henchman look. I eyed them with approval.

Luke and I planned it so that when the villains were a carriage or two away, we'd take our companions and exit the train with the other commuters, walk nonchalantly down the platform and get back onto the train *behind* the guards. Brilliant yet simple, we'd decided.

'Not like James Bond.'

'So true, their plots are waaay too unrealistic.'

Somehow, we managed the manoeuvre twice and by the time we'd gotten to the final stop in France, we were so pumped with adrenaline, fear and excitement we emerged at the station bedraggled, shaking and darting-eyed wrecks. Walking down the platform I found myself waiting for the crack of a dog's jaw on my ankle or a hefty clamp on the shoulder from the bad guys. As we moved toward the turnstiles, Amina's gently shaking hand felt like a small bird in mine. I saw Luke behind us with a bright actor's smile; he was affecting an overly nonchalant John Wayne swagger and passers-by were eyeing him with concern. Dalmar didn't look much better. He looked so out of place, like a piano player at a Screaming Jets concert, all tapered-fingered and gently upright; his eyes were darting but there was a stillness about his body that seemed so completely out of place in the bustling terminal.

I let go of Amina's hand and she dropped back to join her husband and Luke. I took a big breath in, clenched on a winning smile, then sauntered up to the passport guy and began regaling him with explosive excerpts of opinions, stories and lurid smiles. Skippy the bush kangaroo! The recent soccer match that was a travesty of Spanish justice! Do Spanish boys like Australian girls? (Inject lurid smile here.) Behind the bemused guard's shoulder I glimpsed Amina, Dalmar and Luke slip through into French territory – so I turned to follow them.

'Hey!' called the guard.

It felt like everywhere else was in flux and movement but me; my body and the guard's voice hellishly caught in a soundproof room.

I turned back to face him.

'Qué es su número de teléfono?' he grinned, his hands upturned.

It was as if a small piano which (for some reason) had been sitting on my chest lifted off me – and I felt suddenly light and free, and intensely, intensely relieved.

I grinned back at him, clucking my tongue.

'Per-donn-e-may, I am a lesbiano, very sorry.'

He looked at me.

'Not really, but still. Not that there's anything wrong with that. Okay. I might go now. I mean if that's okay?'

So far, so good.

When the guard did let me go I found Amina, Dalmar and Luke grouped behind a big stone pillar in the cavernous station with the tapping of high heels and the hoot of loudspeakers echoing around them. Huddled in our small group, breathless, shining-eyed and trembly, none of us could talk. I don't think any of us believed we'd managed it. We kept staring at each other in turn, taking inventory.

It changed for me then. Because Amina and Dalmar changed. Their soft tired faces, their eyes all spongy from absorbing and absorbing, a whole lifetime of absorbing – changed. They abruptly seemed to stop taking it all in – they were spitting back out. It was as if a crack appeared on their foreheads and grew and widened and split until a fully formed new person stepped out and blinked. I saw the people who had written subversive, strong and proud things, who had chosen to help strangers over their own safety. Who had braved the ocean crossing. I saw immense intelligence. I saw bewilderment and anger. There was fear and incomprehension – and it was all so vivid suddenly. And I saw love, too – that was the biggest one; a boundless and immeasurably deep river of love that existed between them. It was steely-strong and sure, a current that would take a toe off if you went for a swim in it. I hadn't ever properly seen them before that moment.

Then it all seemed suddenly very real.

It was real blood. Real people had hurt them. Real people wanted to hurt them. Physically or with rubber stamps. The boat was real. Amina's haunted eyes were real. They'd seen things I couldn't imagine. They'd been living over an abyss. Occasionally the abyss closed up and there were moments of solid ground like this one at the train station, giving them enough time for the strength and anger and momentum they kept inside to come out.

When I first got to know Amina, I thought because of her acceptance and lack of anger that she was beaten, but she wasn't. Nor was Dalmar. I thought on the train her single tear was the most perfect romantic movie-actress moment, but it wasn't. It was real. They were real. And so were their monsters.

So then, I changed, too. The film dropped away from my eyes and all the bullshit fell away with it. I saw Amina and Dalmar, the sudden strangers. I saw Luke with his ridiculous aviators on, and I saw me. Probably for the first time.

I was a white middle-class girl and I had safety nets strung all around me. In reality all Luke and I had to do was call home and my parents would have swung to the rescue or a concerned ambassador would have explained the delicacies of Spanish sweeteners and helped us out. But Amina and Dalmar didn't have any nets.

So what if our glib movie-style escape had gone pear-shaped? (Which, with our ineptitude, let's be honest, there was a pretty massive chance it would have.) They would have been caught – and sent back to almost certain death. Who would they have called for help? The UN? In Somalia, the UN had been accused of keeping Somalis locked up without trial. Their parents? They were fighting for their own lives. The reality was, there was nobody. No nets, no dial-a-friend, nobody – except two wholly inadequate movie-obsessed Aussie kids. And they deserved a lot better than that. Amina and Dalmar were an honourable, deeply tender pair who spoke up bravely for the broken people. So why wasn't anyone speaking up for them?

I watched Dalmar press his hand on Amina's, nod at Luke and me, then hurry off into the expanse of the terminal to buy the train tickets to Switzerland. When he came back red faced and flushed, he was awkwardly carrying a big cream cake in his arms which he presented to us.

'I don't know how to thank you,' he said. 'It's not an expression. I really don't know how to thank you.' His eyes were wide and they were intensely kind.

I was so horror-struck by my epiphany, so suddenly acutely aware of the risk we'd taken with their lives as we swashbuckled and swaggered and wore aviators; of the intense terror they'd been through versus our ridiculous Indiana notions – and so touched by the cream cake, there was nothing for it but to burst into tears.

It became even more surreal when Amina and Dalmar began comforting me as I waaaed and hiccupped and tried to explain how I finally understood now.

Luke stood with me on the platform and we tearfully and furiously waved back to them as they waved from behind the train window. I remember Dalmar's face had a bemused expression on it, as if he couldn't quite believe what was happening, or maybe it was incredulity at an escape aided by Luke and me.

I don't know what happened to them, or even if they made it to Switzerland, but I know the whole experience changed me. Amina and Dalmar were upright and honourable and even though I learnt that their pain was horribly real and the bloodshed and loss too, their courage and their kindness and their love – that especially – was the most real.

I like to think that Amina raised the safe happy child she'd confessed to wanting and that Dalmar would be watching over them both, growing in happiness and peace. I don't want to think about what would have happened if they'd been caught and sent back. But I believe they'd be all right – they'd been through hell and back and they'd fought monsters; they had the courage of the real heroes, outshining Indiana Jones himself.

LUCKY
KATHRYN HEYMAN

She says to me: 'Tell me everything. Tell me what happened.' When I am silent, staring down at my feet, staring at the strange stain on the grey floor, she says, 'I can't help you if you don't tell me.' Shifting my feet, I angle my toes away from the brown-haired, brown-skinned woman in front of me. She sighs. I sigh. What are we to do? I don't want to tell her everything. I don't want to tell her anything. We wait for a time, she staring at me, me watching the stain at my feet. Opposite the table, the woman sighs again and then pulls her chair back, scraping it against the hard floor. When she leaves the room, I press my hands into the table, flattening my palms against the table. It's a trick I used to teach my students, to help them focus.

This is what I want to say to her: I did not ask for this to happen. I did not make it happen.

But I say nothing. I stare at my feet some more. It takes a long time before the door opens again.

I have never liked boats. When I was a child, I watched the yachts dotting across the water and my father would tell me how lucky I was, how lucky we were, all of us. Lucky indeed; the whole country was lucky. It was my father's mantra; his belly grew round on the pleasure of it. He was an innocent, my father, and I'm glad he missed the signs, grateful – lucky, even – that he believed only in the good of his adoptive country. Sun glinting on the water, the dot of the sails, the smell of salt – lucky, lucky, lucky.

Before he realised what was coming, in our early days together, J wanted to buy a small dinghy and sail it. Wind in our hair, sun on shoulders and so on. Once we – once we had Dusty, though —

The woman stops me there. Head tilted, eyebrow cocked, she says, 'Dusty?'

Yes, I say, Dusty. My —

The woman leans in closer to me, her breath stale on my face. She asks again, 'Dusty?'

Yes, I say, Dusty. My dog.

The woman writes something down and then she looks at me.

Anyway, I say, when we got Dusty we didn't try to do things like that. We stayed on the shore with her. Keeping her safe.

We had a dinner – a while back, before the first of the changes. J cooked – he always cooked. He'd stuffed quail with cashew nuts, I remember that. Made a sweet jelly sauce to pour across it. That was the way we liked to do things: I did the decoration, the surface fluff, and he did the nuts and bolts. There were maybe six of us. It was a small affair. Most of our colleagues had already been priced out of the city; I know I was a lucky one, I knew that all along. My father left his city terrace to me, and don't think I wasn't grateful. Dinners were getting harder, friends and acquaintances trying to travel in from those outer edges of the city. There were reports – casual at first – of concerns about those who weren't born in the country. A general rumbling initially, and then more vociferous statements. Already, then, we'd started to become careful, to look over our shoulders with worry. J more than me. I have always been cavalier.

Halfway through the quail, G – he was one of the teachers – said, 'I've noticed lock-outs on my accounts,' and that was enough to set

J off. 'Oh, god,' he said, 'they're after all your information, that's only the start, if you're less than third generation they'll start locking you out of the city. Don't people read history?' I started to clear up because I didn't think I could bear to listen to it one more time, honestly. He said to me, You don't want to listen, and I told him to keep his voice down but it didn't matter then because the two guests from out of town had already left for their long journey home. Isn't that funny? I can't now for the life of me remember their names. I remember that G and his pretty girlfriend discreetly went outside to look at the flowers and left us inside to argue as loudly as we liked. We had coffee in silence and then G and his pretty girl left and when we closed the door behind them, I said to J, 'You can't just enjoy something, a lovely dinner, wine. It always has to be complicated. Why can't you be happy?'

He said, 'It's got nothing to do with being happy.'

I said, 'You're looking for problems, you're over-thinking. You spoil everything.'

I wish I'd never said that. It wasn't true. But we can't undo what we do, unsay what we have said. And this is not the last of my regrets.

He opened the drawer very quietly – he was drying the forks, he didn't like them to have water marks – and placed each fork inside carefully. He said, 'I'm worried for you, for all of us. If I'm right —'

'You're not right. You can never just accept happiness, accept luck.'

'I'm sorry. I don't want to be right.'

But I was too angry to hear an apology, and too frightened. So I said, 'You do, you'll be happy if you are right. You'll be thrilled to say "I told you so".'

He was not thrilled. He was not happy.

He was right.

No one thinks their country is going to turn against them, no one believes it's possible. Why would I be any different? It was subtle at first, so subtle I didn't notice it. J did. He noticed everything, damn him. Even before the arguments, it was our joke, that I could never slip a surprise into the house without him seeing. Funny. I tried to keep Dusty a surprise at first. Not a chance, though: one look at me and he knew I had something planned. First I showed him the photo. Second, I watched him stare at her picture, his mouth half open, his eyes wet with excitement. He might have been pretending, it's true, but I don't think so. He was never that good an actor.

After the dinner, things changed. There was a – an incident near the university one night. One of my students, in fact. She spent three days in hospital, could barely speak afterwards. One of the radio announcers talked about the case, about the boys who had hurt that poor girl, my student. He said that they were scum, rubbish, nobodies. In the radio announcer's drawling voice, the words came out strung together, the syllables melting into one. That's when they started using the nickname for us: Nobdies.

I was listening to the radio that day. Rare for me to listen to talk radio – I didn't like noise, the unnecessary clutter – and rarer still for me to be sitting in my car with Dusty yapping happily in the back. I didn't normally take her with me, not if I was working, but that morning – it was a Friday morning – I wanted to go and visit the girl in the hospital across town and I thought Dusty might cheer her up. And so there I was, in my little red car, with the voice of that radio announcer – the one who was always getting into fights about something or other – nasaling through my head. I remember reaching my hand over the back seat, stroking Dusty, smiling at her. She looked at me with that quizzical look they get, you know, head on the side, tongue stuck out, and I said something like, Oh you are my best girl, aren't you? Aren't you my best girl? I'm not embarrassed to say that I spoke in one of those bubby-wubby voices. I couldn't help it, with her little tongue poking out. When the announcer said the thing about the nobodies, I thought he meant the young men, the ones who hurt my student. I didn't think he meant us. I didn't think he meant me.

Less than two weeks after the radio announcer introduced his clever little name for us, one of the ministers made the first of the public statements. Something had to be done, that's what he started with, what they always started with. Something had to be done, but where to start? Those like J, whose grandparents had been born here, they were the ones who were safe, the ones who had to be protected. It was an outrage, he said, that those third generations, those whose grandparents had been born on this same soil, it was an outrage that those people had to share resources with newcomers. Upstarts. Nobdies. Those who were second generation born, they were a problem. But first generation, like me: we were thieves, stealing the land itself. We had to be stopped. And that's when they started to move us out of the city, move us out of our jobs. Hand-painted signs started appearing, draped over highway footbridges. First of all the signs said things like *Nobdies go home*. Sometimes they were a little more specific: *Die Nobdies*. Those like me, those with education, those who lived at the heart of the city, we were the ones they wanted to die. The others could just leave. But go where? This was home, this was where we'd been born, it was all we'd ever known.

It comes as a surprise how quickly a whole country can change. I don't have to explain this to you, do I? G and his pretty girlfriend left, even before the ruling that nobdies couldn't live in the city. I don't know why I'm using that word, their word. He was second-generation, G. His father was born in the city hospital next to my university, as an adult he performed surgery in that same building. I used to like that story, envy it. G left while we could still have passports, those of us who weren't third gen; he'd listened to J, that night over the stuffed quail, and made arrangements. By the time they started shipping the nobdies out to the ghettos – I'm not going to call them new towns, we knew what happened there, even those of us who didn't see the scars – we had Dusty and J's belligerence was gone, replaced by his desire to be a protector. He withdrew all our savings, stashed the cash in the bookcase in my study; wrote names of people who could help us if we had to run.

Right in the beginning he booked flights, went that far. That was the week after G left. My passport was still active, I was still optimistic. The curfews hadn't started, the lock-ups hadn't been imagined. Also, I said we didn't need to be protected, didn't want the lists of names, I wasn't going anywhere. We should stay and fight. I said, Fuck them, it's my city.

It was my city.

It was our city.

Another woman comes into the room. They want me to think it's nice, that they're careful in this way, providing me with women. She asks where my identification is, asks me where my father was born, my mother. I stare at her straight in the face, I say: 'They came from here.' Fuck her. I have no need to speak pleasantly any more, I have no need to protect anyone, to speak either truth or lies. Courtesy got me nowhere in this new country that is my old country. Whatever they say, it is my country. The woman writes something down then says, 'So you're third gen?' I stare her, silent, until she adds, 'Do you often imagine things?'

Across the table, the first woman nods at her, smiles at me. She says, 'We're not your enemies.'

But they're not my friends either.

And so J fought. He told his students to stand up for us. When the statement came, the second one, saying that all nobdies were to be shifted out to the new towns, he called on the vice-chancellor of the university to open up the halls of study to those who needed shelter. He lost his job over that one. Before they passed the law decreeing that nobdies couldn't maintain passports, he saw it coming. He saw the work orders coming too; what a gift we were, rounded up and set to work. Others were leaving then, but at night, quietly. Narrow trucks loaded up with goods for the north drove up the highways. If you paid enough, you could be packed into one of the boxes, tucked behind the crates of oranges and bottled water. Word on the street was that if you paid enough, you could get all the way to the tip and from there, any number of fishing boats were ready to make the trip across the water. Even then I said no. Optimism was always my way, my salvation and my crutch. Inherited from my father, this blind belief that things would turn out, that hard work and hope would win, always. So, while J tried to find a way out, I told him that even the new towns could not be so bad. How bad could they be? Worse than a journey in a packing crate to the end of the country? Worse than nights on a boat? Worse than the unknown? Anyway, I told him, I wasn't making that sort of journey with Dusty – and I wouldn't leave her.

Do I need to say all of this? Do I need to make it clear that, egged on by me, it was J who organised the first city blockade, hundreds of citizens, third-gen and nobdies alike, standing together, shouting, 'We are all one, we are the lucky country.' It was a glorious, frightening day, one of those rare sunny winter days where the air temperature is cool but the sun so bright you have to blink away tears.

No one was quite sure how it happened, what turned it. J was standing near the improvised stage, shouting something up to the speaker. There was a flag on the stage – why not? It was our country too – and somehow, something was thrown. Mud? Horse shit? I have no idea, only that it was brown and splattered across the red on the flag, brown dots marking their way across the first of the stars. And then from the other side of the bridge there was a storm of people, everyone shouting, bottles being thrown and the police were there with their megaphones letting the protesters know that they could not, would not, be tolerated and then there was more shouting and then —

It was J who took the first bullet.

Thirteen hundred people stampeded after that, like horses. Hundreds of them ran across his back, across his hands and I could not run back to him, I could not turn back.

He took the first bullet but it wasn't the last.

I took Dusty with me. How could I leave her? Without J, she was all I had, even if she was less than human. I was grateful for J's lists then, and for the cash hidden in my bookcase and for my strong brown walking boots which had seemed so expensive and so foolish.

From my study, I could see the bridge. Most mornings, it was as lovely as they say it is, curving into the sky like a great eye, the harbour glinting beneath it, those white sails still and shining at its corner, a dimple to the bridge's smile. I can't imagine that I will ever look at it again, even in pictures, without seeing the stampede, hearing the crack of bullets.

I can't tell how many of us there were in that crate. I know that there was a woman next to me. Young – younger than me anyhow – she shook with fear or cold, I couldn't be sure which. Three men lifted us in – one of the men had breath that smelled so bad that I wondered if he had eaten a dead cat. One of the men was a boy and the other had grey stains across the front of his shirt. That's all I could tell you about them. My attention was not really on the men, it was on Dusty. Pointing to her, the man with the bad breath said, 'No. It can't come,' and two of my fellow crate-travellers said that was right, Dusty couldn't come, it would be too noisy, too risky, too foolish. My foolish boots housed another stash of notes and that seemed to ease the way for the bad-breath man if not for my fellow travellers.

Darkness is never truly dark, that's what they say. But let me tell you this: if you ever find yourself in a packing container, in the back of a truck, in the night – you will know what darkness is. Beside me, I could feel the stickiness of other people's flesh. At the back of the crates there were large holes for air, and I tried to keep close, to breathe in air that had not first come through someone else's nostrils. Hours passed and I wasn't scared; I wasn't anything. With J gone, I was just moving, keeping moving.

As a child I often suffered from motion sickness – car journeys and flights were marked by my explosions of vomit. It is my abiding memory of family holidays. Odd, then, that in that truck with the smell of more than ten people beside me – and I could smell urine very early on, even before the stop – I felt no illness, no nausea at all. I kept Dusty close to me and although I couldn't see her eyes, I could feel her breath and I whispered to her and stroked her ears and I promised that it would be fine.

The engine of the truck was surprisingly smooth, soothing even, and with the heat inside the crate I must have dozed. My head slipped onto someone's shoulder – I couldn't see who, it was too dark. Dusty was still on my lap when I woke up, but her arm or leg seemed to be pressed under someone else. I felt my way down, trying to push the other person's leg and Dusty started whining, just a little bit. Beneath my legs, the wooden floor of the crate felt burnt with heat and it was while I was trying to adjust my legs, trying to just get a little bit of coolness, that the engine stopped. You could feel the breath being held, the sucking in of sound. Not Dusty, though, she couldn't feel the need for silence – how could she? She wasn't human. She could only feel my panic, the worry I'd kept away all this time beginning to swim up and swallow me whole.

Through the walls of the truck, we could hear the rumble of voices. Jovial sounding, if I were to put a tone on it. Then the truck started again and I could feel all the breath being let out around me. Dusty stopped her little whimpers then and I stroked her back, whispered, Good girl, good girl. But outside there was still shouting, and it seemed like the truck swung around, or just moved a little way – it's harder than you might think, noticing the direction you move in when you can see nothing – and then the engine stopped again. And we all got out of the truck and came here. And that's it. That's my story.

The woman gives me a glass of water. She says, 'We need to write all this down. We need to keep the records.'

I can see officials watching through the interior window. I think they imagine they are in a movie about an important job. They are old enough, all of them, to remember movies and young enough, I suspect, to believe that they have important jobs. To care about their important jobs.

Once more the woman says, 'I can't help you, if you don't tell me what happened.'

I say, 'There is nothing else. That's the end of the story.'

She says, 'But why are you here? How did you get here? Come on, help us out here. We need to fill in the forms.'

Softly, carefully, her companion murmurs, 'We need to know where to put you. We need to know whether you need to go back to the hospital or whether you're ready to —'

I say, 'They opened the doors of the truck. And they found me. And that's all.'

This time they speak together, 'That isn't all though, is it?'

It's stupid that they have rehearsed this.

Maybe it was the engine stopping that made her start up her whimpering again – she'd liked the rumbling of it, the rhythm of that noise and when it stopped again, she started up. However much I patted her and petted her she whined more. Someone near me had urinated; I could feel it warm against my leg, could smell the sour tang. Dusty opened her mouth and started to howl – I guess she could smell it too. They have sensitive noses. Beside me, a man's voice hissed, 'Shut it up, shut it up,' and I said, 'Ssssh, sssh,' as quiet as I could, as much to the man as to Dusty. But it didn't stop her, didn't make it quiet enough and it didn't stop him either. Right in my ear, so close that I could feel the movement of the air through my ear, he whispered, 'Shut the fucking thing up.' Outside the truck we could hear the rumble of voices, the footsteps coming closer, hands banging against the metal truck walls. I know I was shaking; I know Dusty could feel it. I couldn't see the man beside me, but I could feel him tensing, could feel the muscles in his arms contract, and I could feel the shift of movement as he leaned closer and pressed his hand over Dusty's mouth, trying to keep her quiet. I didn't stop him. I didn't stop him. Against the floor of the crate, we could feel the vibrations of the rear truck door as it slid open; we could hear it too, and I could feel the man with his hand against Dusty's face. It worked, she quietened down, she did, and we all held ourselves in and hoped.

Perhaps it was the hoping that worked, or perhaps it was the jovial quality of the driver, the cheery pace of his voice if not his actual words – either way, something worked, and they slid the door closed again, the sharp smack of metal on metal echoing across us. I lifted Dusty to my face, brought her close to nuzzle her, and I could feel, straight away, the lack of movement, the lack of breath. Pressing my nose to her mouth, I listened, I listened, but there was nothing. Against her heart, no beat, no pulse.

So it was my screaming that called them back to us; my screams that cut through to the border guards outside and led them back to the truck door. I kept screaming when they opened the truck door, I kept screaming when they climbed in, I screamed when they pulled the back off the crate and when they pulled us out and I didn't stop screaming when they lifted the gun right into my face. Inside, I am still screaming.

I can see the woman officer's face peering at me, but I'm not sure of the expression. Concern? Curiosity? Distaste?

I say, 'Don't say it. Don't say "she was just a dog".' My throat is closed now, I have used all my words.

The woman nods sympathetically and she says, 'There were no dogs in the truck. There was no dog.'

The other woman adds, 'We need to keep records. It's important that we show due accountability.'

'What was her name?'

I stare at her.

She says again, 'There was no dog in the truck, was there? When you came to us, when they brought you here, still screaming, it was not for a dog, was it? Now tell us who died in that truck.'

I say, 'It was nobody. Nobody.'

I will not give them her name. They can take my passport and my lover and my country and my name. But they cannot take my grief and use it to make their records neat. I will not give them that.

Her hand moves across the page and she nods at the two doctors behind the glass. She says, 'You're lucky it was us that they brought you to. You're lucky that they found you. Those boat trips —'

The other woman repeats the mantra, 'You are, you're lucky.'

Oh, I know, I know. I'm one of the lucky ones.

THE BOAT PROJECT
OUYANG YU

That night
At Fu's place
The man came in lipstick and high-heels
An artist from China
And wondered to me how he could
Get his PR (permanent residence) in Australia
Following is what
I said to him, as a suggestion:

Go and buy a boat
A bad boat
And install yourself in it
Like part of it
Row it ashore
And try
To catch the attention of the coast
Guards
Wear tattered clothes
Don't bring an interpreter
Bring a camera, the video one

And record the whole
Process
When caught
Don't be afraid
Be brave like an asylum
Seeker
Ask them for it
Do
And insist on a Mandarin
Interpreter
By talking Mandarin
Till they are
Confused
Shoot the lot
With your camera
And tell them
When it's time
That it's your boat
Project
A moving
Installation
Then go live
On national TV
In Oz or China
Or both
That's how
You could secure your boat
PR

The high-heeled man
Artist stared at me with his removed lip
Stick and laughed
So much

One of his heels
Came off his
Foot

A good detail, I said
That could be used for the
Benefit of the boat.

ASYLUM: A SECURE PLACE OF REFUGE
ALEX MILLER

'Conditions on board were abominable: the ships overcrowded, and there were insufficient provisions, water and sanitary facilities . . . The British had a difficult time fighting illegal immigration. Some of the boats were caught at sea, towed to the . . . shore, and there passengers arrested. The illegals were then often deported to detention camps . . .'[30] The 'illegals' in this case were not seeking asylum in Australia but were European Jews escaping the Nazis during the Second World War and seeking a secure place of refuge in what was at that time the British-mandated territory of Palestine. Looking back at this cruel treatment by the British of these wartime refugees it is impossible for us to imagine how the British justified to themselves and to their public the inhumanity of their policy. Yet they did, with arguments that now appear to us to be just as hollow and politically expedient as the arguments our present government uses in its attempts to justify to us, the Australian people, its cruel and inhumane treatment of the few thousand desperate and courageous refugees who are seeking refuge in Australia from oppression in their homelands.

I'm one of those Australians my Jangga and Barada friends in the
north call 'the first boat people'. The Aborigines don't make a distinc-
tion between the native born and the migrant that white Australians
sometimes like to make – I have a dear friend here in Castlemaine
who is eighty-six and who whenever I meet her on the street tells me
she is a seventh-generation Australian. To the Jangga and the Barada
people of the Central Highlands and the Bowen Basin in the hinter-
land of North Queensland, those of us who are not Aborigines are
all boat people, no matter how many or how few the generations of
our time here. And we are welcome. The generosity of the Australian
Aborigines is legendary and has often been abused and exploited, but
it persists, and we, the boat people, are still welcome. Sadly, among
many refugees and migrants and their children there is an attitude
of, We're in! You can shut the door now. And they are not alone as it
seems the majority of voters support the government's policy.

We, all of us, the beneficiaries of the persisting Aboriginal generosity, can't find it in our hearts to make a few thousand desperate
refugees welcome here? Evelyn Juers ends her double biography of
Heinrich Mann and Nelly Kroeger-Mann, *House of Exile*, with the
following quotation from the American poet Wallace Stevens: *We
live in a place that is not our own.*[31] Australians, new, old, naturalised
and unnaturalised, with the exception of the Aborigines themselves,
live in a place that is manifestly not their own. Australia is a place of
which we are, by the dubious right of occupation, custodians for the
brief period of our lives. Even if our sense of morality doesn't include
the refugee, we are surely bound by the imperatives of our common
humanity to make welcome here those who seek refuge from tyranny
among us, whoever they are, whatever their religion or their caste.

One of the reasons given by those bureaucrats and military personnel charged with enforcing the policies of the British Mandate in
Palestine during the Second World War was that among the Jewish
refugees there may have been Nazi spies. It is a familiar excuse to
us today. It takes years for our bureaucrats to decide whether the

refugees who we imprison in concentration camps beyond our shores are secretly supporters of the regimes from which they claim to be fleeing. It is an excuse to refuse hospitality to these desperate people. And most Australians are not shamed by it and do not feel deeply betrayed by it. My experience of Australians is of a welcoming and generous people, but this doesn't seem to be true any more. We enjoy the riches of being one of the world's most successful multicultural societies, surely? All refugees and migrants have added to the quality of our lives here. So why don't we feel betrayed and shamed as Australians and as human beings by the cruel and inhuman treatment our government is meting out to refugees? And when we see that both our major political parties share the same views on this question why don't we feel a kind of despair about the failure of our democracy to offer us a choice? I'm sorry I don't have any answers to offer, but only these questions that are forcing me to reconsider what it means to be an Australian.

THE PRIVILEGE OF TRAVEL
FIONA MCGREGOR

Jiva Parthipan's residency has come through. He can now legally leave and re-enter Australia. It has taken about three years. He talks of travelling, to test the waters, but isn't sure where. He wants to avoid London, the city he called home most of his life, lest it upset the process of settling in here. His birthplace Sri Lanka is not on the cards.

We are drinking at the Bavarian Bier Café in Parramatta with a Taiwanese friend of Jiva's from Goldsmiths College in London. Jiva has just pulled off an ambitious dance production down the road at the Riverside Theatre. Featuring scores of dancers from all over that continent, *Dance Africa Dance* is the first in a series of community art projects Jiva is co-ordinating for the NSW Service for the Treatment and Rehabilitation of Torture and Trauma Survivors (STARTTS). By the time you read this, *Baulkham Hills African Ladies Troupe* will have shown at the Belvoir Theatre. Over a period of about three years, there will be more.

We walk to the station for the last train to the city. Jiva has always lived in the inner west, while mostly working in the outer. He describes Newtown as the place he can finally be his often diametrically opposed selves, in a way that London never allowed. Lean, brown, smart as a whip, with a limp and a high unnerving laugh, Jiva has a grip on our culture more perspicacious than many local born. It may be due to the fact that in a short space of time he has worked all over Sydney with people from all over the world. And that his dark skin has precluded the myopic cultural assumptions that even the hippest Brit can have about Oceania. He says 'very' very often, his long, enthusiastic sentences difficult to transcribe. He is exhausted and looking forward to a south coast holiday with his Taiwanese friends, all of them keen to see kangaroos.

When he first came to Sydney, Jiva did not imagine himself as the Community Cultural Development Officer at STARTTS. He had been a full-time artist in Europe, and told us he was looking for funding opportunities. We, the local artists, rued his UK mindset. *Mate, there's no funding in Australia*. As it turned out, Jiva didn't do much art. He began working with refugees. Just over two years later, STARTTS received a grant from the Australia Council for the Arts to roll out this series of workshops, mentoring programs and productions, and Jiva got the job of running it.

'STARTTS does all sorts of work with torture and trauma survivors from a refugee background. The main model is the therapeutic model: counselling, art therapy, psychotherapy, music therapy, etcetera etcetera. There is a parallel team doing community development because it was felt after a while that therapy doesn't exist in a vacuum: people need to be socialised into Australia. Then there is the person who develops the social enterprise of performance, which I am: developing arts and cultural stuff amongst refugees in New South Wales.'

The breadth of the work he does is such that Jiva has trouble clearly defining his position. It is partly funded by Ozco, partly by private sponsors. Ongoing and future projects include dance and circus camps for youth, theatre, film making, capoeira and youth dance classes, an Assyrian dance project, and three choirs – Spanish speaking, Iraqi and South Sudanese.

'I consider myself an ex-artist now,' he laughs. 'Some of the ideas I was always interested in have carried through. Whether you call it social justice, or creating infrastructure – for want of a better word – for multicultural arts. When I first began to perform in England a lot of it was about creating a context for myself which didn't yet exist. Things have changed there and they are changing here and I'm enjoying, as a new migrant, being a part of that change.'

Jiva immigrated to Australia under the clause of Last Remaining Relative. His family had settled in New South Wales years earlier, and having been separated from them for most of his life, Jiva wanted a reunion. At five he had been sent away to boarding school. At fifteen, he was put on a plane to London by his father. The pogrom against Tamils was gathering pace: the Parthipans were in the firing line. Jiva's older sister had already been sent to study medicine in the Ukraine. Such was the urgency of escape that Jiva was put on that plane with nobody to meet him at the destination. This sheltered middle-class boy, Hindu Tamil educated in an English boarding school, flew into space and landed on his feet, via a family on the same flight who took him in.

East London, 1989. Jiva thought all schools had Olympic swimming pools and test match cricket grounds. The shock of Hackney and its grungy black culture, scungy housing estates. Shit food, cold rain, grey on grey. Jiva with his tropical blood, used to home help, dad a doctor mum a nurse, had images torched on his memory of reasons for leaving. Going on holidays to find three heads on sticks outside his parents' house. Bodies floating in the river. From the school grounds, the city in flames. Wads of cash burning. 'We touched them, me and a friend, they just fell apart in our hands.' His uncles were shot, his grandfather killed by a shell. No more platitudes about human values. Life is senseless.

He was also an adolescent craving freedom, evolving an alternative sexuality, so it would be reductive to call the move a disaster. His political escape became personal. He embraced new opportunities, fed the English economy with Dad's stipend and when that was cut off because he didn't study engineering, in true entrepreneurial style, Jiva sold the only thing he had – himself. He finished school, learnt classical Indian dance, stayed *on the game* to pay for university and Goldsmiths, made lifelong friends, taught at St Martins College of Art, developed performances that toured and were lauded. Fair to say he blossomed.

Dance Africa Dance is exciting to watch. A threshold moment, a glimpse of the future. There are scores of performers of all generations, the youngest a three-year-old Sierra Leonean who leaves the venue at the end of the night asleep in a scarf on her mother's back. There are teenage rappers in tracksuits, the songs wry, exuberant, Australian accented. The South Sudanese Women's Performance Group is mourning an octogenarian member who died the day before. Dressed in polka dot skirts and carrying long candy sticks, they sing traditional music composed by group members. They ululate and jump, do call and response, one kicking off her shoes mid-dance. Yet they are a reticent group, and it feels more private ritual than display. An outdoors piece perhaps, done on bare ground, audience in the round.

There is a capoeira group, a Sierra Leonean women's group whose piece includes documentary film and personal stories, there is Afro contemporary dance which incorporates acrobatics. But the most powerful is Martin del Amo's *The Walking Project* featuring ten dancers handpicked from all the other performances. The choreographic masterstroke begins with this casting, for the work is so pared down – no costumes or props, no activity but walking – that it comes to life through sheer force of personality. Martin's solo dance works all featured walking. Up and down the stage; across, around or diagonal; walking fast, walking slow. It could be maddening, or mesmerising, repetitive in the extreme. But when ten very different people, only some professional dancers, all immensely focused, go through their paces within this tight framework, the seemingly mundane activity of walking becomes a vehicle for a whole range of expression. In its obliquity lay revelation. I saw that substance fundamental to all of us. Some call it *spirit*. We say it transcends colour. Maybe, on the other hand, it is indelibly coloured. That is what sings to me, more than neutrality and sameness.

'Martin was not interested in the slightest in the history and background of these people. He was all about, You just turn up on the day and we will work with what we have. It was the most equitable piece in that sense – he's not interested in what happens afterwards, he isn't at all political. It was purely four weeks, three hours a day workshops. And in some ways that creates the most genuine opportunity.'

Martin is an immigrant as well. German born, of part Spanish heritage, he came to Australia almost two decades ago to be with his Australian lover, also a dancer. Knows Jiva from the UK dance scene. His move here was relatively easy, despite the radical demotion gay relationships experienced under John Howard's Department of Immigration.

Expectations of ethnically themed community arts events tend to the folkloric. In the sprawling city of Sydney, divided by lack of public transport, our African population is removed from most of us. (The black Africans, that is; the white are in the affluent centre, with access and movement.) For all my ignorance of Africa, I was grateful to be presented with dance so free of proscriptives. Call me idealistic, but I think all those elements – colour, religion, language, anything that defines culture – are in us no matter what; to drill right down to the core is not to deny them, rather to distil. Transcendence? Or mining? Deep cut mining.

After about a year in Sydney, Jiva created *Last Remaining Relative*, a performative lecture presented at Performance Space's 2010 Liveworks festival. You blinked and missed it because it was on in the middle of the day in the middle of the week. Developed from an earlier piece,

Necessary Journeys, Last Remaining Relative was a witty, inventive account of Jiva's border crossings, from that seminal flight to London to the more recent one here, via performance art tours made into ludicrous ordeals by his ethnicity.

Last Remaining Relative was offered to Parramasala, Parramatta's festival of South Asian arts, but the Anglo-Australian director did not come and see it. A co-producer, also Anglo-Australian, considered it not Indian enough. Jiva shrugs. 'Some festivals are just pursuing an aesthetic, you know. That's okay, that's inevitable. But what we need are more that are willing to go beyond that.'

Having come of age in the UK, Jiva was very alert to the Anglocentricity here. Even the self-declared experimental Liveworks modelled itself on contemporary UK performance, beginning with the UK-coined term 'live art'. Jiva often remarked on its inappropriateness in this region.

But he did not mind the limitations personally: he was ready for a change, so he bade farewell to performance art.

Initially, he worked voluntarily with refugees for a community organisation in western Sydney. Jiva then got a job with Settlement Services International, a private company, as a bilingual worker. He remained there almost a year. 'In hindsight I think it must have been a way of trying to understand my own past, although I didn't think of it like that at the time.' At the coalface, he met people straight out of detention and took them to accommodation, or hospital, whatever they needed. He laughs about the irony of helping people who had just been granted residency, when all he had was a bridging visa. Most of them were Tamil, but there were also Africans and Iranians, whose languages Jiva didn't speak. Many, haunted by trauma, needed to download. 'And there was no support afterwards, no way for me to debrief. It was a very very stressful job.'

In a Redfern pub two months after *Dance Africa Dance*, we talk about the lack of discourse around class in a refugee context. Jiva cites the privilege of his education, saying people from the same background as him who grew up in England had nothing to compare. 'The sheer fact of the confidence it gave me, to go and speak to anybody I wanted to, for instance . . . Most of the Iranians I work with are *hugely* educated. I'm working with a group of musicians at the moment who've all been to the Teheran Conservatory. Their sense of self and culture is huge. Certainly the ones who come here prize the pre-Islamic culture even more so.'

Like Jiva, these are the asylum seekers who could not have taken flight had they not been well off. We wrongly categorise them as underprivileged. The most educated and sympathetic among us are also the most condescending. I had a creeping sense of guilt recently when reading an anthology of refugee writings. I felt more frustrated than aggrieved. Instead of pain, I heard complaint. This could just be a case of amateur writing. It could also be taboo to mention the pathos of class demotion in a country still clinging to an egalitarian ideal, however spurious, characterised most egregiously by the *battler*. You cannot imagine a complex discussion on this topic surviving the airwaves: the floodgates would open to the xenophobes, many of whom are in government.

'And that's why they've got such high expectations for their children,' Jiva adds. 'In one generation they're hoping they'll get to the same level they were before. Or better.'

Boat People: another spurious trope. Most of our ancestors came here on boats: the arduous passage to the other side of the world a linchpin of the battler mystique. Boat people are us. Why then the horror of contemporary boat people? Legitimacy is automatically conveyed to plane arrivals, overshot visas and incorrect papers notwithstanding. But that may be exactly the point, that boats in all their archaic disarray are too close to the bone of our own past poverty and desperation. Is it affluence, and geographic removal, that have made us a race of petty bureaucrats, no matter how arbitrary the rules, and the urgency of crises elsewhere forcing people to leave their countries?

Consider some figures: In 2010–11, Australia received 11491 asylum applications. Less than half of these (5175) were from asylum seekers who arrived by boat. Over the same period, 2696 protection visas were granted to refugees who arrived by boat. This is just 1.3 per cent of the 213409 people who migrated to Australia during that year.

Since 1945, Australia has received about one million migrants per decade.

Since July 2009, New Zealand has been the major source for settlers.

The biggest change therefore would have to be the mindset. Decades ago, most immigrants were invited in to increase the menial workforce. Now most are allowed in if rich and/or 'skilled'. Migration patterns from recently war-torn countries have not produced the sort of solidarity you found post–WW2 from countries like Greece, where whole villages moved, and nobody had much. Jiva talks about the schisms. 'I think you see that very markedly with the Africans and the Sri Lankan Tamils for example. A *large* number of Africans in Australia are from a refugee background, not such privileged backgrounds at all. But when I meet the Nigerians and West Africans they're very clear to tell me that they're *not* refugees and they came here as accountants and so on, and to tell me they don't want to be a part of our organisation because, you know, "we don't need that". And the same with Sri Lankan Tamils. I would say about 25 per cent of them have come from a refugee background, the rest came here as skilled migrants.' There is a diasporic complexity. 'There's a group of Ethiopians I'm working with who lived in a refugee camp in Greece for twelve years, so they all speak fluent Greek,' Jiva laughs.

Most of the regulars are filing into the pub now. A mixture of university students, inner-city bohemians and housos, and working-class blacks. The latter are in the minority.

Jiva remarks that many early Asian immigrants were drawn to this country for the paradoxical reason that long after the White Australia policy was abolished, its mindset has prevailed. Watch local television drama, then go to your local hospital and wonder at the whiteness of the cast. 'Some early Sri Lankan migrants, it might have been because they had a little bit of white blood, and the kind of Singaporean and Hong Kong people who came here, who aspired to the sort of British white ideal . . . I think that's changing, but certainly it remains a strong feature.'

We move up the road when the music gets too loud. Jiva's limp is from an accident that occurred almost a year ago, an awful but not unusual rite of passage for a newcomer. At Coogee Beach he was washed off the rocks, shattering his ankle. There have been several bouts of surgery with enough plates and pins to set off airport security in every capital city. Jiva never complains. Catches public transport everywhere. Often works seven days.

'Oh dear, that's a can of worms,' he winces when I ask his opinion on Australia's methods of dealing with asylum seekers. 'Compared to countries like Canada and New Zealand, I think Australia is very very very very very *limited* in the way they handle asylum seekers. I think privatising and giving up to tender is huuuugely problematic. They're driven by profit. I think generally Canada has been a lot more welcoming of refugees. The population of refugees in Australia is extremely small, but they occupy a big space in people's imagination.'

'Can I be self-critical for a minute?' Jiva asks. 'I think it's amazing the amount of support I get for what I do. A lot of people have been helping and funding. But when I think of the amount of money that is spent on the multicultural arts, it's probably less than the refugee thing. For instance, I think it's incredible that there isn't a youth dance group from western Sydney. There are some organisations there who don't have enough funding, but I can't do their work for them . . . Also, I think it's great we're putting on something at the Belvoir, but they should be putting on more of this sort of thing anyway. More Chinese-Australian plays, more by women, more queer things. Instead of being prodded. The refugee thing becomes the big totem, and that can be problematic. They can think they're ticking everything with it, you know, black, Asian, poor, and so on.

'I think there is a real interest in Australia about African people at the moment, and I'm riding that to a degree. It's a great thing and we need more of it. But within it is a gradient. You're starting to see more black faces on TV, but I think it's also us imagining ourselves as American. Sometimes I want to say, Why don't you want to work with Iraqis or Sri Lankans? Because you think Africans dance better and are sexier to watch?' He suggests it could be yet another iteration of a UK habit, which sees greater representation of black bodies than Asian, despite the size and complexity of the latter community.

Jiva has overcome scepticism about the work he is doing, seeing a bigger future than ever for African performance in Australia. The STARTTS program may be finite, but there are other possibilities on the horizon. 'It can't be a company, but I would like to establish certainly an agency at least. That's what the funding is for, African refugees. I actually think that in the next two years I can create it, not in the same way I first imagined, but I can find a way for it to sustain itself, I'm convinced now. Hence I have to produce a show per year. That's my biggest asset, so I want to find a way of shaping a performance practice on the stage, while exposing the performers to other disciplines.'

I ask Jiva where he's going to travel, when he's going to take a break. 'I don't know.' He laughs his signature high laugh. 'But I have decided I definitely want to stay here. I've decided that next year I'm going to apply for citizenship.'

FIVE POEMS
JUDITH RODRIGUEZ

THERE ARE NO WORDS FOR THIS

Let the young man hang.
Let children lose their trust.
Let them despair and run amok.
And send them back.

Let the woman lose hold of her child
on the deep, among known bodies.
Let oceans take as flotsam
these lives.

1835: a captain – saved –
leaves his shipful of women
to drown off Boulogne, not one
alive, taken off –

his orders being to land them
in New South Wales. What's changed?
Let oceans take them, or slavers.

Or years damn them.

It's simple: they're different. Plus,
illegals, they chose their fates:
there are words for it – human waste.
And the words for us?

SOME POLITICIANS

To have preached even for a moment
that money matters
more than the good it buys;
to have proclaimed the end of caring;
to have unmothered the State
and left orphans to the wind;

to have waged phony battle
on the homeless and fugitive,
the needy come to our door;
to have danced on a tally of the drowned
to have pursued the desperate
for electoral triumph;

these are your names
on the sea-bed at our shore gate
behind razor wire
among the fatherless
the trapped and the destitute
and among the separated families.

TAMPA: CAPTAIN ARNE RINAAN

looked down on the deck. 'You could see it from
the bridge, they started to be restless, started
looking at the stars, the wind direction changed,
everything changed.'

On deck in the dark
between containers
families are asleep.
They have passage.
Outcast panic is past
and shipwreck past.
God's compass is set
for the ancient land of Beach,
Australia.

High on the bridge
their world's heartbeat
god can glance down
storeys to the pit.
His hand to save
his will to landfall
holds firm, they sleep.

Till a shadow
crosses the screens,
a contrary will clamps
its hand on his –
and these know
who learned to steer
by stars, smelt winds,
do not forget powers

that change course,
that coerce and condemn.

Lost or saved
turning in their sleep
in the belly of the whale
the ship's turning
wakes them, they know
it all, their universe
turns in the waters
and the continents turn
to inurn them –

Their lit beach
of the captain's will to save
flares and recedes
bleeds a trace
into voids of hate
is gone –

They rouse, they leap up –

Round them powers move – tides
of legislation rise
on the expensively shod and exercised
feet of politicians
in the artfully pitched and liquored
tones of politicians
in the skateboard arena
minds of politicians

making their mark
keeping their footing

saving their skins
figuring the gradient
of the electoral chicane
turning their trick
and professionally
mouthing family
chanting security
painting a picture
about difference

And however the people
rail and insist on a course
and however the captain in his honour
prevails in his course
they are lost on these seas
and this sand

And for long, long
under the lash of chance
they will find no landfall
beached in a container
for as many years as it takes

the scorn of commandants
in Australia.

WILLIAM STREET: ERIC VADARLIS

wept. '[This is] open game [season] on refugees.
If they come near our shores, the government
is going to push them out, tow them out, drag

them out. I can't believe this is happening in this
country.'
It is open season on refugees
and some are fairer game than others.
Their lawyer is weeping in William Street.

You can hardly expect an MP to greet
A muslim, a spic and a black as brothers.
Illegal's the word for refugees.

The PM tells us, expect a fleet
of indigent terrorists under cover.
They'll blow up your neighbourhood street by
street.

Fugitives jailed by our northern seas –
election-tactics for those who govern,
Canberra-deaf to refugees.

What of the forerunners they might meet?
'No more must come' – that's a Bosnian mother,
twelve years safe on her Melbourne street.

Baiting illegals is strategy.
Africans, Asians and such – why bother?
It is open season on refugees
And the bleeding hearts on William Street.

THE ASYLUM SEEKERS

Bearing your loss

however you can
in fear in hope
to our fearful ports
NO PLACE
my abasement
Your cry in my hearing
your children your children
the salt waste
these depths these deaths
my abasement
Your feet in my shallows
your hands at my shore
my guns at your face
inquisition
NO PLACE
your plea in my ear
your need in my sight
rights and denial
undoing of lives
NO PLACE
my guards in your path
your grief in my soul
the pledges broken
time passing time passing
my abasement

FROM *ALL THAT I AM*
ANNA FUNDER

A NOTE:

My novel *All That I Am* is about four young people who are forced to flee the Hitler regime in 1933. They find an uneasy and, as it turns out, unsafe refuge in London.

I started writing the book in 2006. At that time, my conception of my country had been shattered by Australia's treatment of asylum seekers. I can admit now that I experienced this as a kind of personal disillusion, bordering on despair. It shocked me to realise how much of my self-conception was tied up with my love for and pride in my country. This emotion lasted about four years, and I took it with me into the writing of the novel, which is about people who love their country but despair of it, and who are refugees.

Was I really so naïve before? My love for and pride in my country were not ignorant. I had some knowledge of cruel aspects of our history, foremost among them the mistreatment of Aboriginal people. But I had also let myself believe, rightly I still think, in Australia's respect for human rights, for the law both domestic and international, and in the globally unparalleled success of multiculturalism on our soil. I had worked in international law for the Australian government and seen at close quarters our attempts to implement our international human rights obligations. I had, in fact, been a small part of them.

Australia's treatment of asylum seekers forced me to change my conception of my country.

The specific episodes are well known. To mention just a few from those days: the Tampa affair in August 2001; the mass drownings of the passengers from the SIEV X in October of that year; the 'Children Overboard' government slander of asylum seekers; the forcible placement of asylum seekers on remote islands in order to deny them their rights under international law; the establishment of chains of privately operated remote and suburban detention camps around the nation to hold children, women and men indefinitely and without adequate legal recourse. A dozen years on, the camps are still there, and they are still full.

These events were catastrophic for the people involved. But I still can't quite account for the depth of my disillusion-bordering-on-despair. I am a little ashamed of it. Part of me would like to blame a certain dewy-eyed, progressive-but-patriotic, inner-city Whitlamite 1970s childhood. Or perhaps the residual lawyers' faith in human rights standards in the face of massive, real-world evidence of their breach (evidence I eventually left the law to write about). Or even some kind of quasi-inherited, late-enlightenment conviction that countries and human beings are, essentially, on the improve.

In my defence I can only say that it was possibly the eerie and terrible familiarity of some of the stories, and indeed some of the rhetoric, that cut me to the quick.

Let's take, for example, the so-called *Tampa* affair. In August 2001, to gain political approval among the electorate, the Howard government refused permission for a boat carrying asylum seekers to land in Australia. The *Tampa* was boarded by government troops and turned around to the Pacific island of Nauru. The government named this tactic the 'Pacific Solution'. In October of the same year the government created propagandistic lies to the effect that asylum seekers on a boat had threatened to sacrifice their children by throwing them overboard to drown, in order to force Australian vessels to act. This came to be called the 'Children Overboard' affair.

I was struck first, of course, by the horror the people seeking asylum had likely been through, and the horror of Australia's treatment of them. But also by other things. I was writing a novel set during the rise to power and early years of the Nazi regime in Germany. That regime scapegoated a specific cultural group, the Jews, including by spreading propagandistic lies that Jews murdered their own children in strange rituals. It considered sending the entire Jewish population to a remote island, and then, most horrifically, it implemented what it called the 'Final Solution' to this self-created 'problem'.

As I was researching this background to the novel and bringing my characters into being, I watched the Australian government create a scapegoat of a group, making its members feared by the domestic population as unscrupulous would-be child killers, in order to gain popularity and win an election. I read about its 'Pacific Solution', which turned people into a 'problem' to be 'solved' by their removal from our territory and protection. I saw innocent people being incarcerated in camps with the tacit approval of an electoral majority. I saw in both my research and my reality the same kind of politically calculated, legalised disregard for the life of another human being.

These parallel worlds, the inner one of my writing and the outer one of my country, met most acutely when I discovered the 1939 story of a boat of Jewish asylum seekers no country would take.

The story of the *St Louis* is incorporated into *All That I Am* in the extracts below. These scenes take place in the Mayflower Hotel, New York City. In them, Ernst Toller, a famous playwright, poet and former political prisoner, is dictating amendments to his autobiography *I Was a German*, a book he now sees as self-serving and full of holes. In particular (like most statesmen of his era) he left out the love of his life, Dora Fabian. Dora had worked for him as his secretary; she later became his editor, muse and saviour.

But Dora is now gone. Toller has another secretary to take his shorthand. Her name is Clara, and Clara's brother is on the *St Louis*. Paul is a fictional character, but he is on a real boat.

On 13 May 1939 the *St Louis* left Hamburg carrying 937 passengers, mostly German Jews, fleeing persecution under the Hitler regime. Some of them had already been interned in concentration camps and released. Many were single members of families that could afford to pay passage for only one person, and had had to choose whom to save.

Part of the fare included payment to the Cuban government for a landing authorisation which would, apparently, allow them into Cuba. But when the *St Louis* arrived in Havana harbour, it was not allowed to dock, and no one was permitted to land. Desperate negotiations took place. A proposal arose to offload the asylum seekers at the Isle of Pines. It failed, along with every other plea. Cuba, the United States and Canada all turned the ship away.

During the return journey to Europe the frantic negotiations escalated, trying to avert the ship having to return its passengers to Germany. In the end, other countries were found which would take the asylum seekers: 228 went to Great Britain, 181 to the Netherlands, 224 to France and 214 to Belgium.

Hitler invaded Western Europe on 10 May 1940. By June 1940 all of the former *St Louis* passengers who were still in continental Europe found themselves again under Nazi rule. (Eighty-seven had managed to emigrate to other countries). Two hundred and fifty-four of them died after the invasion, mostly in the killing camps of Auschwitz and Sobibor. (Of those who had been accepted into Britain, most were alive at the war's end in 1945.)[32]

In 1939 when President Roosevelt did not accept the refugees, he was dealing domestically with heated anti-immigrant and anti-Semitic sentiments. Today, the refusal to give refuge to the Jews on the *St Louis* has become a source of shame in US history and a much debated stain on Roosevelt's record.

The idea of turning away a ship of Jews seeking to escape the Nazis is shocking to us now, because we know a great deal about the persecution they were facing, as well as the subsequent genocide. It would probably seem to most of us that the domestic political concerns of the US president should not have outweighed a moral obligation to offer asylum to the passengers on the *St Louis*. But such a view is partly a matter of hindsight; at the time, clearly these domestic political considerations outweighed the moral obligation to save another human being.

But now we have better tools, tools that can assist us to see beyond the domestic political pressures of the day. After the war and the Holocaust the United Nations was established in an attempt to prevent such catastrophic events. Its earliest tasks were to draft conventions which would embody internationally adopted standards for the treatment of human beings in peace, in war and for refugees. The UN Convention on the Status of Refugees came into force in 1951. Australia is a party to that convention.

In the Convention on the Status of Refugees we have the tools – and the obligation – to make an assessment of refugee status and protect accordingly, regardless of the blinkers our current situation puts on us. We do not need to wait for the 20/20 vision of hindsight.

Australia is currently in breach of our human rights obligations to asylum seekers under that convention. Sadly, we do not need to wait for the historical record to condemn us. We can do that now.

At the end of *All That I Am*, Ruth, Dora's cousin, holds Toller's book, stuffed with typewritten paper containing the amendments about Dora, on her lap. She reads Toller's words: 'Must people have no imagination,' he wrote. 'If they could imagine the sufferings of others, they would not make them suffer so.' In that moment

it occurs to her that '[i]magining the life of another is an act of
compassion as holy as any.' But then another thought comes into
her head. She realises that 'Toller, great as he was, is not right. It is
not that people lack an imagination. It is that they stop themselves
using it. Because once you have imagined such suffering, how can
you still do nothing?'

This anthology of writing is an act of imagining the lives of
others, and as such an act of compassion as holy as any. It is an act
designed to make sure we do not stop ourselves from imagining,
properly and in every human detail, the plight of asylum seekers in this country. And it is an act designed to make sure that we
do not stop there: that we do something. We need to honour our
obligations to them, and to ourselves.

TOLLER

'No mail.' Clara is standing in the tiny tiled foyer to this room, closing the door behind her. She wears a creamy dress, belted at the waist.
I check quickly – I am dressed too.

What she means is, there is no news. We are both waiting, each day,
for news. I have written three times to my sister Hertha in Germany,
with no response. I know in my bones they have taken her away, and
her husband and my nephew Harry, who is seventeen. Clara's parents
have managed to get the money together to put her younger brother
Paul – but not themselves – on the *St Louis*, a ship full of Jews escaping Europe for Cuba. And then, we hope, for here. The *St Louis* is due
in Havana next week.

Clara brings the other letters over to the table and I look up at
her clear, open face. I do not doubt that some part of her is racked
with worry for her parents. But she can, like most people, contain

it. Whereas, depending on my frame of mind, mine can engulf me. Right now I can feel the sorrows expanding their black spread under my ribs, ready to pull me down. They are stronger, this time, than they have ever been.

But when she sits and I look closer, I see that Clara is biting her bottom lip. Small, grey-blue shadows have appeared under her eyes and she seems thinner, cheekbones sharper. I get a sudden sense of what she will be like at forty, her life half led: fully, first-generation American, with perfect-toothed children and a past that includes, once, long ago, listening to a washed-up old revolutionary from another world settling the account of his life.

I wish there were something I could do to help her parents, but there is nothing. All I can do is try to explain.

'It is not possible to understand Hitler,' I say, 'unless you understand his hatred. And that began with us.' I light the first cigar of the day, inhale its black heat. 'What he is doing now will obliterate the memory of progressive Germany for a century. And, I am quite sure, of me along with it.'

*

It's eight a.m. Two knocks at my door and she comes straight in these days.

Clara's hand is unsteady, holding out the *New York Times*. Her voice is clotted with anxiety. 'Paul's boat has reached Havana harbour but no one can get off. Cuba won't let them dock – the government is demanding huge sums. Where can anyone get that from? I don't —'

I take the paper from her. The headline is 'Refugee Ship on Approach'. She doesn't wait for me to read it.

'They were meant to stay as tourists in Cuba, awaiting a visa for America.' I can hear her effort to control her voice, to make this a rational matter of entry permits paid for and honoured, to convince herself that the world is reasonable and her fears cannot be real. 'Paul has a landing document – my parents paid for it with the ticket – now the Cuban President has cancelled them all. I don't understand —'

'They'll give them visas,' I say. 'Or some kind of permit.'

Clara pinches her nose together, closes her eyes and swallows hard.

'They're hardly going to turn away a whole ship of people,' I say, 'now, are they?'

She smiles a little, as if, yes, what a silly, black thought. Then her face clouds over again. 'There are letters to the editor,' she points at the paper, 'against letting them land here if Cuba turns them away. Saying there are not enough jobs for our own kind —'

'Are there letters in favour too?'

'I think so . . .' She sits, picks at a thread on her sleeve. 'Our own kind,' she repeats.

'You have to ignore that,' I say. 'I'll write a letter too. Let's do it now.'

I scan the article. There is a photograph of the SS *St Louis* in Havana harbour. It looks oddly festive, a string of flags flying from bow to stern. But it is surrounded by a ring of police boats. Behind those are small craft from which relatives and friends already saved wave at their loved ones. The Jewish Joint Distribution Committee, the piece says, is going down there to try to negotiate something for the refugees with the Cuban government. The US government has gone very quiet. The Canadians have rejected the refugees outright. And in Europe, Hitler is making the most of the situation, saying if the whole world is refusing to accept the Jews, how can Germany be blamed for their fate?

We write an open letter to the president, in the name of international brotherhood and our own humanity. I write: 'To be given the chance to save someone and refuse it must be, in anyone's religion, a cardinal sin . . .'

After Clara types it, she calls a boy to deliver it to the paper. When she sits again she takes a deep breath and smooths her skirt over her knees. 'Do you think letters can make a difference?' she asks. Her green eyes are riven with pain and hope.

I pull as much power as I can from somewhere inside me, from the actor, the orator, the hope-pedlar and the charlatan. 'Yes,' I say. 'Yes, I do.'

*

The photograph in the paper shows the SS *St Louis* lit up at night like a Christmas tree in Havana harbour, by searchlights from police boats and by the lamps dangling from its decks to stop people jumping. I also read my own letter, demanding that 'this nation founded by those fleeing persecution accept now these refugees fleeing from inhumanity, from a barbarism that seeks to make war against us all'.

Same old story. What did Auden say? He could no longer believe in our better nature. The blue-eyed rabbi in our village at Samotschin used to talk to me as though I were a grown person, even when I was just a boy. We must believe in God, he told me, because if we don't we will have to believe in man, and then we will only be disappointed.

When she comes in she's wearing the same clothes, though I know it's a new day. Her face is lightly powdered; the red scrape on her forehead has faded. She is very pale. She puts my ticket down on the table.

'They're saying at the shipping office there have been suicides on the boat,' she says, just holding it in. 'They are saying the captain has had to institute a suicide watch. I can't get a telegram to Paul, they won't let them have any contact with relatives, so we can't know —'

I get up and take her elbow, guide her to the comfortable chair. 'Have you seen today's *New York Times*?'

'No.'

'There's a new plan. To let them land at the Isle of Pines. Maybe to make a Jewish colony there.' I can see relief and hope tumbling into her, then a backwash of despair. 'It's hard that he is so close, isn't it?' She nods. 'But,' I touch her shoulder, 'it might just turn out okay.'

'Okay,' she echoes. She turns automatically to her bag for her pad and pencil.

'Mail today?'

'Oh. I forgot. I'll go now.'

When she returns – still no news from my sister – we resume.

*

This morning it's pelting down outside, early summer rain. When Clara walks in, her hair wet, clothes wet, it takes me a moment to register that she is also crying.

'The *St Louis* is going back to Europe.' Her arms are flung loose, dark strands plastered to her forehead. 'The coastguard fired a shot —' She chokes. 'Off Florida.'

There has been nothing but silence from President Roosevelt.

'Paul was so close, and now, and now . . .' She sits and weeps, head hung over her lap. I lean forward and place my hands on hers till they too are wet, and she gets a handkerchief from her bag.

'The captain seems like a good man,' I say. 'He will try to dock in Antwerp or Lisbon or somewhere. It won't be straight back to Germany.'

Hope-pedlar, snake-oil merchant – who am I to know? I can't remember how anyone gives comfort any more. Clara looks up, sniffs. She believes me, because the alternative is unthinkable. She wipes her eyes while I nod, pants on fire.

THE SEA
EVA HORNUNG

Abd al-Rahman was beyond exhaustion. His body shook in the air-conditioned room. An Indonesian official who knew a few words of Arabic wrapped a blanket around his shoulders and motioned kindly to the plastic seat, then excused himself with open hands to go to the others. Nothing seemed real. Abd al-Rahman looked as if through a film at the faces around him in the room, recognising no one. So few! He closed his eyes and imagined turning, dreamily, to feel for Zahra at his side, to reach for struggling Siham on her lap, a movement that would dispel this impossible room with its lost faces. He opened his eyes again. He knew absolutely that Zahra and Siham would not be there.

He remembered suddenly that when he first met Zahra he had mistaken her for a dead person. His chest burned and suddenly he was weeping in front of all the people. She was gone. He had not had time to finish fighting with her and to begin simply loving her.

Abd al-Rahman saw a bundle of black cloth sodden in the water with trapped air raising it in small slick humps out of the green sea. He saw a hand, suddenly, poke stiffly out of the water and then disappear and realised with horror that it was a woman, face down in the water.

He pulled off his sandals with a sick lurch in his stomach. What if it was a body, old, putrid? Worse, what if it was seconds too late and he tried to revive her without success? What if her relatives had drowned her, forcing a young head under? He waded out but at that moment the shapeless bundle leapt up and he uttered a small scream. Her slick head rose, hijab plastered from brow to breast and her black balto billowing wide around her, and then she turned lurid green goggles his way. She barely registered him standing there in the shallows, then dived again, floating away as a shapeless weighted bundle of black cloth.

Zahra was not like other women. He knew that from the moment he saw her wet, cloth-covered head rise from the water. She stopped snorkelling after she married him, even though his engineering contracts had taken him to Egypt and they lived at that time in Sharm al-Shaykh on the Red Sea coast. He didn't prohibit it, but, privately embarrassed by how foolish she looked, teased her mercilessly about it. He had been so young and self-conscious. He had never asked her what she saw. After such teasing, she would never have told him. And he was so young and stupid, then, that if she had told him something wonderful, he would have been jealous, so she was wise to keep her secrets from him.

He had the power to keep her in the house, to insist that she wore even gloves on the street, to recall her from university. He could demand her service. He could demand her body. In the moment these things gave him a heightened pleasure, but it was fleeting and he was, when she complied, ashamed. He wanted a fight.

She never fought but she always won. She withheld what felt to him like everything he yearned for but he could not have said what it was. She could withhold herself even as he grasped her body and reached as deeply into it as was humanly possible. She could withhold the world and have him live in the shadowlands of his own resentment and pettiness. She could cut him down with one sentence.

'You, Abd al-Rahman, are like the little boy who sets a chicken alight because he needs to cry.'

Zahra was his adversary, his other half. Siham was his joy, the arrow between them. He watched Zahra's amusement at Siham's preference for him, at her crazy, excessive adoration of him. He felt praised by that amusement, basked in it. He imagined Siham's passion and demonstrative love as the expression of everything Zahra felt for him but never showed, either to him or Siham, and he felt Zahra's warmth towards him carried from her to him in Siham's importunate hands. *Men trust their wives after the arrival of children*, his mother had said and he realised that this meant something deeper than he had imagined. Siham was Zahra's emissary. And as father of Siham, Abd al-Rahman thought of himself as a man his wife could like, even love.

Their worst fight started with the littlest thing. Zahra wanted Siham to finish her cereal and Abd al-Rahman, when Zahra wasn't looking, grinned at Siham, hid the plate behind the sofa and wiped her delighted little face, all as though she had finished. They had often fought over his indulging Siham. He thought she should run wild, do anything she wanted, mainly because he loved her pleasure, but also he thought she should be playful, not like her mother. Zahra smacked Siham frequently, partly, he was sure, to annoy him. Zahra wanted Siham to be good, to have discipline and restraint. She never said so, but Abd al-Rahman knew from her pursed lips at Siham's shrieks. When Siham jumped or ran, Zahra would clutch her by the arm and force her to walk quietly by her mother's side.

Zahra found the cereal and immediately put Siham back in the high chair, strapped her in despite the child's writhing, and looked coldly, challengingly at Abd al-Rahman. Siham didn't stop screaming until she fell asleep.

He could never fully reconstruct what happened over the next three days. It was a twilight of twisted, unbalanced misery and rage.

After three days they stepped over the threshold between wounding each other and into the dark realm of wounding a marriage.

He could remember clearly her white face when she said:

'You, Abd al-Rahman, would fuck your mother if you thought you could find yourself in her cunt.'

And he did remember that he divorced her. And took Siham from her until the obligatory time passed and he could remarry her.

His last touch of her was squeezing her hand on the lurching deck, in the moment that people fell against each other, clutching at the timbers, and others cried out in horror as three children fell over the side into the water.

He had looked at Zahra's white face, her eyes huge and dark, and wondered what he, Abd al-Rahman, could give to reassure her. He squeezed her hand.

It had begun to rain and the deck was slippery. He could hear children sobbing in terror below. Then suddenly there was a bucking shudder underfoot, and water rushed about his knees. And then there was no boat, only a ravenous sucking sound, and seething water filled with tumbled people, ripping them all from each other. There was screaming, screaming everywhere. He was in water, his body twirled by unseen forces, roiling up from beneath him. Siham had been on his hip, her arms twined about his neck, trading her warm fearful whimpers for his murmured reassurances. He could still feel where her arms had been, burned into his neck, despite the cold water. She had to be near! He felt for her, floundered for her, churning the water beneath him with his arms. He gulped mouthfuls of fuel and vomited as he sank, snatching at wet empty cloth in the heavy cold. 'Siham, Zahra!' he shouted, hoarsely, thinking, *even here, she will not turn to me*. He began sobbing in terror, feeling the terrible vision of the sea like an impenetrable heaviness on his eyes. He sank, held his breath in the cold pressure of the water, feeling frantically for them, and then he didn't know which way was up. When his head broke the surface, he

was shrieking her name. Siham had to be with her. The rain spattered
the fuel and water about his face and for a while he could see nothing.

There must have been hundreds of men, women and children
floating or flailing about. A man near Abd al-Rahman, sobbing with
the effort, held two baby boys high on his shoulders, but one of them
was already dead, a milky fluid running from his nose and mouth.
Abd al-Rahman could hear prayers but could not spare his breath for
more than Zahra's name. He hadn't known he could still swim, but,
threshing, he stayed afloat. He moved slowly from clump to clump,
more and more frantic as darkness fell and the cold gripped him from
below. His throat was burning, and each drowned child he found
brought a heavy darkness over his eyes. A man in a life jacket drifted by
him in the twilight and clutched at him briefly, babbling for forgive-
ness, then suddenly released him and floated away. Abd al-Rahman
could hear his voice in the darkness, sobbing out strange words and
phrases with no meaning.

He grabbed at women in the dark, hearing their gasps, their gur-
gles, screaming breathlessly for Zahra. Then, exhausted, he held onto
one woman, even though he knew she was dead and knew she was
not Zahra. He held her body lightly, not wanting to demean her, and
then, when he could, he released her and held onto a large piece of
wood. The sea around him slowly stilled and the mounds of cloth
drifted away in the darkness, or sank.

Dawn found him still in a flotilla of junk and bodies, his eyes
peeled open and crusted with salt. He could see one or two survivors,
all men. Zahra and Siham were gone.

In the dawn light, a half-naked woman floated by him, her fuel-
soaked clothes draped over her head and her bloated belly half-covered
by a stained wet shift. He would have averted his gaze but near her
hand floated a baby, white-blue with fine white ribs and a sunken
belly, but as tiny as red Siham had been at her birth. Over the baby's
belly ran a shocking thick blue cord. His eye followed it down into
the water where it trailed whitish skeins of flesh in the currents, then

travelled unwillingly to where it reappeared as a blue coil over the woman's naked thigh and disappeared between her legs. He suddenly didn't care whether he lived or died. He stared, gasping, shaking his head crazily from side to side, shaking his hand on the water's surface to try to unsee this. He couldn't turn away. He shuddered as they bobbed together with him, and then he managed to scrape his eyes closed.

Zahra didn't cry out in childbirth. He stood outside the room. His mother had said, She will cry out, my son, a woman does. She will scream. She will abuse you. I screamed abuse upon your father. Take it as an honour.

But she didn't cry out. Later, holding his darling Siham, disarmed by the wonder of such sudden fatherhood, he looked into Zahra's eyes. He remembered being shocked by how ancient they seemed in her young face. He felt foolish with his excitement and questions.

'Why didn't you cry out, darling?' he asked, unable to stop himself. 'I wouldn't have minded.'

He had wanted to hear what an unguarded woman, what Zahra in pain, would accuse, would abuse him with. What secrets he would find revealed in birth. He had even felt that his part, father, eavesdropper, had been somehow denied him. He had wanted to hear Siham's coming from that remote world inside a woman's body to this, his world.

She said, 'I knew it was not real pain.'

He had let himself misunderstand her.

He began to weep. He opened his eyes, reached out and clasped the dead woman's hand firmly and drew her and the baby to him. He was whispering his mother's name, and Zahra's, over and over. He pulled her sodden Afghan chador down over her body, covering that terrible cord, and he lifted the cold baby and laid it face down to her chest. He could feel the will of God stern and calm all about him, pressing down on his hands and face and on all the mess in the sea.

The weight was just enough, or the moment had come. The woman and her child sank and quickly disappeared. His last sight of them in the blue water was her pale, broad, pockmarked face and the tiny glimmer of silver flesh like a small fish seemingly living at her chest. Something in him stilled and he felt himself farewell Zahra and his baby in the way one feels oneself faint, everything draining from his body, downwards. He laid his cheek to the wood and stared at the wreckage in the shining sea. He could wait in these slowly warming waters forever. He knew it would all hurt too much to bear, later, but now he felt a blissful nothing, as if his life had reached all horror and glory and could encompass no more.

A FOLLY OF HISTORY
TOM KENEALLY

No one shall be subjected to arbitrary arrest, detention or exile.

Universal Declaration of Human Rights, Article 9

A story from, in some ways, a more honourable time:

Sir Robert Jackson might be the noblest Australian of them all. He had been an Australian naval officer who became involved in the international effort to feed the Arab population of the fraught Middle East in World War II. Then he was appointed Secretary-General of the UN Relief and Rehabilitation Administration (UNRRA) from 1944 to 1948. He knew that Europe by war's end would be full of Displaced Persons – in other words, people without documents, a condition which is now, in Australia, depicted as something between a crime and an arch stratagem. Some of the DPs were former concentration camp prisoners, others were deportees conscripted from outside Germany to work in factories, others refugees from the Baltic states or western Poland or Czechoslovakia. Some were ex-POWs and in a small margin of cases, some had been active Fascists but kept that fact quiet. In any case, UNRRA was the body that looked after the displaced persons camps. 'At the end of the war, apart from the tragic survivors of the concentration camps in Germany,' Jackson wrote, 'we had eight-and-a-half million Displaced Persons – you know, flotsam and jetsam of the war.' So he visited Australia and went to see Ben Chifley, Australian Prime Minister, a man with large public schemes in mind (the Snowy River Scheme, for example).

Chifley asked how many UNRRA wanted him to accept, and Robert Jackson asked, 'Well, sir, can you take 100000?' Chifley asked why Australia should take 100000, but ultimately yielded. He did say (I would like to believe for humour's sake), 'Hold on though, not too many Poles! We don't want another Buffalo City over here.'

One hundred and seventy thousand displaced persons came to Australia between 1947 and 1952, bearing their United Nations Displaced Persons/Refugee identity cards. According to Jackson, Chifley's alacrity in accepting DPs had global repercussions. Jackson attributes the eventual solution of the DP crisis in part to 'Mr Chifley's immense contribution at that point'. He himself, through his good-will and skills, placed the DPs in new lives, in new countries, within a few short years.

I don't want to make things sound too noble. Displaced persons were attractive to the Commonwealth only in part on humanitarian grounds. They were also to be cheap labour. But Chifley had enough imagination, in those days of White Anglo-Australia, to admit a number of previously un-encountered languages and faces into the country.

These events reflect on 2013, when a world problem of the displaced again exists. But it seems that in 2013, at an emotional level, refugees are somehow apparently a threat *uniquely* involving, above all other nations, Australia. And because we are uniquely threatened, we must be uniquely tough. It is as if we believe the asylum seekers, the day they fled home, had the intention to impose themselves on Australia, and on Australia alone. The term 'international cooperation', of the kind Robert Jackson sought, is therefore not often heard in the modern discourse. Nor do governments assure us loudly that they are working with the UN High Commission for Refugees to solve a world crisis. In fact, the UNHCR has become something of a byword for unrealistic objectives and pallid but intrusive do-goodery. Most terms used publicly in Australia are to do with showing the refugees of the world what's what, and putting them in their place. And their place is Christmas Island, Nauru, Manus Island, etc., etc.

As John Menadue, former secretary of the Department of Immigration, argues, if detentions and severe conditions are put in place by Labor or Coalition governments to deter asylum seekers, they will not work. Australian governments have assumed that people can be frightened out of trying to escape terror or likelihood of death. They seem also to assume that people trying to flee barbarism have read Department of Immigration press releases. And last of all, they must believe the smugglers will conscientiously inform their desperate clients of what present Australian policy is.

There was a significantly different approach to resettlement of refugees in the post–Vietnam War era. I once spoke to a Vietnamese man who arrived by one of the early boats from Vietnam in the 1970s. It was a craft with a handful of young men aboard and a school atlas for navigation. They made landfall at Nightcliff, a suburb of Darwin, and going ashore next morning, inquired of a fisherman where the nearest police station was. He pointed it out and asked, 'What's the matter, mate? Someone steal your dinghy?'

More and more boats of Vietnamese arrived without inducing any hysteria. Processing went ahead in a civilised way under – shock horror, for Labor folk! – the usurper of Gough Whitlam, Malcolm Fraser. Towards the boats of the 1970s and early 1980s, Fraser assumed no pseudo-Churchillian pompousness, and nor did the Opposition.

As a result of Fraser's humanity, I recently saw a Vietnamese boat person of that era telling his story of escape to a class of school children at the City of Sydney Library. The massive majority of us now respect his narrative. His journey is a saga. But we don't respect the stories of contemporary asylum seekers. They are not depicted by government, or by most media, as admirable and desperate escapees. They are not described as being 'game as Ned Kelly', as in fact they must be. They are depicted as evasive chancers who have gone to the trouble of trying to impose on our better natures. And some are without papers (like the DPs of old). What a racket that is! They've destroyed them so they can fake their nationality. Or else they should have gone around to a government that hated them, and wanted to detain or kill them, and asked a state they feared to hand them the favour of a passport.

You've been very patient, but I hope you'll let me impose on you one more case of historic sanity in immigration matters. More recently than Fraser, Bob Hawke publicly wept over the massacre of protesters in Tiananmen Square in 1989, and declared that 42000 Chinese students then in Australia could stay here if they chose. That is, nearly three times the record number of boat people in the last business year, 2011–2012, were to be absorbed in one stroke. These was no need for detention, and no taking away of rights of movement or employment or medical treatment. There were no gross delays. In 1989, the PM decided, and Immigration issued permanent visas. That's how fast and well these things can be attended to under the humane intentions of a government!

In what many of us think of as a sad era, 1996 to 2013, there have been no such stories of decency. When, between 1996 and2007, a mere 13 000 asylum seekers arrived by boat, Australia was put in a lather of fury and anxiety by them. In that period the boat people represented less than 5 per cent of all asylum seekers – the others arrived by plane. Yet our popular imagination was influenced by the 5 per cent – the images of flotillas of the unwanted, the undesirable, the supposedly hostile. We were encouraged to feel a sense of invasion and violation. I find it hard to blame the mass of us, who were surrounded by blaring voices warning us at all waking hours that this was the onslaught, the greatest crisis since the Japanese advanced over the Owen Stanleys. When the resultant government policies regarding boat people were severe, many of us were grateful, and slept better.

Thus, for the sake of 13000 hapless voyagers between 1996 and 2008, thousands of opinion pieces – many of them hysterical in tone – and hours of TV and crassest radio, were deployed. For the sake of the scatter of powerless arrivals, an expensive off-shore and on-shore system was created. Apart from detention centres where people who were our responsibility were guarded by employees of a foreign security company, there were, for many of those released after years of detention, the so-called temporary protection visas. 'Temporary protection' in this case was an abuse of language, since these visas – like detention itself – put asylum seekers in limbo, without work, without entitlements, without a place in society. Their mental health, damaged by detention, was undermined further by the non-personhood inherent in the temporary protection visa.

Above all, for the sake of the boat people, the government cringed and weaselled, was exalted and cast out. Ultimately, as I'll explain in a minute, whether pre- or post-2013, we gave the vast majority of the boat people residency, and thousands of them are now our fellow citizens. They have been required, though, to come into our community not only by way of oppression in their country of origin, but also by way of long imprisonment and soul-bruising restrictions here. Brave Australia, country of Bradman, the Diggers and Henry Lawson, but forced to cower before the advance of the lost and scared and wretched!

The pattern was set by 2008 and – as we know – was soon revived after a brief hopeful hiatus following the 2008 change of government. At the time of writing this, as part of the renewed hysteria, the present government has decided to remove the right to work from those asylum seekers granted bridging visas. And the return of the crippling temporary protection visa is again foreshadowed by a confident Opposition.

Bruce Kaye and his wife are Australians who 'host' asylum seekers for six weeks after their release from detention. They have complained that when the asylum seeker goes out into the general community under the work prohibition, he or she is forced into poverty or the black economy. The government receives no tax from the person holding the bridging visa, but that doesn't count beside the need to signal toughness. 'The new policy from August last year [2012],' writes Kaye, 'may look tough in the current political games of one-upmanship, but it is inhumane and cruel and it simply will not achieve any effective settlement process for these people.' Bruce Kaye's last utterance could be applied to the whole system: 'it is inhumane and cruel and it simply will not achieve any effective settlement process . . .'

Just in case we're misunderstood, let me say confidently that no writer who contributes to this book wants people to risk their lives with people smugglers and their ill-maintained vessels. According to an expert I spoke to recently, once Australian territorial waters are reached, the captains of such vessels now often escape back towards Indonesia on an accompanying vessel, lighter, faster but safer, leaving the adolescent crew to take the ill-equipped and ill-founded vessel on towards unpredictable peril on the coast. We all remember and mourn for the desperate, drowning asylum seekers in the churning surf of Christmas Island. Many of these boats sink before they can get as far as to intrude themselves on our sight. Late in 2012, a ship bearing thirty-three Hazara men from Afghanistan and Pakistan sank. The Hazaras were in the open sea for over three days, only one surviving. They seem to have been voyagers on their own behalf in an obviously unsafe boat, but I suppose one could call the person who sold them the boat a species of smuggler.

Were those thirty-three lost Hazaras queue-jumpers? Or could they even find a queue to join – in other words, was there even an Australian consulate-general in their region for them to apply to? But they are not the only ones who would die without managing to impose themselves on our good nature. Earlier in the year, in June, seventy-five died when a boat carrying 200 people capsized half-way between Indonesia and Christmas Island. And on 30 August that year, 105 bound for Australia were drowned off the Indonesian coast. These are three mere examples from 2012, not an exhaustive list. But for those reasons alone, it would be wonderful if we could discover a means to diminish people-smuggling. Stamping it out seems an impossibility, given the geography and the cash involved. And it is not generally understood that people smugglers are also involved in greasing the wheels, in ticketing and advice, for those who arrive by plane.

Perhaps one way of diminishing the trade is to have a range of better alternative processes on the ground. The Malaysian Solution, by which Australia would accept 4000 'processed' refugees in exchange for 800 boat people, whose rights in Malaysia were guaranteed, was seen by some advocates as the best of many options – not perfect, but satisfactory. It was, however, struck down by the High Court. In any case, we can wonder if the Australian Coalition really wants to see boat arrival numbers stemmed yet. According to Wikileaks, a Coalition official told the American embassy that no one on his side of politics wanted the boats to stop; that they were political gold.

And yet most of the boat folk ultimately end up living among us. From 2008 to 2011, 48000 asylum seekers came by air and under 15000 by boat. This means that three out of four arrivals were by air. Yet by March 2011 there were 6500 'irregular maritime arrivals' in detention, and only 56 'unauthorised air arrivals'. It would be germane to ask why the boat people are punished more than the plane people. Is it for a genuine administrative reason we can't perceive? Or is it for no reason other than that national hysteria focuses on the boat, and the boat is graphic, and provides the better and most disturbing and most politically useful footage?

So, to repeat – I hope not too didactically – the great contradiction is that 80 per cent of boat arrivals are recognised in the end as genuine refugees, as against fewer than three in ten plane arrivals. For example, of 1254 boat people processed on Christmas Island between July 2009 and January 2010, only 110 were rejected for refugee status; and this pattern is fairly uniform.

It is true that as I write, an electorally threatened Labor government in power is under pressure from an Opposition who harry it savagely, as do Murdoch newspapers and radio and television. It is true also that since 2008, when the Labor Party came to office, more than 30000 boat people have arrived, for 17000 arrived in 2012 alone. Thus, the present government is accused by the Opposition of being soft and inefficient. But no account is taken of the fact that these increased numbers reflect, at least in some part, new international wars and dispossessions. There seems even to be a growing confidence on the part of smugglers, a confidence which will not necessarily be likely to be dented too severely by Opposition promises to turn the boats around if it's at all safe to do it. The smugglers' answer is surely to defeat that by employing kamikaze boats; that is, boats good only for one crossing and designed to be appropriately leaky when encountered.

Sadly, the argument that the problem is both multi-faceted and not merely domestic but international is one which is sneered at in this dispute. In any case, whatever the cause, 278 boats brought those above-mentioned 17000 boat people, and that number is close to equivalent to those coming by plane. Hence, if Labor thinks it's stopping the problem by being tough – well, it isn't working. Having been suckered into the confidence trick of themselves giving the question greater urgency and publicity, they are – in their own terms – failing. As Labor has so often done during and since the Howard years, they have sold their souls to no electoral purpose.

Now the system blunders along, carrying its captives, whose individual detention costs are equivalent to those of a university education; granting rights – such as medical treatment – to some, denying them to others; uncertain about the refinements of policy; lambasted by a hostile press and condemned by many in the wider world, including – for its Manus Island policy not least – the UNHCR. A tragic and grossly unjust oversight was the case of the Tamil detainee Shooty Vidakan, who suicided while still locked up more than six months *after* being granted refugee status. (Hawke's Chinese students of 1989 had to face no such mistakes or delays.) In the cases of a number of more recent Tamil asylum seekers from Sri Lanka, the method was to strong-arm them into returning to a country dangerous to their welfare but, according to the government's self-deluding perception, with which every foreign editor on earth disagrees, suddenly stable, and eminently kind to the Tamil minority. And we still hold children in sundry abusive forms of detention – according to Amnesty, some seven hundred in 2010.

There seems no imminent finish to these abuses, as little as is their benefit for the present government. The system is maintained in honour of its own absurdity. The asylum seekers yearn for humane treatment, and we yearn for some sort of national honour. But both hopes have been crushed under the wheels of this asinine and callous policy.*

*As this book goes to press I am horrified to receive figures from the organisation ChilOut that show we now have the highest number of children in detention we have ever had in the modern era – over 1000. This figure does not include those children held on Manus Island, nor the further 923 held in the domestic detention system. The argument that these young should not be separated from their parents, and that it is this fact that requires their detention, is not an excuse, but a reason to abandon the system. Until then, Australia remains a nation that is committed to locking up children for no crime but that of blood descent from asylum-seeker parents. It is not the history of modern refugeeism that has required this of us. It is where we have chosen to take ourselves, and we are content to watch our politicians announce these arrangements with a demeanour of civic piety and earnest moderation. We who apologised to the Stolen Generations will have much to apologise for to those among these children who ultimately become Australian. Apology, however, will validate but not ease the present pain.

FLIGHT
EVA HORNUNG

The shell of a downed American bomber rested on its side in the yellow earth of the empty mound just a couple of houses away from Akram's best friend Yusuf's place. After Akram's parents were killed, he moved in with Yusuf's family, and the two boys went down to the bomber whenever they could. Every weekend they climbed into the crushed cockpit and flew the plane high into the sky in great wheeling spirals, in aerobatic displays, competing with the kites. They stared at their quarter far below, laughing at how tiny and insignificant it had become. The bombsite where Akram's home had been was just a tiny hole, like a gap in a row of teeth, and the streets were thin wriggly threads between the clumps of houses joining his place to Yusuf's.

On their first flight, they concentrated on getting the controls right and getting the engine sounding as it should, and were exhilarated just by the sky itself. But on the second, they were charmed by the effect they had on the people far below. They waved to Uncle Hamid and Auntie Halima, laughing, and when Hamid yelled at them to get out of it and get back home and help Yusuf's mother, they couldn't hear him over the engine noise. They could just see his mouth moving far in the distance. They looked at each other and laughed. Iman, Yusuf's younger sister, ran out of their house, looking tiny, and just waved to them in great excitement and Akram decided then and there that he would marry her when he grew up.

Eventually Uncle Hamid was able to get them down out of the sky by running up the mound towards the plane with a big stick.

Akram was usually pilot because Yusuf was very nice to him these days. Yusuf was co-pilot, gunner and instructor, which made up for it. They became proficient at take-offs and landings, at aerobatics and at buzzing friends and giving them the scare of their lives. It was time for more.

'Perfect day for it,' Akram said, scanning the sky to the west, and Yusuf nodded, knowing that, before long, he would find out what 'it' was. They gunned the engines and zoomed up into the sky as usual, but this time Akram veered purposefully right and headed with resolve towards Jordanian airspace. He communicated cryptically with Jordanian air traffic control, received the go-ahead and flew at high altitude over the border to Israel.

'Bomb Sharon!' Yusuf shouted excitedly over the engine noise. But neither of them knew exactly where the Knesset or Mossad HQ were.

'It moves about. In a different building each day,' Akram said, and that put an end to that.

To the discerning eyes of Iraq's two finest, Jewish settlements stood out from the air. They were orderly. The roofs were all the same colour and they had green gardens with fountains wasting the water while all around the Palestinian dwellings were higgledy-piggledy, many colours and shapes, and the gardens were dead and parched. They bombed the crap out of the settlements and then flew back home, evading the helicopter gunships in brilliant swooshes, and dodging the F16s with a skill that drew gasps of admiration from the Israelis themselves. Their names were added to the list of Israel's most wanted.

It was a good day.

The plane had been there for about a year and, for a while, had worn slogans and rested as a lop-sided, broken-winged war memorial, somehow cheering to everyone even with the savage sound of F16s overhead. But as life got harder in their quarter, the plane itself was slowly eaten.

Every week it shrank. Bits of metal were sawn off and sold. In what seemed no time, the two broken wings were gone, and the downed plane's breastbone was eaten away. All the wires and bits of glass had vanished. In the cockpit they had to sling a wheat sack between some struts to make a seat. Each flight was harder, dogged by mechanical problems and sudden scary engine cut-outs and out-of-control spirals to a few metres above ground when Akram's frantic tinkerings would bring the welcome roar out of an unpromising splutter.

Then their school closed because Sheikh Hasan had to look after his family just like everybody else, and they went out flying every day.

One day, the plane was completely gone. Yusuf and Akram had to build a plane on the mound out of bits of wood, flying what looked like a cross into the blue sky, waving to everyone below, and dropping pebbles as tiny bombs. Every day they had to dismantle it again, or the wings and fuselage would have disappeared just as the original bomber had. They could not get to Israel now without mishap, and only evaded the fighter planes hunting them by accidental near crashes and Allah being with them.

Then one day they arrived at the mound with nothing. Their sticks had been burnt for firewood and Yusuf's mother had grabbed her broom off them as they sneaked out of the door, screaming at them and then bursting into tears.

Akram drew a large plane in the sand. It took him an hour and a half, with Yusuf reminding him that there were struts here, flaps there, buttons on the console here and there, and checking everything everywhere as officiously and seriously as he could. Yusuf scratched 'Made in al-Iraq' in the side, and they grinned at each other. They dug two little seats into the earth and wet the earth in front of them to make the pilot and co-pilot's operation stations. Yusuf filled its virgin tanks with fuel and then ran to get his sister while Akram guarded the plane, his hand resting lovingly on the clean, smooth lines of its perfect wing.

It was a perfect plane, completely undamaged, as yet unflown. Straight from the factory. He got in, carefully.

'*Bismillah al-Rahman al-Rahim*,' he said softly, and started it up. The engine was a flawless roar, instantaneous. It had none of those worrying little burbles and choking sounds that gave you a scare in mid-flight. It had none of those little moments that made you slap the dash, or kiss it, or tap it sharply at a special spot, or pray out loud. He knew its engines would never cut out and drop them in a sickening, exciting free fall towards the ground. It was perfect.

Yusuf came running up the mound with Iman, tugging her by the hand.

'Where's the plane, Yusuf? Where's the plane?' Iman was calling.

'Here,' said Yusuf, 'but you have to squeeze into this little space behind the seats, because there are only two and we're the pilots.'

Iman stepped in carefully and crouched down, her eyes shining. She had brought the food, which was going to get them into a lot of trouble. She had some stale bread with herbs on it, some cold cooked rice and some sheep's fat in a plastic bag. Akram didn't look at her. He was the pilot and would go without food if he had to. He punched buttons, checked the console and, as Yusuf fastened his harness, began to taxi off. The take-off was incredible and they all slammed back into their seats.

'We forgot bombs!' Yusuf shouted suddenly over Akram's roar, jumping up to get out. Akram pulled him back into his seat.

'We don't need bombs this time,' Akram cut the engines quickly to say and then continued. They soared up into the blue, past the smoke, past the kites, past the crows. It was an impossibly long time before Akram levelled out, higher than they had ever flown before. Their quarter disappeared below them and Baghdad itself was lost to them. All they could see was celestial blue and a white herd of sun-drenched clouds passing under them. Akram didn't speak until at his chosen altitude, then he double-checked the instrument panel, sat back, cut the engines and looked at them both conspiratorially as he glided.

'The satellites can still see us,' Yusuf said. Akram pressed a button on the dash that he had drawn after Yusuf left.

'Not any more!'

They all stared at each other in delight.

'Where are we going?' Iman shouted joyously.

'Australia!' Akram said, and it flooded his chest with happiness to see their mouths fall open.

And away they flew.

ACKNOWLEDGEMENTS

The compilation of this anthology was very much reliant on the goodwill and support of the literary community and those administering it. We were overwhelmed by the enthusiastic and creative response.

Particular thanks to Fiona Inglis whose invaluable expertise, wisdom and support were indispensable to this project.

Warm thanks to Margaret Connolly for her encouragement and excellent advice.

To Kate Grenville, Richard Flanagan, Alexis Wright, Robyn Davidson, Anne Deveson and Drusilla Modjeska, who all agreed to contribute at the outset but due to circumstances beyond their control and our short run-up time had to regretfully withdraw. They remained very supportive of the project.

To Meredith McKinney for her creative input, permission, enthusiasm and patience. Her suggestion for the extract was perfect. She wrote of her mother, Judith Wright, 'I do think Mum would have been wholeheartedly behind the idea of the anthology and all too happy to share the story, which did always haunt her.'

To Kate and Rosie Lilly for their kind permission to use their mother's poem.

To Ngareta Rossell for her support and suggestion of the perfect title.

To Debra Adelaide for her valuable advice and encouragement.

To all those other friends and colleagues who supported this anthology from the beginning: Fenella Souter, Annette Hughes, Angela Bowne, Mark Goudkamp, Ian Rintoul, Sharon Rundle, Lyneve Rappell, Christine Olsen, Abdul Karim Hekmat, Mohsen Soltani Zand, Rachel Buckley, Roslyn Arnold, Francis Milne, Pamela Hewitt.

To those who made our work easier: Tami Heaton, Tom Thompson, Jane Schwager, Jenny Darling, Grace Heifetz and Angelo Loukakis.

To Penguin and staff for their enthusiasm for this book – in particular Cate Blake, who has been a pleasure to work with, and Ben Ball.

To Amruta Slee for her interest and support.

To my family, as always my husband Danny, daughters Bella and Josie and granddaughters Siona and Sabela.

Above all our deepest thanks and gratitude to the writers who gave us this extraordinary anthology.

'Homeland' by John Tranter published in *Homeland: Twenty-six Australian Writers Compose an Idea of Homeland*, ed. George Papaellinas, Allen & Unwin, Sydney, 1991.

Elliot Perlman's 'While the Drum Beats, "Stop the Boats" ' is a version of a speech Perlman gave in February 2012 at the Wheeler Centre Gala in Melbourne.

Sue Woolfe wishes to thank Dr Bruce Gardiner of Sydney University for his guidance in her research for 'The True Story of My Father'.

'Exodus' by Dorothy Hewett published in her collection *Halfway up the Mountain*, Fremantle Arts Centre Press, Fremantle, 2001.

The People Smuggler by Robin de Crespigny published by Penguin Group (Australia), 2012.

Gail Jones' 'The Ocean' employs certain details from the account of the Tampa events outlined in David Marr and Marian Wilkinson's *Dark Victory*, Allen & Unwin, Sydney, 2003.

'Immigrant Voyage' by Les Murray published in his collection *Ethnic Radio*, Angus & Robertson, Sydney, 1978.

'The Company of Lovers' by Judith Wright is from *A Human Pattern: Selected Poems*, ETT Imprint, Sydney, 2010.

'Tender Mercies' by Rosie Scott published in *Fear Factor: Terror Incognito*, ed. Sharon Rundle and Meenakshi Bharat, Picador, India, 2009.

All That I Am by Anna Funder published by Penguin Group (Australia), Melbourne, 2011.

'The Sea' and 'Flight' by Eva Hornung published in her collection *Mahjar*, Allen & Unwin, Sydney, 2003.

'Some Politicians' by Judith Rodriguez appeared in the FAW anthology *Said the Rat: Writers at the Water Rat 2000–2002*, ed. Jennifer Harrison and Phil Ilton, FAW/Black Pepper Press, Melbourne, 2003. 'The Asylum Seekers' appeared in both *Said the Rat* and *Acting from the Heart: Australian Advocates for Asylum Seekers Tell Their Stories*, ed. Sarah Mares and Lousise Newman, Finch Publishing, Sydney, 2007. The other three poems are from a sequence Judith Rodriguez hasn't completed about incidents in the whole asylum-seeker saga. The quotes are from press reports in *The Age*.

CONTRIBUTORS

DEBRA ADELAIDE is the author of three novels including *The Household Guide to Dying* (2008). Her latest book is a collection of short fiction, *Letter to George Clooney*. She is associate professor in the creative writing program at the University of Technology, Sydney.

GERALDINE BROOKS is an Australian-born journalist and novelist who grew up in the western suburbs of Sydney. She worked for some years as an award-winning foreign correspondent covering crises in the Middle East, Africa and the Balkans, before becoming an internationally acclaimed, bestselling novelist. Her non-fiction works – *Nine Parts of Desire* (1994) and *Foreign Correspondence* (1997) – and four novels – *Year of Wonders* (2001), *March* (2005), *People of the Book* (2008) and *Caleb's Crossing* (2011) – have won numerous awards including Australian Book of the Year, Literary Fiction Book of the Year, the Nita B. Kibble Literary Award and the Peggy V. Helmerich Distinguished Author Award. In 2006 her novel *March* won the Pulitzer Prize. Brooks' novels are all based on historical events; she is 'sublimely proficient at both the details of language and the dynamics of storytelling', with a 'reputation as one of our most supple and insightful novelists'. (Jane Smiley, *New York Times*)

ROBIN DE CRESPIGNY is a Sydney filmmaker and a former directing lecturer at the Australian Film, Television and Radio School. In 2008 she began writing a screenplay about the life of Ali Al Jenabi, which became the book *The People Smuggler*. Since its launch at the Sydney Writers' Festival in 2012, where it was the highest selling Australian book at the festival, *The People Smuggler* has won Best Non-Fiction at the Queensland Literary Awards, the Human Rights Award for Literature, the Alex Buzo Prize from the Waverley Library 'Nib' Awards, and was one of three finalists for the Walkley Book Award. In 2013 it was longlisted for the Stella Prize.

ANNA FUNDER'S novel *All That I Am* won the 2012 Miles Literary Award and many other Australian awards. Her non-fiction book *Stasiland* won the Samuel Johnson Prize. Both have been international bestsellers.

RAIMOND GAITA is Professorial Fellow in the Melbourne Law School and the Faculty of Arts at the University of Melbourne and Professor Emeritus of Moral Philosophy at King's College London. He is a Fellow of the Australian Academy of the Humanities. Gaita's books include: *Good and Evil: An Absolute Conception*, *Romulus, My Father*, which was made into a feature film of the same name, *A Common Humanity: Thinking About Love and Truth and Justice*, *The Philosopher's Dog*, *Breach of Trust: Truth, Morality and Politics*, and, as editor and contributor, *Gaza: Morality, Law and Politics* and *Muslims and Multiculturalism*. His most recent book is *After Romulus*.

RODNEY HALL has twice won the Miles Franklin Award. His novels have been published in the USA, the UK and in many translations. He arrived in Australia in 1949 as a child migrant at the age of thirteen.

DOROTHY HEWETT was born in the Western Australian town of Wickepin. Her career as a writer spanned fiction, poetry, plays and articles for which she received numerous awards and fellowships throughout her life. Her contribution to Australian literature was recognised with an Order of Australia medal (AM) in 1986. Her publishing record is vast and includes three novels, a first volume of memoirs, *Wild Card* (the second volume was in process at the time of her death), fifteen plays, anthologies of poetry, radio and screen plays, short stories, musicals, librettos and articles for Australian and overseas journals. In addition, Hewett and her works have been the subject of much analysis and review by other authors.

It is difficult to separate Hewett's writing from her persona. Her early bohemian lifestyle and political and social activism earned her a reputation as an unrepentant rebel. Students, political colleagues from both sides of politics, theatre people and literati alike were drawn to her outgoing personality and vast intellect. Hewett's flamboyant image and creative output never waned.

Dorothy Hewett died in Springwood, New South Wales, on 25 August 2002, survived by husband Merv Lilley and five of her children.

KATHRYN HEYMAN is the author of five novels, including *The Accomplice* and *Captain Starlight's Apprentice*, published internationally and in translation. She has won an Arts Council of England Writers Award, the Wingate and the Southern Arts Awards, and has been nominated for the Orange Prize, the Scottish Writer of the Year Award, the Edinburgh Fringe Critic's Award, the Kibble Award and the Western Australian Premier's Book Awards. She's written several radio plays for BBC radio, including adaptations of her own work, and has taught creative writing for the University of Glasgow and the University of Oxford. Heyman is the senior judge for the 2013 NSW Premier's Literary Awards. Her most recent novel, *Floodline*, was published in September 2013 by Allen & Unwin.

EVA HORNUNG is an Australian writer. She has won many awards for her fiction. Her latest novel, *Dog Boy*, won the Prime Minister's Literary Award in 2010 and has been translated into fifteen languages worldwide. In the past she travelled extensively in the Middle

East and she now runs a small farm in the Adelaide Hills.

STEPHANIE JOHNSON is one of New Zealand's best-known writers. She has published ten novels, several collections of poetry and short stories. Her awards include the Deutz Medal for Fiction at the Montana Awards for her novel *The Shag Incident*, shortlistings for the same award for her novels *Belief* and *The Whistler*, the Katherine Mansfield Fellowship in Menton and the Auckland University Literary Fellowship.

Johnson's novels have been published in the UK, the USA and Australia and *Music from a Distant Room* and *John Tomb's Head* were both longlisted for the International IMPAC Dublin Literary Award. Her US publisher St Martin's Press heralded *Belief* as 'the US debut of a remarkable writer with a vivid evocation of a bygone way of life'.

Johnson is a past winner of the Bruce Mason Playwright's Award and several of her plays have gone into professional production. She has also written for television. She co-founded and for some years directed the highly successful Auckland Writers and Readers Festival. Her latest novel is the bestselling *The Writing Class*. Johnson lived in Australia for some years and is married to the Australian film editor Tim Woodhouse.

GAIL JONES is the author of two books of short stories and five novels, the most recent of which is *Five Bells*. She is professor in the Writing and Society Research Centre at the University of Western Sydney and a proud member of PEN.

TOM KENEALLY was born in 1935 and his first novel was published in 1964. Since then he has written a considerable number of novels and non-fiction works. His novels include *The Chant of Jimmie Blacksmith*, *Schindler's Ark* and *The People's Train*. He has won the Miles Franklin Award, the Booker Prize, the *Los Angeles Times* Prize and the Mondello International Prize; has been made a Literary Lion of the New York

Public Library, a Fellow of the American Academy and a recipient of
the University of California gold medal; and is now the subject of a
55 cent Australian stamp. He has held various academic posts in the
United States, but lives in Sydney.

DENISE LEITH is the author of the novel *What Remains* and two non-
fiction books, *The Politics of Power: Freeport in Suharto's Indonesia* and
Bearing Witness: The Lives of War Correspondents and Photojournalists.
She has a PhD in international relations with a special interest in
the politics of war, American foreign policy, the United Nations and
human rights. She served on the committee of International PEN
Sydney, sharing in the 2004 Human Rights and Equal Opportunity
Community Award for the work the organisation did with writers
held in Australian detention centres.

FIONA MCGREGOR is a Sydney writer and performance artist. She has
published five books, mostly fiction, and writes essays, articles and
reviews. She has won and been shortlisted for various literary prizes, her
most recent novel *Indelible Ink* winning *Age* Book of the Year. In 2011 at
Artspace, she completed *Water Series*, a series of multidisciplinary performances inspired by water. She is currently working on a novel.

ALEX MILLER is the author of eleven novels. His most recent novel is
Coal Creek, published by Allen & Unwin in October 2013. Miller's
novels are published internationally and widely in translation. He is
twice winner of Australia's premier literary prize, the Miles Franklin
Literary Award, and is an overall winner of the Commonwealth
Writers Prize. He has won numerous other literary awards includ-
ing, on two occasions, the Christina Stead Prize for Fiction in the
NSW Premier's Awards (2001 and 2011) and the *Age* Book of the Year
Award in 2011, and was awarded the prestigious Melbourne Prize for
Literature in 2012. Miller is a recipient of the Centenary Medal for
services to Australian society and the Manning Clark Medal for an

outstanding contribution to Australian culture. Miller is a Fellow of the Australian Academy of the Humanities.

LES MURRAY is Australia's leading poet. He lives in Bunyah, near Taree, in New South Wales. He has published some thirty books. His work is studied in schools and universities around Australia and has been translated into many foreign languages. In 1996 he was awarded the TS Eliot Prize for Poetry, in 1999 the Queen's Gold Medal for Poetry, and in 2004 the Mondello Prize.

OUYANG YU came to Australia at the age of thirty-five, and, by fifty-seven, has published sixty-seven books of poetry, fiction, non-fiction, literary translation and criticism in English and Chinese languages, including his award-winning novel *The Eastern Slope Chronicle* (2002); his collection of poetry in English, *The Kingsbury Tales* (2008); his collection of Chinese poetry, *Slow Motion* (2009); his book of creative non-fiction, *On the Smell of an Oily Rag: Speaking English, Thinking Chinese and Living Australian* (2008); his second novel, *The English Class* (2010), which won the Community Relations Commission Award in the 2011 NSW Premier's Literary Awards, as well as being shortlisted for the 2011 Christina Stead Prize for Fiction and the 2011 Western Australian and Queensland premier's awards; his book of literary criticism, *Chinese in Australian Fiction: 1888–1988* (2008); and his translation in Chinese, *The Fatal Shore* (forthcoming in 2013).

He was nominated one of the top one hundred most influential Melbournians for the year 2011 as well as one of the top ten most influential Chinese writers in the Chinese diaspora.

Ouyang is now professor of English and the Siyuan Scholar at Shanghai Institute of Foreign Trade, China.

ELLIOT PERLMAN'S *Three Dollars* won the *Age* Book of the Year, the Betty Trask Prize (UK) and the Fellowship of Australian Writers' Book of the Year Award, and was shortlisted for the John Llewellyn-

Rhys/*Mail On Sunday* Book of the Year Award (UK) as well as for the Miles Franklin Literary Award. He co-wrote the screenplay for the film of *Three Dollars*, which received the Australian Film Critics Circle Award for Best Adapted Screenplay as well as the AFI Award for Best Adapted Screenplay. *The Reasons I Won't Be Coming* was a national bestseller in the US, where it was named a *New York Times Book Review* 'Editors' Choice', and received the Steele Rudd Award. *Seven Types of Ambiguity* was a critically acclaimed bestseller in France and the USA and was shortlisted for the Miles Franklin Award and the Queensland Premier's Award for Fiction.

Perlman is a recipient of the Queensland Premier's Award for Advancing Public Debate and has been described by the *Times Literary Supplement* (UK) as 'Australia's outstanding social novelist', by *Le Nouvel Observateur* (France) as the 'Zola d'Australie' and by *Lire* (France) as 'the classic of tomorrow', one of the '50 most important writers in the world'. His most recent book is the novel *The Street Sweeper*.

JUDITH RODRIGUEZ's collections include *New and Selected Poems* (University of Queensland Press) and, more recently, *The Cold* (National Library of Australia), and chapbooks *Terror: Poems* (2002) and *Manatee* (2008). *The Hanging of Minnie Thwaites* – a long ballad with historical account and lyrics – was issued by Arcade Books in 2012. She has collaborated with Robyn Archer on the play *Poor Johanna*, and with Sydney composer Moya Henderson on the opera *Lindy*, produced by Opera Australia in the Sydney Opera House in 2002. The editor of several anthologies, during the 1990s she edited Penguin Books' Australian poetry list. She is an Honorary Fellow of Deakin University, active in the Melbourne Shakespeare Society and involved in the work of International PEN.

KIM SCOTT's most recent novel is *That Deadman Dance*. Kim is proud to be one among those who call themselves Noongar, and is closely involved in an Indigenous language revitalisation project which has resulted in the publication of two bilingual picture books, *Mamang* and *Noongar Mambara Bakitj* (UWA Publishing). Kim is currently Professor of Writing at Curtin University.

ROSIE SCOTT is an internationally published award-winning writer who has published six novels, and a collection each of short stories, poems and essays. Her play *Say Thank You to the Lady* was the basis for a film which won several international awards.

She and Tom Keneally co-edited a PEN anthology of writers in detention, earning them a nomination for the Human Rights Medal and helping to gain PEN the Human Rights Community Award. She was appointed a permanent member of the Council of the Australian Society of Authors, is a recipient of the Sydney PEN Award and is a lifetime member of PEN. She is a co-founder of Women for Wik. In 2012 she was nominated as one of the one hundred most influential people in Sydney in education – for her mentoring, teaching and the work she has done in public education about asylum seekers.

Her novel *Faith Singer* was on the list of '50 Essential Reads by Contemporary Authors' compiled by the Orange Prize committee, *The Guardian* and the Hay Festival.

JOHN TRANTER is a Doctor of Creative Arts and an Honorary Associate in the University of Sydney School of Letters, Arts and Media and an honorary member of the Australian Academy of the Humanities.

He has published more than twenty collections of verse. His latest book, *Starlight: 150 Poems*, won the *Age* Book of the Year poetry award and the Queensland Premier's Award for Poetry, both in 2011.

He is the founding editor of the free internet magazine *Jacket*. He has a large and detailed homepage at johntranter.com and a journal at johntranter.net.

CHRISTOS TSIOLKAS is the author of the novels *Loaded*, *The Jesus Man*,

Dead Europe, *The Slap* and, his most recent, *Barracuda*. His work has been adapted for the screen by filmmakers Ana Kokkinos and Tony Krawitz. The mini-series adaptation of *The Slap* was produced by Matchbox Films for the ABC. Tsiolkas also co-wrote the dialogue for *Jump Cuts: An Autobiography* with Sasha Soldatow and has written a monograph on Fred Schepisi's *The Devil's Playground* for Currency Press's Australian Screen Classics series. He is also a playwright, script writer and critic. Tsiolkas lives in Melbourne with his partner Wayne van der Stelt.

BELLA VENDRAMINI wrote the bestselling, critically acclaimed autobiographies *Biting the Big Apple* and its sequel *Naked in Public*. She's been nominated twice for the Cosmopolitan Fun and Fearless Woman of the Year Award (writer category) by *Cosmopolitan* magazine and her first book is now being made into a feature film. After graduating from the Conservatorium at the Lee Strasberg Institute in New York City she worked as an actor, film producer and journalist. She is now based in Sydney where she is working on her next book.

'Bella is the belle of the ball . . . and now the belle of books.' – Quentin Tarantino.

SUE WOOLFE's bestselling, prize-winning, internationally published novel about mathematics and motherhood, *Leaning Towards Infinity*, was described by Fay Weldon as 'nourishing' and 'glorious'. Her stage version of it was workshopped in New York and produced at the Ensemble Theatre, Sydney.

She also adapted for the professional stage another novel, *Painted Woman*, published in Australia in 1989 and now in translation in France; with a composer she's adapting her 2003 novel about genetics research and autism, *The Secret Cure*, into an opera. Her most recent novel, *The Oldest Song in the World*, is set in the remote desert of Australia. She has also published many short stories and articles.

Her interest in the creating mind is reflected in her non-fiction:

with Kate Grenville she wrote *Making Stories: How Ten Australian Novels Were Written* (Allen & Unwin), and in 2007 she published *The Mystery of the Cleaning Lady: A Writer Looks at Creativity and Neuroscience* (UWA Press). She has taught creative writing since 2004 at Sydney University, and she is currently helping to conduct creativity research at NIDA.

Woolfe is one of the two co-founders of the world's first author-owned, author-run epublishing website, Wuthering Ink.

JUDITH WRIGHT (1915–2000) was one of Australia's finest poets, and a tireless advocate of the rights of Australia's natural world and its first people. She was born in New England, and moved to Tamborine Mountain in Queensland in her late twenties. In the early 1960s she helped found one of Australia's earliest conservation groups, and after her move to Braidwood in NSW in 1975 she became a founding member of the Aboriginal Treaty Committee.

She published eleven volumes of poetry, as well as literary criticism, children's books and several collections of essays. She was the recipient of numerous prizes, including the Britannica Australia Award, the Robert Frost Memorial Award and the Queen's Medal for Poetry.

ARNOLD ZABLE is a writer, novelist, storyteller and human rights advocate. His books include the memoir *Jewels and Ashes*; *The Fig Tree*, a collection of true stories; and three novels, *Café Scheherazade*, *Scraps of Heaven* and *Sea of Many Returns*. His most recent book, *Violin Lessons*, continues his exploration of themes of exile and displacement with stories spanning the globe. Zable is the author of numerous stories, columns, features and essays, and is a co-author of *Kan Yama Kan*, a play in which asylum seekers tell their stories. He has worked on a range of cross-cultural projects and conducted numerous writing workshops for asylum seekers, refugees, immigrants, the homeless, the deaf, problem gamblers, survivors of the Black Saturday bushfires and other groups, using story as a means of self-understanding. Born in Wellington, New Zealand, Zable grew up in Melbourne and has lived and worked in New York, India, China, South-East Asia, Papua New Guinea and throughout Europe. He is the president of the Melbourne centre of International PEN, an ambassador of the Asylum Seeker Resource Centre, and has a doctorate from the School of Creative Arts, Melbourne University, where he has been appointed a Vice-Chancellor's Fellow.

NOTES

1   Mearns, Andrew, *The Bitter Cry of Outcast London*, originally published as a pamphlet 1883, republished by Leicester University Press, 1970, p. 59.

2   Ibid., p. 64.

3   Ibid., p. 58.

4   Loc. cit.

5   Ibid., p. 73.

6   Ibid., p. 58.

7   From the *Pall Mall Gazette* of 16 October 1883, quoted in Schults, Raymond L., *Crusader in Babylon: W.T. Stead and the* Pall Mall Gazette, University of Nebraska Press, 1972, p. 50.

8   London, Jack, *The People of the Abyss*, first published in UK 1903, republished by Journeyman Press, 1977, p. 111.

9   Mearns, Andrew, op. cit., p. 67.

10 London, Jack, op. cit., p. 37.

11 Ibid., p. 11.

12 Ibid., p. 122.

13 Ibid., p. 123.

14 Weil, Simone, 'Human Personality', *Simone Weil: An Anthology*, Penguin Books, 2005, p. 71

15 Ibid., p. 83.

16 Levi, Primo, *If This is a Man*, Sabacus, 1987, pp. 172–3.

17 Weil, Simone, *The Need for Roots*, Routledge, 1978, p. 7.

18 Le Guin, Ursula, *The Earthsea Trilogy*. Puffin Books, 1984, pp. 162–3.

19 Perera, Suvendrini, *Australia and the Insular Imagination: Beaches, Borders, Boats, and Bodies*, Palgrave Macmillan, 2009, p. 648.

20 Brown, Hazel and Scott, Kim, *Kayang and Me*, Fremantle Press, 2005, pp. 41–42.

21 Birch, Tony, 'The Last Refuge of the UnAustralian', *UTS Review* 7, no. 1, 2001, p. 21.

22 Hodge, Bob and Mishra, Vijay, *Darkside of the Dream: Australian Literature and the Postcolonial Mind*, Allen & Unwin, 1991, p. xiii–xiv.

23 Philpott, Simon, 'Fear of the Dark: Indonesia and the Australian National Imagination', *Australian Journal of International Affairs* 55, no. 3, 2001, pp. 371–88.

24 Birch, Tony, op. cit.

25 Hodson, Michael, 'Government Lies Again – Tiwi Islanders', *Green Left Weekly*, 2003.

26 Diamond, Jared, *Guns, Germs and Steel: A Short History of Everybody*, Random House, 1998, p. 321.

27 Shellam, Tiffany, *Shaking Hands on the Fringe: Negotiating the Aboriginal World at King George's Sound*, UWA Press, 2009, p. 249.

28 Agamben, Giorgio, *Means without End: Notes on Politics*, trans. Vincenzo Binetti and Cesare Casarino, University of Minnesota Press, 2000, pp. 16–7.

29 Le Guin, Ursula, op. cit., p. 164.

30 Segev, Tom, *One Palestine, Complete: Jews and Arabs Under the British Mandate*, trans. Haim Watzman, Abacus, 2000, p. 459.

31 Juers, Evelyn, *House of Exile: The Lives and Times of Heinrich Mann and Nelly Kroeger-Mann*, Giramondo, 2008, p. 370.

32 Ogilvie, Sarah and Miller, Scott, *Refuge Denied: The* St Louis *Passengers and the Holocaust*, United States Holocaust Memorial Museum, 2010.